WORDSWORTH'S
VAGRANT MUSE

WORDSWORTH'S
VAGRANT MUSE

Poetry, Poverty and Power

G A R Y   H A R R I S O N

Wayne State University Press   Detroit

Copyright © 1994 by Wayne State University Press, Detroit, Michigan 48202. All rights are reserved. No part of this book may be reproduced without formal permission. Manufactured in the United States of America.

99   98   97   96   95   94   5   4   3   2   1

Library of Congress Cataloging-in-Publication Data

Harrison, Gary Lee.
    Wordsworth's vagrant muse : poetry, poverty, and power / Gary Harrison.
        p.   cm.
    Includes bibliographical references and index.
    ISBN 0-8143-2481-9 (alk. paper)
    1. Wordsworth, William, 1770–1850—Political and social views.
2. Political poetry, English—History and criticism.   3. Power
(Social sciences) in literature.   4. Poverty in literature.
I. Title.
PR5892.P64H37   1994
821'.7—dc20   94-17136

Designer: Mark C. Howell

For my parents

Contents

List of Plates

Acknowledgments

Parts of Chapters Three and Five appear in different form in "Words-worth's Leech Gatherer: Liminal Power and the 'Spirit of Indepen-dence,' " *ELH* 56 (Summer 1989): 327–50; Chapter Two appears in different form in "Spec(tac)ular Reversals: The Politics of the Sublime and Wordsworth's Transfiguration of the Rustic Poor," *Criticism* 34 (Fall 1992): 563–590; and parts of Chapter Five appear in different form in "Wordsworth's 'The Old Cumberland Beggar': The Economy of Charity in Late Eighteenth-Century Britain," *Criticism* 30 (Winter 1988): 23–42. The editors of these publications have granted permission to use and adapt these materials for this book. Permissions for illustrations that appear in the book have been kindly granted by the following: The Huntington Library and Art Gallery (Plates 2–6), San Marino, Califor-nia; the Lilly Library (Plate 1), Indiana University, Bloomington, Indi-ana; and Dover Publications, Inc. (Cover).

For supporting various stages of my research, I wish to thank the following: the Andrew W. Mellon Foundation, the Huntington Li-brary, the Research Allocations Committee of the University of New Mexico, and the Whiting Foundation. In addition, I am happy to thank the staffs at the following libraries for their courteous and timely assis-tance: The Huntington Library and Art Gallery, San Marino, Califor-nia; the Lilly Library, Indiana University, Bloomington, Indiana; and Green Library, Stanford University, Stanford, California.

I am most grateful to my colleague Michael Fischer, who gener-ously took time to read early drafts of each chapter, and to Michael Scrivener, who read the complete manuscript in a previous draft, for their helpful suggestions. I am indebted to Herbert Lindenberger, under whose guidance I first embarked upon a study of Wordsworth and the representa-tions of the poor, and to Stephen M. Parrish, in whose Wordsworth semi-nar I many years ago first directed my close attention to some of the works I discuss here. Through the long course of this study, I have benefitted from conversation with and encouragement from Barbara Gelpi, Jerrold Hogle, Alan Liu, Ann Mellor, Lucio Ruotolo, Tom Richards, R L Widmann, Paul Davis, Carolyn Woodward and Patricia Clark Smith. Thanks too to my colleagues in the Western Conference on British Studies who have commented on the many papers on Wordsworth I have given there over the last few years. For help in tracking down prints, editing the final draft and preparing the manuscript, I appreciate the exacting assistance of SueAnn Schatz and the guidance of my editor, Lynn Trease, at Wayne State University Press. My final and deepest thanks go to my long-time friend Jack MacDonald and to my family—Marlys, Miranda and Jeremy—for their patience, love and support over the course of this project. More than any others they know what it has meant for me to rediscover the utopian horizon of Wordsworth's work. They have, to paraphrase Gregory Corso, helped me gather the dream.

List of Abbreviations

This book uses the following abbreviations for frequently cited works and editions. (For complete citations, consult the Works Cited List.)

ASP   *Adventures on Salisbury Plain* (1795-c.1799). In *SPP* 123–54.

CPW   George Crabbe, *The Complete Poetical Works*. 3 vols. Ed. Norma Dalrymple-Champneys and Arthur Pollard.

EY   *The Letters of William and Dorothy Wordsworth: The Early Years 1787–1805*. Ed. Ernest De Selincourt. 2nd ed. Rev. Chester L. Shaver.

MY   *The Letters of William and Dorothy Wordsworth: The Middle Years. Part 1, 1806–1811*. Ed. Ernest De Selincourt. Rev. Mary Moorman.

PR   George Crabbe, *The Parish Register*. In *CPW* 1.212–80.

PW   *The Poetical Works of William Wordsworth*. 5 vols. Ed. Ernest De Selincourt and Helen Darbishire.

Poems   *Poems, in Two Volumes and Other Poems, 1800–1807 by William Wordsworth*. Ed. Jared Curtis.

Prelude   *William Wordsworth: The Prelude 1799, 1805, 1850*. Ed. Jonathan Wordsworth, M. H. Abrams and Stephen Gill. (Unless otherwise noted, all citations are from the 1805 version of *The Prelude*.)

PrW   *The Prose Works of William Wordsworth*. 3 vols. Ed. W. J. B. Owen and J. W. Smyser.

RBBR   John O. Hayden. *Romantic Bards and British Reviewers*.

RCP   *The Ruined Cottage and The Pedlar by William Wordsworth*. Ed. James Butler.

SP   William Wordsworth, *Salisbury Plain* (1793–94). In *SPP* 21–38.

SPP   *The Salisbury Plain Poems of William Wordsworth*. Ed. Stephen Gill.

Village George Crabbe, *The Village*. In *CPW* 1.157–74.

Introduction

Frederick Morton Eden's groundbreaking three-volume treatise on the Poor Laws, *The State of the Poor* (1797), demonstrates the extent to which poverty, the poor and the Poor Laws had become central concerns in the England of Edmund Burke, William Pitt and George III. Referring to the period between 1753, when Henry Fielding published his "Proposal for making an effectual provision for the Poor," and 1797, the year his own treatise appeared and the year William Wordsworth finished *The Borderers* and the first draft of *The Ruined Cottage*, Eden remarks: "The Poor Laws seem to have attracted very general attention, both in and out of Parliament" (1: 317–18). The last decade of the eighteenth century was a time of social, political and economic crisis throughout Britain, and the debate over the Poor Laws focuses many of the issues that divided England at the time, including questions about Parliamentary reform, population, wages and education. The high cost of war with France, poor harvests, enclosures and the commercialization of all sectors of the economy brought spiraling high prices, large-scale agricultural unemployment, intermittent food shortages, social discontent and increasingly tense oppositions between a more highly organized right and left. In the aftermath of the storming of the Bastille and the Reign of Terror, the Pitt administration introduced a series of repressive acts limiting the freedom of the press, restricting political organization, and muting public debate and protest. England was a divided nation in the 1790s, and this division permeated all aspects of English social, political and cultural life. If the storming of Joseph Priestley's Birmingham residence in 1791 and suspension of habeas corpus in 1794 find cultural analogues in the popularity of Gillray's patriotic prints and the reactionary tales of Hannah More and Samuel Jackson Pratt, the storming of the homes of noted crimps in London and the acquittal of Hardy, Tooke, Thelwall and Holcroft in 1794 find their cultural analogues in inflammatory broadsides supporting the doctrines of Paine and the French Revolution, Blake's minor prophecies and *The Four Zoas*, and Wordsworth's *Salisbury Plain*.

By the middle part of the decade, of course, Pitt's alarm, bolstered in the cries of church and king supporters, raised the spectre of an English revolution on the model of France; after France's foiled attempts to invade England in December 1797 and February 1798, the conservative reaction received widespread support. As E. P. Thompson so elegantly noted in "Disenchantment or Default: A Lay Sermon," in this wave of patriotism, as Coleridge's "France: An Ode" testifies, many British intellectuals and reformers cooled to or altogether repudiated the principles of the French Revolution with which they had previously sympathized. It was into this atmosphere of political and social conflict that many writers, printmakers, painters and poets introduced countless representations of the poor, divided between the industrious and the idle, the virtuous and the profligate, the rustic and the urban, and the deserving and undeserving. Since these categories and criteria are predominant features in widely disseminated and unabashedly tendentious narratives directed at both the poor and their so-called betters, literature from this period written about poverty and the poor, poems and paintings that depicted laborers as part of a rural or urban scene, could not be, and should not be, perceived as politically neutral or purely formal media for aesthetic experience.

In *Wordsworth's Vagrant Muse: Poetry, Poverty and Power*, I show how a few key poems from Wordsworth's early years constitute a direct engagement with and intervention into the politics of poverty and reform that swept the social, political and cultural landscape during the 1790s in England. In contrast to George MacLean Harper's claim that Wordsworth's poetry was not at all "charged with a temporal alloy" (1: 3), my book joins other recent studies of Wordsworth to show that, on the contrary, the temporal was the very metal out of which Wordsworth's poetry was forged. Wordsworth's poetry of encounter with vagrants and solitaries reproduces and empowers in literary form, elaborates and diffuses in its aesthetic texture, features of a discourse on poverty that shaped the attitudes toward the poor well into the nineteenth century— a discourse that informed discussions about poverty, poor relief and political power for the poor, who by the definition in place during the time of Wordsworth's early poems, meant those who had to work for a living.[1] Inhabited as they are with vagrants, beggars, discharged soldiers, pedlars and paupers, Wordsworth's early narrative poems directly engage what Theodor Adorno would call the "social bustle" of the 1790s, which centered around poverty—a subject linked inextricably with the politics of reform, the war with France, and the steady industrial transformation of English social and cultural practices. In "Lyric Poetry and Society," Adorno notes: "The tenderest most fragile forms must be touched by, even brought together with precisely that social bustle from which the ideals of our traditional conception of poetry have sought to protect them" (56). My project here is precisely to integrate Wordsworth's poetry into those controversies from which his poetry emerged and which have been largely lost to the modern reader removed from the overriding concerns of the late eighteenth century.

While I concentrate primarily upon the representation of the poor in Wordsworth's poetry, I also discuss other cultural works of the time, including the poetry of William Cowper and George Crabbe; the paintings and prints of Francis Wheatley, Robert Sayer and Thomas Bewick; the narrative tracts and tales of Anna Barbauld, Hannah More, Sarah Trimmer and Mary Wollstonecraft; and the political treatises of Jeremy Bentham, William Godwin, Thomas Malthus and Joseph Townsend. To borrow a metaphor from Alan Liu's *Wordsworth: The Sense of History*, my study opens the aperture of a camera focused upon the administrative and disciplinary function of the representations of the poor, especially in Wordsworth's poetry, while at the same time taking into view the utopian function of the agrarian idyll that his poetry invokes (23). What Ernst Bloch would call the utopian surplus of that idyll, as realized among some working-class readers of the nineteenth century, shows the radical potential of those representations to confer a sense of legitimacy and dignity upon an emergent working class. In this latter point, my work diverges from that of some recent critics, such as Marjorie Levinson, Jerome McGann, John Williams, and to a lesser degree James Chandler and David Simpson, who argue with varying degrees of emphasis that Wordsworth's poetry betrays a lack of sympathy for, or that his work rigidly reaffirms bourgeois attitudes toward, the poor.[2]

I choose Wordsworth as the key figure in my study because the early, formative years of his poetic career bridge a critical era of intensive social, economic, political and cultural change. As much as, if not more than, any of his contemporaries, Wordsworth took part intellectually, emotionally and physically (he went through crises of ideology, self-doubt and illness during the 1790s) in the economic and social reformation of the English subject in this decade of crisis. As an index to this transformation, Wordsworth's work offers a site for the cultural critic to register the dynamic interplay between the poetic text and the book of the world, that volume of conflicted stories that a culture tells about itself in a given historical moment. By placing Wordsworth's work into the broader discursive system of representing the poor I accomplish a double purpose: to track the modulations of the discourse on poverty as it moves through the late eighteenth century and to demonstrate the socio-political significance of Wordsworth's poetry as a vital force in the debate over the Poor Laws and the condition of the English poor and their relief at a time of socio-economic transformation and crisis in the 1790s and again in the 1830s.

The formal ambiguities deriving from the transitional moment of social, political and cultural ferment in the 1790s typify Wordsworth's poetry, which, while couched in an iconoclastic poetics that argues for transgressing cultural boundaries, appears to reinforce the ideological and social boundaries it purports to break down. Drawing upon both pastoral and picturesque conventions even as it denounces them, Wordsworth's poetry is implicated in an ideology that confirms and perpetuates the pauperization of the agricultural laborer and the idealization of rustic poverty that interferes with genuine concern over the welfare of the poor. Nonetheless, as I will show, Wordsworth's poetry problematizes the ideology of poverty even as it invokes the constitutive features of the discourse on poverty; his work does more than simply confirm what Raymond Williams in *The Country and the City* called the "rentier vision" of the rising middle classes and gentry (46). In the *Salisbury Plain* poems, *The Ruined Cottage*, *Lyrical Ballads*, "Resolution and Independence" and "The Old Cumberland Beggar," in particular, Wordsworth inverts the terms of the eighteenth-century loco-descriptive or pastoral spectacle of poverty associated with that privileged vision. Instead of meeting rustic paupers as distant aesthetic objects, Wordsworth's reader encounters the poor as mirrors of his or her own precarious subjectivity and as reminders of the fragility of the reader's own social status. Wordsworth's poetic spectacle, then, disturbs the complacency of the spectator-reader and places him or her in a position of uncertainty that opens the borders of the aesthetic to the onslaught of the social and political. If Wordsworth's poetry removes the poor into a marginal space, it does so in such a way as to invest those marginals with a certain, if ambiguously realized, power— a power that radicals and reactionaries alike have claimed as their own.

Exploring both sides of this dialectic, looking at Wordsworth from above and from below, I argue that despite its complicity in the middle-class idealization of the rural poor and castigation of the urban poor, Wordsworth's poetry nonetheless destabilizes the complacency of those who were not poor by placing them in a position of risk relative to the indigent vagrants and laborers in his poetry who fix a chastising gaze upon the reader. In the resultant face-to-face encounter between reader and vagrant a kind of status reversal takes place, in which the poor are at once dignified and invested with affective and moral power while those who are not poor are confronted with a disturbing sign of their own economic precariousness and possible pauperization. While many of the vagrants in Wordsworth's poetry function as repositories of conventional moral value, the early poems that focus upon poverty and the poor reverse the conventional relationship between the reader and the aesthetically objectified pauper. Inverting the relations of power in a space and moment of liminal power, Wordsworth's vagrants display a troubling tension between their apparent deference to normative values and their uncanny tendency to subvert and undermine the customary authority of the reader. In this disruption of social expectations of the reading contract, Wordsworth's poetry thus qualifies and questions, if sometimes tentatively, the latent paternalism of his work.

David Simpson, who more than most contemporary critics attempts to read Wordsworth's poetry dialectically, begins his *Wordsworth's Historical Imagination* by reminding us that "many of Wordsworth's poems address themselves to fairly precise events and circumstances," including "the condition of England" and "the plight of the poor" (2). Simpson rightly believes that many of Wordsworth's poems are positioned "as a polemical commentary upon the condition of England" (2).[3] Alerting us to the potential critical power of Wordsworth's depiction of poverty, Simpson writes that Wordsworth's poetry shows that "poverty *does* have a brutalizing effect on most of us." Simpson cites as examples the poor man's abandonment of his family in "The Last of the Flock" and Robert's psychological breakdown in *The Ruined Cottage*, the latter of which is "marked by a complex awareness of the terrible effect of unemployment on the moral and domestic life" (192). One could add many other poems here, such as "Point Rash-Judgment," "Simon Lee," "Goody Blake and Harry Gill," and "Michael," among others, in which the present circumstances of the indigent heroes or heroines fall painfully short of the life of cheer and health promised in the pastoral-georgic and in the discourse on poverty as a reward for their lives of industry and thrift. The old laborer of "Point Rash-Judgment," for example, leads a life of desperation even though it is clear that he put in a life of labor; Simon Lee and Ruth can barely survive despite their willful determination: "Tis little, very little—all / That they can do between them" (55–56). Their labor has not fulfilled the promise of economic gain, of domestic comfort; nor is it clear just how they are to survive beyond the moment. In these poems Wordsworth's presentation of the laboring poor evokes the ideology of industriousness only to disrupt its simple pattern of moral and socio-economic development touted in the discourse on poverty.

In discussing the "politics of sympathy" in Wordsworth's poetry, Simpson has described furthermore how Wordsworth's "Michael" and "The Old Cumberland Beggar" function, however obliquely, as critiques of various proposals, including Bentham's and Pitt's, to reform the Poor Laws (*Wordsworth's Historical Imagination* 169–72). Since many of these reforms were proposed in the mid-1790s, it should not surprise us to see Wordsworth developing his most trenchant critique of the Poor Law reforms in the poems he was writing between 1795 and 1800, especially in *Lyrical Ballads* and the early drafts of *Salisbury Plain* and *The Ruined Cottage*. While certainly not Jacobin poems such as the kind Shelley would produce in "The Mask of Anarchy" or like those that Chartist poets, such as Thomas Hood or Ernest Jones, would later pen to rouse the indignation of the working men (and I use the masculine pronoun advisedly) of England, Wordsworth's poems of the mid-1790s deliberately criticize the dehumanization of the rural poor that Wordsworth, like many of his contemporaries, believed would be the consequence of the centralization and bureaucratization of Poor Law administration.

Simpson's reading of Wordsworth's attraction to, and contempt for, a vagrant kind of freedom in "Gipsies" supports my thesis that Wordsworth finds in the indigents of his poetry the site for a troubling, yet sympathetic, identification. In different personae such as the self-reliant leech gatherer, the hard-working Margaret and Robert of *The Ruined Cottage*, and the indefatigable Simon Lee, Wordsworth's poetry embodies in rustic characters not only the rougher edges of poverty—Simon Lee's weakness, Robert and Margaret's self destructive despair—but the preeminent virtues of the polite reader of the "middling orders": industry, thrift and independence. In their normative perfection, Wordsworth's laborers and indigents become what Ian Hunter calls "moral objects"—"a projection or correlate of the reader's moral self and personality" (245). When we consider the suffering so common to Wordsworth's poor in light of the suffering which his poetry posits as the common, universal link among all human beings, high or low, we can see that it blurs the boundaries between the poor and those who are not poor in a way that radically challenged the prevailing assumptions of his contemporaries. Indeed, his representations of the poor make possible, if they do not necessitate, an uneasy literary identification between the spectator and the "working poor"—a disturbing awareness that in a society purportedly open to talents yet subject to irrecoverable losses, the middle classes might well be reduced themselves to manual labor—or worse, to vagrancy and poverty.[4]

While we may question whether the literary identification enacted in Wordsworth's poetry actually promotes social intercourse between members of different classes or redefines the actual practice of charity, evidence that the representations of the poor in his poetry effect a general insensitivity for the poor is so far lacking. On the contrary, some evidence shows that just as the Sunday school and charity school movements failed to produce a yielding and deferent working class in Britain, the idealized representations of the poor in Crabbe, Cowper and Wordsworth also failed to inculcate the poor with prescribed moral values or cause their so-called betters to turn their backs on them.[5] Precisely because the relationship of his solitary vagrants to traditional modes of production and the relationship between the vagrants and Wordsworth's readers is so problematic, ambiguous and contradictory, his work readily lends itself to appropriation by those whose interests may be to subvert, rather than support, the status quo. Indeed, the precarious balance between the repressive ideology and the anticipatory or utopian surplus in his work has enabled readers of various political persuasions to strategically deploy Wordsworth's representations of the poor to serve contradictory and even antithetical political ends: to inculcate deference and moral virtue in the poor, or to instill in them an enabling sense of dignity and political power.

When we place Wordsworth's representations of the poor among the myriad treatises, poems and paintings of and about the poor and poverty in the late eighteenth century, what emerges is a body of poetry that shares certain normative conventions about poverty, discursive strategies for talking about the poor, fears and idealisms about paupers and peasants, and yet transforms certain features of the discourse on poverty to break both poetic and social decorum, thereby presenting images of the poor that were to his contemporaries ambiguous and alarming for some, curious and calming for others. The value of Wordsworth's poetry, I believe, rests in its ability to open itself dialectically to these variant readings; or, to restate my position in terms of the utopian function, in its double vision of social alienation and natural harmony, Wordsworth's poetry produces a kind of utopian surplus that, despite its complicity and origin in middle-class ideology, can be harnessed by the subordinate classes as a means of self-empowerment and a stimulus to hope that enables real change—hope in its most positive sense. Here I mean to follow Bloch in distinguishing between hope as an anticipatory gaze that grasps the actual potentials of contingent material conditions—that is, hope founded on probabilities—as distinct from hope as fanciful or mere longing that ignores those probabilities altogether. Bloch suggests that literature and art produced within the dominant ideology may function to distribute surplus utopic ideals to groups other than those who originate those works out of conscious or unconscious self-interest. If I may quote at length:

> Ideologies, as the ruling ideas of an age are, in Marx's striking phrase, the ideas of the ruling class; but since even the latter is self-alienated ideologies also incorporated, apart from the interest in presenting the well-being of one's own class as that of humanity as a whole, that yearning and overhauling image of a world without alienation, that above all passes for culture in the bourgeoisie, and that showed the utopian function at work partly also in that class which otherwise felt happy in its alienation. It is obvious that this function truly, indeed almost entirely, animated the still revolutionary ideologies of such classes. Without the utopian function, no spiritual surplus at all is explicable over and above what has been attained and thus exists, however full this surplus may be of appearance instead of preappearance. Therefore, every act of anticipating identifies itself to the utopian function, and the latter seizes on all possible substance in the surplus of the former. (*Principle of Hope* 1: 150)

In pointing to the utopian character of Wordsworth's poetry, *Wordsworth's Vagrant Muse* departs from recent criticism that sees Wordsworth's poetry as a poetry of historical denial. In my view, recent criticism has largely overlooked the utopian character of Wordsworth's work, even as such criticism has usefully cautioned us against ignoring the complicity of Wordsworth's poetry in its ideological moment. Such criticism has offered a useful corrective to studies that ignore ideology altogether and read Wordsworth's work—or romantic literature in general—as a revolutionary literature. While Wordsworth's poetry does indeed attenuate the conflicted socio-political positions on which it devolves, it does not altogether erase or displace those conflicts, as one might infer from approaching Wordsworth through the doors of "Tintern Abbey," as they have been opened by Levinson and McGann. McGann, for example, argues that the "method" of "The Ruined Cottage," "Tintern Abbey" and, by implication, other Wordsworth poems, is to "replace an image and landscape of contradiction with one dominated by 'the power / Of harmony' " (*Romantic Ideology* 86). Similarly, Levinson's *Wordsworth's Great Period Poems* and Liu's *Wordsworth: The Sense of History*, from sympathetic but divergent critical positions, argue that Wordsworth's poetry enacts a partially successful project of denial—a denial of the material conditions of its production and of its history . While I believe it is important that we recognize, in the words of Levinson's "The New Historicism: Back to the Future," the "helpless complicity of his [Wordsworth's] critique with the object of its contempt" (35), it is equally important that we recognize, as I argue throughout this book, the power of that critique to call that complicity into question.

As an academic from a working-class background whose entry into academia derives in part through my own early, if naive, encounter with Wordsworth's poetry, I have been troubled by the power of contemporary criticism, in the name of a radical project, to silence the radical potentials of Wordsworth's dialectical poetry and neglect the largely hostile and politically motivated early reception of Wordsworth's early poetry. That reception, as I will discuss further in the final section of this book, took Wordsworth to task on the grounds of violating both aesthetic *and* social decorum. Moreover, in many cases, those attacks came from people, like Francis Jeffrey, who in their own time were considered to be political liberals. If Wordsworth's poetry were the instrument of repression and reaction, of denial and displacement that we have made it out to be, why would middle-class, liberal critics attack it with such vengeance? Moreover, why would some working-class readers in the Victorian period attribute to Wordsworth the power to help them realize their independence and recognize their right to reject and combat middle-class ideology? To answer these questions we need to re-engage the dialectic of Wordsworth's poetry and hence move beyond a critical moment that rightly countered a criticism that overemphasized the revolutionary qualities of Wordsworth's poetry, but only by neglecting to remember the real threat that such poetry posed to entrenched social and political interests in the early nineteenth century. In my view, we have yet fully to recognize the historicity and dialectical nature of Wordsworth's poetry. Cautiously engaging the spirit of the romantic attempt to reconcile opposites, I hope to move beyond the totalizing positions that tend to exaggerate Wordsworth's conservatism, on the one hand, and his radicalism, on the other. Instead, I hope to show that in its dialectic between ideology and utopia, reaction and revolution, Wordsworth's early poetry of encounter unsettles rather than affirms the conventional relations of production; it not only challenges its middle-class readers to recognize the basic humanity of the poor, but challenges its working-class readers to realize their right to an equal share of human dignity and political power.

I begin my approach to Wordsworth with an overview of the ways of seeing and speaking about poverty during the late eighteenth century. Setting the representations of the poor in the works of moral reformers, such as More and Malthus, alongside those of painters, such as Gainsborough and Wheatley, and poets, such as Cowper and Pratt, I identify the features of what one might call the "discourse on poverty." From these eighteenth-century versions of poverty, I turn to observe a transformation of the agrarian idyll—the mythic naturalization of poverty—as it enters into a new set of social and political relations in the 1790s. In the work of Crabbe and Wordsworth, in particular, the agrarian idyll takes on a critical, if not utopian, function and power which it is easy for contemporary readers to overlook.

To bring out the critical aspects of their poetry, I discuss the differences between eighteenth-century and early nineteenth-century representations of the poor in the poetry of Cowper and Wordsworth. This contrast focuses upon the shift in spatial perspective on the poor in the poetry of Cowper and Wordsworth and in the picturesque theory of William Gilpin and Uvedale Price. While many recent critics have discussed the politics of the picturesque, my chapter concentrates on the deepening of a move from high to low. While other critics have shown how the picturesque moves the eye from high to middle ground, I argue that Wordsworth's early poetry escorts the spectator to an even lower ground, so that in some of his poetry—as in "Resolution and Independence" or "Point Rash-Judgment"—the spectator becomes subject to the gaze of the indigent Other. Thus reversing the status of spectator and pauper, Wordsworth's liminal poetry places the privileged subjectivity and social status of the spectator into question—a subversive consequence, if not strategy, that I discuss at length in Chapter Three.

I turn in Chapters Three through Five to explore the dialectical possibilities of Wordsworth's sublime vagrants in the poetry of 1795 to 1802. Wordsworth's poetry participates in the essentially binary moral system that governs the discourse on poverty; this system divides the poor into the deserving and undeserving, based upon their relation to production. As I show, writers as diverse as Wollstonecraft and Crabbe relied upon "industriousness" as an ideologeme by which to signal the moral worth of their characters and as a guarantor of their readers' sympathy with such characters. While Wordsworth and Crabbe both criticize the habitual abuse of simple categories, such as idleness and industry, in promoting unfounded judgments about the poor and in maintaining a social distance between the poor and their benefactors, both poets nonetheless rely upon these categories to earn sympathy for their indigent characters. While Crabbe's poetry—somewhat contrary to our familiar way of thinking—interpellates the industrious poor as moral objects, Wordsworth's poetry facilitates a sympathetic identification between the reader—who is also enjoined to industry—and the industrious pauper. Indeed, in Wordsworth's poetry of encounter, rural industry becomes a sign of inclusion; the industriousness of the poor becomes a self-reflexive projection of middle-class values that complicates the relationship between the bourgeois reader and the rustic poor represented in the poetry. Contrary to social and poetic conventions, poems like *Salisbury Plain* and *The Ruined Cottage* refuse to blame indigence upon the laziness and profligacy of the poor, as Wordsworth's contemporaries were wont to do; and though the female vagrant, the discharged sailor, Margaret and Robert display the virtues of industry and forbearance expected of the poor, these poems locate the causes of destitution in social, political and economic conditions beyond the immediate control of the laboring poor. Therefore, although the discourse on poverty governs to some degree the representation of the poor in Wordsworth's poetry, it does not utterly negate Wordsworth's critique of the social conditions, events and policies that exacerbate poverty.

In turning to "Resolution and Independence," the focus of Chapter Four, I discuss Wordsworth's tendency—one might say compulsion—to seek out surrogate figures for the poet among marginal or liminal figures, like the leech gatherer. Wordsworth's vagrant muse, as I call it, is affiliated with the eighteenth-century invention of the English bard and minstrel tradition. Eighteenth-century antiquarian-critics link the native genius of the bard (including Homer) and the minstrel with "honest poverty," a critical move which leads to a new language of authenticity in the "artless tale" and to the popularity—albeit short-lived—of "peasant poetry." This cultural valuation of poverty as a sign of poetic truth and authenticity informs Wordsworth's identification with, and cultivation of, marginality and exile as a sign of value and affective power for the poet, an identification which reaches its greatest intensity in "Resolution and Independence."

In the old leech gatherer of "Resolution and Independence," Wordsworth creates a figuration of the socio-economic precariousness of the poet confronted with the uncertainties of the marketplace. The leech gatherer invites an uneasy identification between Wordsworth and the indigent leech gatherer, an identification that the poem tries to deny by attempting unsuccessfully to limn the leech gatherer's history into a timeless and indeterminate realm. The identification between Wordsworth and the leech gatherer, however, is not entirely negative. In the moral virtue and economic resilience of the leech gatherer Wordsworth discovers the values of the poet, himself marginalized in the anonymity of the literary marketplace, cut off from the localized charity of the system of patronage. Developing the associations between poverty and the authenticity of the poet begun in eighteenth-century depictions of Homer, the English bards and minstrels, Wordsworth claims for himself that empowering marginality familiar to later conceptions of the poet as exile from Baudelaire to the Beats.

From the question of literary identification, I turn in the next chapter to reexamine the problem of charity in "The Old Cumberland Beggar," a subject already explored by Edward Bostetter, Heather Glen, James Chandler, David Simpson and others. Rather more like Simpson than the other critics here, I take up the challenge to realize some utopian potential in what critics have perceived as Wordsworth's most blatantly condescending poem. Though the poem invokes an idealized agrarian community that recalls the imagined ease and sympathetic bonding of the "domestic affections" in a system of benevolent paternalism, it also serves as a good example of romantic anti-capitalism. Imagining the historical transformations taking place in the practices and policies of charity in England in the late eighteenth century, "The Old Cumberland Beggar" reads as a deliberate intervention into the debate over Poor Law reform and challenges the dehumanizing assumptions that underlie the social engineering envisioned by Malthus and Bentham. In the idealized economy of gift exchange that the old Cumberland beggar keeps in motion, the poem functions as a critique of the "progressive" reform of the Poor Laws that would transform the system of poor relief into an alienated form of commodity and cash exchange, a reform that would culminate in the hated Poor Law Amendment Act of 1834.

Wordsworth's critique of the Poor Law Amendment Act foreshadowed in "The Old Cumberland Beggar" anticipates my final chapter—a kind of historical postscript to those preceding—which discusses the fate of Wordsworth's polarized or dialectical "social text" among its nineteenth-century readers. Occupying various reading communities with different social agendas and political interests, these readers realized both the utopian and the reactionary potentialities of Wordsworth's poetry about the poor. In this all too brief essay, I begin to map out how different interpretive communities have recognized and actualized the polyvalence of Wordsworth's social text to serve quite incompatible political interests. While early reviewers were concerned with the accuracy of Wordsworth's representations of the poor, readers from the 1830s and beyond began to question how they could deploy Wordsworth's poetry as a guide to moral and social practices. Among some readers, such as the founders of the Wordsworth Society, which included Matthew Arnold, Wordsworth's text became a testament to deep religious and moral truth; to middle-class readers, like William Howitt and George Eliot, the same text served as a guide to moderate social reform and the moral transformation of the working class; to some working-class readers, like William Thomson, editor of *The Chartist Circular*, Wordsworth's text became an instrument in the struggle for political and human rights for the oppressed. In this final section, which I conceive of here as a preliminary sketch to inspire further research and study, I offer, then, some evidence that both the reactionary and the utopian potentials of Wordsworth's work have been recognized and realized in the discursive practices of its readers.

1

The Discourse on Poverty and the Agrarian Idyll in Late Eighteenth-Century England

It was a sweet view—sweet to the eye and the mind. English verdure, English culture, English comfort, seen under a sun bright, without being oppressive.

Jane Austen, Emma

Economic and social historians generally agree that the rise of population and the massive redistribution of land through private acquisition and enclosure between 1650 and 1800 took a heavy toll on the customary relations of production in the English countryside, largely to the detriment of those at the bottom two tiers of the classical triad of landlord, tenant farmer and landless wage earner making up the social landscape of rural England. Not that such loss was new to the late eighteenth century. According to Alan Armstrong's *Farmworkers in England and Wales*, recent research suggests that the major period of decline for tenant farmers in general took place between 1660 and 1760, when agricultural and land prices were low (34). During the reign of George III, when Parliamentary acts of enclosure were extensive (some 3,724 acts of enclosure between 1760–1829), rising prices helped to offset losses so that "dispossessed small farmers probably did not greatly augment the numbers competing for wage-paid employment in the agricultural sector" (35).

While this research usefully tempers the idealized view of early social historians such as the Hammonds, we must not let economic analysis alone serve as a measure of social and cultural perceptions and feelings. Armstrong concedes that wages were down in the latter half of the eighteenth century and that the experience and memory of farm laborers during this time would have led them to compare their lot unfavorably to the comparative "golden age" of their grandfathers (33). The recorded personal observations of those affected by change in rural England often belie the sweeping observations and statistical generalizations of economic history. Thus, as Armstrong observes, Samuel Lewthwaite of Cumberland could blame the enclosure of Skelton Common in 1770 and the consequent "destruction" of the commoners for a lack of increase in population; and Arthur Young, one of the foremost observers of agricultural life in England during this period, would complain in a letter of 12 June 1786 that "in many cases the poor had unquestionably been injured" (qtd. in Armstrong 37). As Dorothy Marshall observes in *Industrial England*, even the simplest changes could have considerable psychological impact upon those who saw outside forces transforming their way of life: "For many the shock of seeing the old landmarks and the old practices disappear was psychological rather than material . . . " (72). Losing the ability to keep "a pig, a few hens" or the right to collect wood from the commons, however immaterial from our point of view, would have "caused bitter resentment" among those who relied upon the commons to supplement their meager subsistence (73). Thus, if the many people between the ranks of tenant farmer and landless wage earner were not competely "swept away" in the force of economic and social change, as W. A. Armstrong would have it (88), the combined forces of population growth, loss of land, demand for wage labor and increasing prices nonetheless had a marked impact upon the lives of those at the margins. In Peter Mathias's cautious formulation, these forces "put great pressure on the small proprietors of land, the peasantry and those lower down the social structure in the countryside" (55).

Accompanying this extensive transformation of the socio-economic landscape of rural England was an equally extensive transformation of the habitus and sense of identity of those who occupied that landscape. Torn loose from the moral economies of agrarian society and assimilating values and everyday practices amenable to the new economic structure, those who lived and worked in the countryside struggled to adopt and adapt to new practical demands.[1] In "Patrician Society, Plebeian Culture," Thompson explains how the gentry became increasingly dependent upon a theatrics of power, as they withdrew from their customary and paternal responsibilities toward their tenants and laborers. As flat wages replaced such non-monetary perquisites, "economic rationalization nibbled (and had long been nibbling) through the bonds of paternalism" (384–85). While some gains were made in the relative independence of the laborers that such rationalization brought about, as Thompson notes, much of that independence amounted to little more than a new precariousness and uncertainty about their maintenance and subsistence (386).

Those who could not find adequate wage labor to substitute for their loss of customary tenant rights often found themselves among the growing ranks of rural or urban poor, many of whom turned to their parishes for support.[2] Demanding more money for support of its poor, each parish had to increase the burden upon its ratepayers. This heightened demand led to a proliferation of proposals for changes in the management and delivery of poor relief, still fundamentally structured by the Elizabethan Poor Law, which had been variously amended since its inception in acts passed from 1597 to 1601. No one, it seems, could escape the problem of poverty, leading the author of *A Compendium of the Laws Respecting the Poor* (1803) to declare that the nexus of poverty and the Poor Laws, "from the nature of the subject, affects in greater or smaller degree, almost every member of the community" (i).

As social and economic relations changed, so too did the cultural practices and myths that had supported the older system. From roughly 1760 onward, we can discern what Clifford Geertz calls a "flurry of semiotic activity" that erupts when major incongruities develop between social practices and the master narratives or discourses that naturalize or legitimate those practices. In the *Interpretation of Cultures* Geertz recognizes that in "these very discontinuities . . . we shall find some of the primary driving forces in change" (144). Burke's England serves as his example of a moment when the "hallowed opinions and rules of life come into question" and "the search for systematic ideological formulations, either to reinforce them or to replace them, flourishes" (218). In the various works that support, challenge, ignore or set up alternatives to reform the Poor Laws, one sees a proliferation of narratives about poverty and charity, many of which seem to be out of joint with the actual changes taking place. Confronted with new social and economic practices, some writers and artists sympathetic to the agricultural poor protested such changes in a reactionary insistence upon the integrity of the old ways; others more accepting of change attempted a dialectical adaptation or synthesis of the old to the new; while others, more rarely, introduced a new way of seeing and speaking about the rural countryside and its relations of production. The debates over poor relief, proposals for social reform, theories of political economy and population, and paintings and poetry about the rustic poor fall with great variety along this continuum between ideology and utopia, between situationally incongruent positions that either lag behind or anticipate social change (Mannheim 203). More often than not, however, as in the case of William Godwin, Thomas Gainsborough and William Wordsworth, to name but a few notable examples, ideological and utopian positions are present together in a kind of unstable relationship in the late eighteenth- and early nineteenth-century discourse on poverty.

For purposes of this analysis, we can isolate two major discursive strategies, both imbedded in the discourse on poverty and the overlapping "agrarian idyll," that produce this tension between ideology and utopia. The first, a strategy of containment rooted in the aristocratic conventions of the pastoral and the georgic, involves a "rustification" of poverty, a displacement of poverty into a scriptural space that attenuates its shock and violence. The second, a strategy of normalization rooted in middle-class conventions of capitalism and industry, involves the writing of values, like thrift, patience and industriousness, onto the working-class body. The cost of these strategies, however, was a blurring of social

boundaries. As agricultural labor violates the sacred *otium* of the aristocratic pastoral, the conventions separating the leisured from the laboring
orders begin to blur; as the poor appropriate thrift and industriousness
as positive values, confusion similarly arises about what separates the
"middling" from the "lower" orders. Thus in the discourse on poverty in
the late eighteenth century, the center and periphery marked out by
conventional poetic and social discourses collapse; distinctions blur as a
new scriptural economy keeps pace with the new moral and industrial
economy.

I

In the multitude of works directly or indirectly concerned with poverty,
writers from William Cowper and George Crabbe to Anna Barbauld
and Hannah More drew attention to, but at the same maintained their
distance from, the poor. As literacy grew among the working poor, a
morality industry emerged in Britain that attempted to foster better
social relations among the classes without disturbing the "subordination
of the ranks." Under the cloak of a socially integrating benevolence and
sympathy, many of these works enjoined the poor to become, in Burke's
words, "satisfied, laborious and obedient" and to recognize "that happiness that is to be found by virtue in all conditions" (*Reflections* 124).
While certain groups emerged specifically to address the issue of morality for the poor—such as the Sunday School Society (1785), the Society
for Bettering the Condition of the Poor (1796), and the National Society
(1809)—and while there was considerable disagreement over how, and
how far, to educate the poor and relieve their suffering, even the most
radical of reformers of the Poor Laws did not escape a paternalistic
sense of superiority over the "lower orders." Although Evangelical reformers such as Richard and Maria Edgeworth, Hannah More and Sarah Trimmer display their paternalism most blatantly and tendentiously,
even radical reformers such as Joseph Priestley, Richard Price, William
Godwin and Mary Wollstonecraft display a sort of unwitting acceptance
of, and satisfaction with, the subordination of the poor. With the more
conservative Evangelicals, radicals and reformers alike submit to the
prescriptive and condescending assumptions about the relations of production implicit in the discourse on poverty.

The debate over literacy that gained frequency after 1750, when
the need for a better educated, minimally literate, working class became
evident, offers a particularly revealing site from which to excavate both
the features and the ideological limitations of the discourse on poverty
governing the scriptural possibilities of both reactionaries and reformers. From 1750 through the early nineteenth century, lay and clerical
philanthropists founded numerous societies and schools, primarily to

educate the working classes in basic literacy and to inculcate in them those Christian values that would promote discipline and the habits of industriousness, self help and deference to authority—both religious and secular. There was even a proposal in Dr. Townson's *The Poor Man's Moralist* (1799) to engrave and paint moral slogans on the drinking jugs, saucers, handkerchiefs and other everyday items used by the working classes in order to deter the "depravity" of the poor and to remind them of their social station. As the *Anti-Jacobin Review* (1800) noted in its enthusiastic review of the fourth edition of Townson's work, this simple method of saturating the working-class mind with useful information would effect a symptomatic cure of the ills of poverty "without disturbing the present order of things" (208).

The middle classes, especially the Evangelicals, wanted to use education to keep the poor in a position of social subordination, while at the same time making them economically independent. One of the founding principles of the Sunday schools, for example, as stated in John Liddon's *General Religious Instruction* (1792), was to ensure that each individual learn "to fill up that place which Providence has assigned him," because "a well-instructed Christian peasantry will constitute the support and happiness of the nation" (qtd. in Laqueur 191). In *Sketches of the History of Man* (1802), Henry Home, Lord Kames, complains that charity schools, whose mission was primarily to teach religious piety, social deference and gratitude—hardly a radical agenda—would be "more hurtful than beneficial: young persons who continue there so long as to read and write fluently become too delicate for hard labour and too proud for ordinary labour" (2: 46). He goes on to explain that "knowledge is a dangerous acquisition to the labouring poor: the more of it that is possessed by a shepherd, a ploughman, or any drudge, the less fitted is he to labour with content" (2: 46). Similarly, Sarah Trimmer's *Reflections upon the Education of Children in Charity Schools* (1792) argues that the poor should receive only limited education to ensure they accept their place in society:

> [H]owever desirable it may be to rescue the lower kinds of people from that deplorable state of ignorance in which the greatest part of them were for a long time suffered to remain, it cannot be right to train them *all* in a way which will most probably raise their ideas above the very lowest occupations of life, and disqualify them for those servile offices which must be filled by some of the members of the community, and in which they may be equally happy with the highest, if they will do their duty. (7)

Despite her exceptional awareness of the social imbalance resulting from unequal education, in *The Oeconomy of Charity* (1787) Trimmer restricts the curriculum for the children of the poor; their instruction should prepare them "merely in such a knowledge of the English language as shall enable them to read the scriptures; in the plain duties of Christianity; and in those modes of conduct which their station requires" (37). Social intercourse between girls of different classes would reestablish "concord" and proper social subordination among the classes. Endorsing what Daniel Defoe called the "Great Chain of Subordination," Trimmer claims that the welfare of both rich and poor "depend[s] in a great measure on their mutual interchange of good offices, and [God] has ordained to each peculiar duties: to all in superior stations, justice, humanity, condescension and charity: to the poor, honesty, diligence, humility, and gratitude" (3–4). While admitting both reading and writing into her curriculum for the poor, Trimmer balks at any design to transform society: "Far be it from me to propose anything that may have a tendency to destroy the subordination of ranks, which is requisite in all civilized societies or to lessen the respect of the poor for their superiors" (60).

According to the Evangelicals, education would not only lead the poor to accept their station in life and give them the moral values and virtues recommended by their betters, it would also prevent them from falling prey to radical thought. As Thomas Bernard, a major supporter of the Society for Bettering the Condition of the Poor, puts it:

> [A]mid the tremendous convulsions which have for some time agitated Europe, let us reflect how much of the evil is to be attributed to an improvident neglect in the education of the poor; a neglect which has left them a defenceless prey to the sophistry and delusion of the teachers of infidelity, and of the disseminators of sedition. Ignorant, unprincipled, incapable of giving a reason for their faith, or of explaining the reason of civil order and society, to what miseries have not the poor in many parts of Europe been exposed. (66–67)

Similarly, in his *Treatise on Indigence*, Patrick Colquhoun, Glasgow merchant turned London police magistrate and a friend and follower of Jeremy Bentham, insists upon maintaining the social hierarchy even as he recommends a national system of education for the poor:

> Let it not be conceived for a moment, that it is the object of the author to recommend a system of education for the poor that shall pass the bounds of their condition in society. Nothing is aimed at beyond what is necessary to constitute a channel to religious and moral instruction. To exceed that point would be utopian, impolitic, and dangerous, since it would confound the ranks of society, upon which the general happiness of the lower orders, no less than that of those in more elevated stations, depends. (148)

As late as 1818 Robert Southey would summarize in similar terms the conventional reasons for educating the poor: "Give us an educated population—fed from their childhood with the milk of sound doctrine, not dry-nursed in dissent—taught to fear God and honor the king, to know their duty toward their fellow creatures and their creator . . ." (97).

Hannah More, whom J. C. D. Clark calls "a champion of the established order," believed that the poor should remain passive recipients rather than become producers of knowledge and opinion (*English Society* 246). More's Mrs. Jones of *The Sunday School*, one of the many mouthpieces for More's theories about education, attempts to get a subscription from the reluctant farmer Hoskins by explaining the political value of education for the poor: "I, farmer, think that to teach good principles to the lower classes, is the most likely way to save the country. Now, in order to do this we must teach them to read" (*Works* 1: 130). As for what they will read, Mrs. Jones assures the farmer that it won't be the "loose songs and ballads" such as those he has hung around his kitchen; it will be the Bible: "Now the whole extent of learning which we intend to give the poor, is only to enable them to read the Bible. . . . The knowledge of that book and its practical influence on the heart, is the best security you can have, both for the industry and obedience of your servants" (*Works* 1: 130). While agreeing that the poor needed to learn to read, More insisted that they receive no instruction in writing. As she explained to Dr. Beadon, Bishop of Bath and Wales: "My plan of instruction is extremely simple and limited. They learn, on week days, such coarse works as may fit them for servants. I allow of no writing for the poor. My object is not to make fanatics, but to train up the lower classes in habits of industry and piety" (*Memoirs of Hannah More* 2: 72).

While one would expect the ideologists of the morality industry to advocate industriousness, deference, duty and resignation for the poor, it is perhaps surprising to see the champions of reform taking up almost identical positions. Indeed, More's concern about full education for the poor found such unlikely sympathizers as Richard Price, Joseph Priestley, and even Mary Wollstonecraft. Steeped as they were in the principles of the French Enlightenment, these Dissenters and reformers saw education more often as a means of social control than as an instrument of genuine enlightenment for the poor. Although most of the Dissenting radicals wanted to raise the agricultural poor up from ignorance, most did not want to empower them to rise too high on the social ladder. While recommending the poor receive some education, for example, Priestley's *Miscellaneous Observations Relating to Education* (1778) would set a limit to that education in order to accommodate the poor to their station: "Advice to persons in the lowest classes of life, with respect to the education of their children, is necessarily limited to a few articles, such as a care to give them habits of industry, sobriety, honesty, and other virtues, and, if possible, to have them taught to read and write. For in their mode of life . . . they have very little to command" (59). Never recognizing that the social conditions governing the poor might lead to a substantial change in their living conditions or their livelihood, Priestley, like Trimmer, advocated merely an education that would teach the poor to accept their circumstances, if not with gratitude, at least with content. Priestley puts it this way:

> If . . . those who have the poorest prospects in life can be taught contentment in their station, and a firm belief in the wisdom and goodness of Providence that has so disposed of them, and consequently apply themselves with assiduity and cheerfulness to the discharge of their proper duties, they may be almost as happy, even in this world, as the most virtuous of their superiors, and unspeakably happier than the generality of them whose tempers and dispositions by no means suit their more exalted stations, and who have not virtue in proportion to their wealth. (*Observations* 29)

For both the moralists and reformers of the "middling orders," literacy was welcome as a means to inculcate specific values and behavior among the working poor, but only so long as limits were maintained upon that instruction in order to ensure social stability and avoid the dangerous threat of working-class dissension, if not insurrection. Trimmer, More and Priestley all share a common epistemological lens through which to view the poor; they draw upon a discourse which posits the middle classes as the superintendents of the poor, who must be kept temperate, industrious and deferent to their superiors.

As Jean Baudrillard claims in *The Mirror of Production*, despite its apparent opposition to capitalist modes of production, revolutionary discourse may reproduce the very forms it purports to critique. Moreover, the content of classical revolutionary (and one might add reformist) critique adopts productivity for its self-legitimation. Thus, Marx and Engels emphasized the productive potential of the post-revolutionary economy, just as early socialist thinkers, like Robert Owen, attempted to reorganize the means, only to serve the same ends, of economic production. In each case, the promise of some utopic community—posited as a Golden Age of the past or as a New Age to come—helped to frame and justify the political and economic transformations needed to build the new society. In the late eighteenth century, both apologists for and critics of the industrialization and capitalization of the English countryside found common ground in the virtue of labor, accepted as a kind of transcendent and undeniable value for people in any social class, but especially for those among the middling and lower orders. The industriousness of the poor was by far the primary concern of the middle-class moralists, who treated it as the key to all other virtues. As John Barrell has observed, in late eighteenth-century England " '[i]ndustry' was the chief virtue a poor man could display"; consumers of art and literature came to "demand," to use Barrell's term, industriousness as a premium feature in literary and aesthetic representations of the poor (*Dark Side* 20). From Joseph Townsend's *Dissertation upon the Poor Laws* (1786) to Frederick Eden's *The State of the Poor* (1797), Mary Wollstonecraft's *Original Stories from Real Life* (1788) to Hannah More's *Cheap Repository Tracts* (1795–98), William Wordsworth's *Lyrical Ballads* (1798) to George Crabbe's *The Parish Register* (1807), the moral and economic value of the poor was thus constructed in terms of a relation to production. The constitutive features of the good or "deserving" poor included preeminently their industriousness, followed by independence, honesty and deference to authority—religious, political and economic. Both "industry" and "independence"—perhaps better known to Wordsworth's contemporaries as "the spirit of independence"—appear in the discourse on poverty as *a priori* constituents of human worth, as natural and inevitable determinants of human value and dignity; yet each of these concepts registers only the value of persons in relation to some unspoken standard of productivity. The discourse on poverty masks the subvening sign of production, to which these categories defer, as it confers a premium upon the industrious poor: a sense of dignity. Generally considered to be productive members of society who would refuse to accept poor relief even under the most abject conditions, the industrious poor were considered, ironically, those who best deserved respect and charity from those who were not poor. The idle poor, on the other hand, those who could not or would not work, were considered to be the undeserving poor. Because the discourse on poverty named profligacy, drunkenness and licentiousness as the causes of all idleness, the "idle" poor were considered to be objects of contempt, were not eligible for private charity (which would only encourage their profligacy), and so fell upon the parish and the workhouse for a grudging relief. Thus, the industrious poor gained a privileged place in the discourse on poverty, an ontological sense of human value which naturalizes the socioeconomic calculus upon which it depends.

These binary and determinate categories within the discourse on poverty governed virtually every analysis and representation of the poor—both urban and rural—in the late eighteenth and early nineteenth centuries; and it is clear to anyone who has followed the discussion about homelessness in Europe and the United States that they persist even today. Throughout the eighteenth century, as William Hogarth's series of the "Idle and the Industrious Apprentice," Thomas Morland's series called "Industry and Idleness," and the publications of Hannah More and others through the Cheap Repository Tract Society suggest, cultural production operated to censure the idle and praise the industrious, spinning out endless warnings about the punishment for waste and the rewards for productivity. As More cautioned in her *Strictures on the Modern System of Female Education* (1799): "Life is but a short day; but it is a working day" (1: 117).

As moralists and reformers called upon the growing numbers of poor to eschew idleness and take upon themselves habits of industry, the poor soon found that appealing to their industry provided a quick source of legitimacy. Consequently, as Reinhard Bendix has noted, during the eighteenth century both "the workers and their spokesmen . . . made an emphatic distinction between the *idle* and the *industrious* poor, and . . . stressed the major contribution which the latter made to the welfare of the nation" (40). Nonetheless, while the many works praising benevolent paternalism emphasized the cheerful, wholesome and economically beneficial labor of the rustic poor, the actual value of their industriousness was beginning to change. As industrial practices triumphed over customary moral economies, the emphasis upon hard work gave way to an emphasis upon worker output. As Bendix observes, the "claim to recognition" conferred upon and expected by the industrous worker, "who shunned the sin of indolence even as he accepted the burden of poverty," began to erode with the advance of industrialization (40). That is, workers came to be valued less for their industriousness and more for their industrial output, less for the ontological value of their labor and more for the economic values of the commodities they produced. Moreover, as poverty was less often attributed to the inevitable, natural and necessary workings of Providence and more to the purported profligacy and idleness of the poor themselves, the role of charity and poor relief came more sharply into question. Overall, in the wake of the age of benevolence and reform, a harsher, more cynical view of the poor began to displace the paternalistic, but tolerant, view of the poor as a group whose want was decreed by Providence and whose needs should be supplemented by their economic, if not moral, superiors.

Of course, even the providential legitimation of poverty did not prevent its practitioners from appearing callous and coldhearted, as the notorious case of Soame Jenyns proves. In *A Free Inquiry into the Nature and Origin of Evil* (1756), Jenyns argues that God created poverty as the natural condition for those at the lower rungs of the social ladder. Since poverty was necessary, Jenyns's infamous argument goes, any intervention to abolish it or improve the living conditions and especially the understanding of the poor threatened to break apart the social fabric. Like Trimmer and More after him, Jenyns recommends only a strictly limited degree of literacy for the poor, since, in his words: "Ignorance, or the want of knowledge and literature, the appointed lot of all born to poverty, and the drudgeries of life, is the only opiate capable of infusing that insensibility which can enable them to endure the miseries of the one, and the fatigues of the other" (34). Carrying his argument so far as to suggest that the well-to-do should therefore accept the benefits they gain from the disadvantage of the laboring poor, Jenyns of course provoked the wrath of Samuel Johnson, who attacked Jenyns's blatant callousness in the *Literary Magazine* (1757). Nonetheless, despite Johnson's thorough thrashing of the treatise, Jenyns's view of poverty as the natural and inevitable, God-given condition of the laboring poor continued to surface throughout the late eighteenth century, most notably in popular works like Jonas Hanway's *Virtue in Humble Life* (1774), William Paley's *Reasons for Contentment* (1792), Hannah More's stories and poems in *Cheap Repository Tracts* (1795–98), and Edmund Burke's *Thoughts and Details on Scarcity* (1795), among many others.

In his *Natural Theology* (1802), Paley explained that "the poor, that is, they who seek their subsistence by constant manual labor, must still form the mass of the community; otherwise the necessary labor of life could not be carried on; the work would not be done, which the wants of mankind, in a state of civilisation, and still more in a state of refinement, require to be done" (284). Though the unequal distribution of property, according to Paley's *Principles of Moral and Political Philosophy* (1785) is an evil, "it is an evil, which flows from those rules, concerning the acquisition and disposal of property, by which men are incited to industry, and the object of their industry is made secure and valuable" (95). Thus Paley, like Malthus and Townsend affiliates the doctrine of providential poverty with an account of the political economy of poverty. In *Natural Theology*, he writes: "A world furnished with advantages on one side, and beset with difficulties, wants, and inconveniencies on the other, is the proper abode of free, rational, and active natures, being the fittest to stimulate and exercise their faculties" (276). Moreover, like the natural law theorists, Paley links poverty to the pressures of population: "Mankind will in every country breed up to a certain point of distress," in which provision "will pass beyond the line of plenty and will continue to increase till checked by the difficulty of procuring subsistence. Such difficulty therefore, along with its attendant circumstances, must be found in every old country: and these circumstances constitute what we call poverty, which necessarily imposes labor, servitude, restraint" (*Natural Theology* 276–77). For these writers, to use Barrell's phrase, poverty is "nothing else than the stimulus provided by God to our industry and self-improvement" (*Dark Side* 86).

Nonetheless, though Paley's doctrine of property legitimates the gap between rich and poor as the inevitable workings of Providence, Paley believes that no person should be denied "a sufficiency for his subsistence, or the means of procuring it" (*Principles* 203). This right to subsistence is founded upon natural law, in that the division of the commons "was made and consented to, upon the expectation and condition, that every one should have left a sufficiency for his subsistence, or the means of procuring it" (*Principles* 203). Thus, Paley enjoined those who were not poor to assist those who were: "When the partition of propriety is rigidly maintained against the claims of indigence and distress, it is maintained in opposition to the intention of those who made it, and to his, who is the Supreme Proprietor of every thing, and who has filled the world with plenteousness for the sustenation and comfort of all whom he sends into it" (*Principles* 203–4). Paley, then, represents a kind of compromise between benevolent paternalism and natural law theory, for he is unwilling to abandon the poor to their own deserts. Others, like Malthus and Townsend, had few qualms about dismissing society's responsibility to the poor.

Malthus placed the burden of welfare not on the rich but squarely on the poor themselves. As he puts it in the second edition of the *Essay on Population* (1803), "they [the poor] are themselves the cause of their poverty; . . . the means of redress are in their own hands and in the hands of no other persons whatever" (qtd. in Himmelfarb 118). Townsend's *A Dissertation on the Poor Laws* also reflects the harsher attitude that we see in Malthus and that came to dominate the view of political economists up through the time of the New Poor Law. For Townsend,

> It seems to be a law of nature, that the poor should be to a certain degree improvident, that there may always be some to fulfill the most servile, the most sordid, and the most ignoble offices in the community. The stock of human happiness is thereby much increased, whilst the more delicate are not only relieved from drudgery, and freed from those occasional employments which would make them miserable, but are left at liberty, without interruption, to pursue those callings which are suited to their various dispositions, and most useful to the state. (35)

Townsend believed that hunger was Providence's greatest incentive to put the poor dutifully to work, and he advises legislators that poverty works to affirm the natural bonds and obligations of society, among the first of which "stands the relation of a servant to his master" (26). "The first duty required from a servant," Townsend explains, "is prompt, chearful, and hearty obedience" (26), and in order to get that obedience no more effective incentive exists than hunger: "The wisest legislator will never be able to devise a more equitable, a more effectual, or in any respect a more suitable punishment, than hunger is for a disobedient servant. Hunger will tame the fiercest animals, it will teach decency and civility, obedience and subjection, to the most brutish, the most obstinate, and the most perverse" (27).

As I will discuss further in Chapter Four, Malthus's *Essay on the Principle of Population* (1798) also argues that want is a great incentive to labor and to genius. Malthus reverts to the language of physico-

theology—as he puts it, reasoning "from nature up to nature's God"—
for his vindication of poverty:

> This view of the state of man on earth will not seem to be
> unattended with probability, if, judging from the little experi-
> ence we have of the nature of mind, it shall appear, upon investi-
> gation, that the phenomena around us, and the various events
> of human life, seem peculiarly calculated to promote this great
> end [the development of the human mind]: and especially, if,
> upon this supposition, we can account, even to our own narrow
> understanding, for many of those roughnesses and inequalities
> in life, which querulous man too frequently makes the subject of
> his complaint against the God of nature. (356)

Want, then, in Malthus's final analysis, "[c]ould not be withdrawn from
the mass of mankind without producing a general and fatal torpor, destructive of all the germs of future improvement" (359). Since one of the
"gracious designs of Providence" that keeps the social machine in motion is the principle of population developing faster than food supply,
"want and its consequent misery are the desolation and waste necessary
to stimulate industry and even imagination" (361). In this context, Arthur Young's infamous and Bounderby-like injunction stands out as only
a rather more straightforward, or one of the more brutally blunt, examples of this pervasive doctrine: "Everyone but an Idiot knows that the
lower class must be kept poor or they will never be industrious" (qtd. in
Jarrett 80).

Young's anxiety about the increasing possibility that through
their works the poor (meaning in the eighteenth century anyone who
had to work for a living; that is, by logical extension, anyone whose
wealth did not derive from some form of landed property) might move
up out of their station shows the degree to which he both understood
and feared the power of a new economic system to disrupt the fixities
of the old. The only way to keep the poor "in their place" (and so keep
the natural aristocrat in his) was to deny them wages that would allow
them to exchange their labor or the products of their labor for new
social positions that would destabilize the chain of subordination—that
system of permanent, as opposed to temporal, identities. If labor is no
longer simply a productive activity but a commodity that can be bought
and sold, or withheld at will to renegotiate its value, the once naturalized social hierarchy is exposed as arbitrary and subject to unpredictable mutation. Moreover, the laborer—or, more powerfully and
threateningly, a collective entity of united laborers—is now free to
contest his or her relationship with his or her former master. In
the controversy surrounding Burke's *Reflections on the Revolution in
France* (1790), a reviewer of Wollstonecraft's *A Vindication of the*

Rights of Man (1791) raises the spectre of just such a scenario. In *The Gentleman's Magazine* (February 1791), we read: "The Scripture every where keeps up the distinction of rich and poor; but Mrs. W's millenium is to restore mankind to the level of the golden age" (153). The reviewer accuses Wollstonecraft and other radical reformers of intending "to poison and inflame the minds of the lower class of his Majesty's subjects to violate their subordination and obedience" (154). In *Thoughts and Details on Scarcity* (1795), Burke made his own reply to the radical reformers, affirming the need for subordinance and obedience among the poor, whose condition of poverty cannot, indeed should not, be helped. Burke writes: "We, the people, ought to be made sensible, that it is not by breaking the laws of commerce, which are the laws of nature, and consequently the laws of God, that we are to place our hope of softening the Divine displeasure to remove any calamity under which we suffer" (*Works* 7: 404). To show that he meant what he said, Burke advocated small charity to the laboring poor, but he would tolerate no public protest over their abject conditions: "Let compassion be shown in action . . . but let there be no lamentation of their condition. It is no relief to their miserable circumstances; it is only an insult to their miserable understanding. . . . Patience, labor, sobriety, frugality, and religion, should be recommended to them; all the rest is downright fraud. It is horrible to call them 'The *once happy* labourer' " (*Works* 7: 377–78).

This fear of social insubordination prompted not only a rain of aspersions on Wollstonecraft and others, but numerous appeals for landlords to restore their customary practice of benevolent paternalism. The benevolent landlord and his grateful industrious laborer were conspicuous figures of the agrarian idyll as it approached the contested field of politics in the 1790s. From George Crabbe's encomium in Book II of *The Village* (1783) on the benevolent Duke of Rutland, to Hannah More's *Thoughts on the Importance of the Manners of the Great to General Society* (1788), to the precious panegyrics to aristocratic benevolence in Samuel Jackson Pratt's *Bread, or the Poor* (1801), the doctrine of *in loco parentis* was peddled as an insurance against instability. Interpellating the laborer as a natural subordinate to the natural aristocrat, such works testified to a growing if repressed awareness that such was not indeed the case. Thus the agrarian idyll became increasingly bound up with nostalgic revisions of the feudal past, which led eventually to the more conservative elements of what Robert Sayre and Michael Löwy in "Figures of Romantic Anticapitalism" call "restitutionist romanticism" (40), characterized by an uncritical nostalgia for pre-capitalist socio-cultural formations that saw its greatest flowering in the Young England movement of the 1840s—itself born out of the crisis between labor and capital—with its relish for chivalric spectacle and romantic feudalism.

II

The determinate categories of industry and idleness and the binary structure of industrialist morality upon which they depend cross over the boundaries between the social, aesthetic and economic spheres. In literature, art, social treatises and popular middle-class journals, the discourse on poverty informed both aesthetic and social practice, not only creating an idealized pauper for popular aesthetic consumption, but also setting up the criteria by which to judge the actual poor. While many works concerning the rural poor criticized the colonization of the countryside by urban and industrial values and practices, the attempt to rescue the traditional values of the country by isolating them in a rustic landscape and by emphasizing the industriousness, thrift and contentment of the rural poor actually helped to fix those industrial values onto the body of the rural working poor. Indeed, by inscribing industriousness—or its obverse, idleness—as the premier value of the poor, the discourse on poverty placed the rustic poor under a yoke of production. Even as painters and writers drew upon the myth of the countryside as a sanctuary of stability and simplicity, they were incorporating into the inhabitants of that ostensible site of repose values congruent with the industrialism and capitalism to which they were often opposed. Thus, the familiar representations of both the urban and rural poor demonstrate the interdependent strategies of containment and normalization.

Ann Bermingham observes in *Landscape and Ideology* that "when the countryside—or at least large portions of it—was becoming unrecognizable, and dramatically marked by historical change, it was offered as the image of the homely, the stable, the ahistorical" (9). Yet the thrifty and industrious plowmen, milkmaids and laborers who occupied those homely spaces in the paintings of Thomas Gainsborough, the prints of Francis Wheatley, the poems of Samuel Jackson Pratt and the tales of Maria Edgeworth served to embody in idealized and sentimentalized forms the very work discipline from which the country was to be a refuge. The precious scenes of domestic bliss, cheerful toil and beatific simplicity that characterize the representations of the poor in Gainsborough, Wheatley, Pratt and Edgeworth, to name only a few, portray English rural life as a kind of indigenous Eden. As Barrell has observed of Gainsborough, this idyllic portrait of rural harmony satisfied "a demand to see the rural life portrayed as it ought to be, decent and edifying, even if it is not" (*Dark Side* 63). With notable exceptions like Thomas Bewick and George Morland, who produced more realistic representations of the poor, writers and artists after 1760 drew upon a complex set of iconographic and narrative strategies that constitute what Mikhail Bakhtin calls the agrarian idyll in order to depict the rural poor as pleasing objects for aesthetic gratification or as instructive objects for moral edification. Indeed, as the numbers of urban and rural poor increased and became more troublesome, a polished, second-order spectacle of poverty began to absorb the attention of the polite classes. With a wide array of simulated poverty designed to meet their expectations for an image of a cheerful, healthy and contented peasantry, the polite classes could indulge both their curiosity about and sympathy for the poor in a pleasing spectacle of rustic poverty without troubling themselves too much about the actual conditions of the poor.

In landscape painting, genre painting, popular prints and literary works, the harsher outlines of poverty faded into the background or were obscured by highly stylized and sentimental portraits of the poor, such as Gainsborough's and Wheatley's. As Sean Shesgreen has recently observed in his *The Criers and Hawkers of London*, the moralized and sanitized spectacle of poverty for which Gainsborough and Wheatley came to be celebrated replaced the more graphic realism of down-to-earth observations of the poor like those found in Marcellus Laroon's *Cryes of the City of London* (1687). Indeed, the fate of Laroon's *Cryes* in the hands of its eighteenth-century publishers provides a graphic example of the way in which the agrarian idyll held sway over the visual arts in late eighteenth-century England.

Shesgreen documents the conversion of Laroon's *Cries* from a series of realistic images of street criers into a collection of highly stylized and sentimental portraits targeted for the children's book market. Henry Overton published four editions of Laroon's *Cryes* in their original form between 1711 and 1733. When Robert Sayer took possession of the Overton firm in 1751, he acquired the plates for Laroon's *Cryes* and decided to publish them in altered form as a six-part serial. Under the direction of Sayer, Laroon's stark depictions of London street vendors and paupers with their hard, black-and-white outlines were transformed into pretty pictures for the consumption, as Shesgreen speculates, of "bourgeois uncles" who bought the book "as a gift—typically avuncular—for their nieces" (42). Sayer's alterations to the plates were substantial. The ragged clothes of the vendor women were replaced with finer yet more revealing garments; the stark white backgrounds to each vendor were filled in with conventional landscapes; and verbal allusions to anything that might offend young ladies' taste, such as the plates of "The London Curtezan" and "Madame Creswell," were deleted.[3]

"Dainty Sweet Nosegays" (Plate 1) demonstrates the bucolic quality of Sayer's alterations. The highly conventionalized landscape obliterates completely Laroon's depiction of the bleakness and emptiness of urban poverty, substituting instead a rustic poverty that better suited the eighteenth-century consumer's sensibility. In an inversion of Wordsworth's formula in the *Prelude* (1850) of "by distance ruralised" (1.89), the ragged street crier is ruralised into distance; that is, the highly

N.º 1. Part 2. of the London Cries.— in 12 Prints.

F. Boucher Del: *P. Angier S.*

Dainty Sweet Nosegays.

Printed for Rob.t Sayer opposite Fetter Lane Fleet Street.

Plate 1: "Dainty Sweet Nosegays."
Robert Sayer, *The Cries of London, in Six Parts* (after Marcellus Laroon).
Courtesy of The Lilly Library, Indiana University, Bloomington, Indiana.

idiosyncratic street characters of Laroon's original plates become "types and emblems," to invoke Wordsworth again, of a generalized idea of Poverty. The female criers, well illustrated by "Dainty Sweet Nosegays," were made to conform to what might be called the trope of rustic décolletage. While overt allusions to female sexuality were expunged, the women vendors were made to be more erotic with enhanced busts and lowered necklines. Such eroticized images apparently appealed to the convention of the bashful coyness of the English country girl, a convention both parodied and popularized by John Gay's *The Shepherd's Week* and which, as Barrell has noted, had become a fixture of "the comic ideal of rural life" by the middle part of the eighteenth century (*Dark Side* 58). Barrell notes that dating from the publication of *The Shepherd's Week*, "the countryside of England was . . . considered to be populated by desirable girls who, though they might be hoped to distribute their favours with some freedom, did so with a bashful sincerity which added to their charm . . ." (*Dark Side* 58). Although Sayer kept what poet John Scott calls the "cottage Marians, in their torn array" (qtd. in Barrell 63) to titillate the male buyers of Laroon's heavily revised suite, such suggestive figures presumably were not intended to serve as models for the young ladies who ultimately received the book.

In their rustification of poverty Sayer's revisions to Laroon's *Cryes* take part in a larger network of aesthetic and literary representations of the poor at the close of the eighteenth century. Sayer's alterations to Laroon's prints appeal to conventions drawn from the agrarian idyll and point forward to the pastoral sentimentality of paintings like Reynolds's *The Cottagers* (1788), Gainsborough's cottage scenes of the 1780s, and Wheatley's *Cries of London* and even more bucolic *Four Times of the Day* (1799). As with these works, Sayer's revisions to Laroon's *Cryes* place urban poverty into a rural setting, where its harder edges can be blunted, where the spectator's eye—hardly offended by the elegant simplicity of the reconstituted costermongers—can find relief or refuge by fixing on the landscape. Shesgreen rightly says, "With these precious, insipid, and highly finished prints, the ensemble abandons the depiction of city life and embraces the pastoral. . . . In espousing the arcadian and the bucolic, the suite becomes a document in the history of artistic banality, anticipating by a short time Francis Wheatley's influential *Cries of London*, the nadir of the genre" (41). This nadir is marked by the lack of any effort to depict the poor realistically and an attempt to glut the market with confectionary images of sentimentalized poverty to satisfy the growing late eighteenth-century taste for paupers shorn of their dirt and rags—in the terms of Anna Barbauld, shorn of "their squalor and mean employments" ("Inquiry" 222). Wheatley's "Two bunches a penny primroses, two bunches a penny" (Plate 2) portrays the eroticized country Marian in a vignette that evokes the childhood innocence and domestic simplicity associated with the countryside.

Plate 2: "Two bunches a penny primroses, two bunches a penny."
Francis Wheatley, *The Cries of London*; engraved by L. Schiavonetti. By
permission from The Huntington Library, San Marino, California.

Even in the engraving we can see how the chiaroscura heightens the contrast between country and city as the light falls on the cherubic faces of the young woman, her brother and sister, with their baskets of wild-flowers. The urban landscape, itself stylized, recedes in the shadowy background; a dichotomy is established between the mechanical auster-ity of the city and the organic bloom of the country. Even an early twentieth-century critic could be moved to fancy by such examples of what he called Wheatley's "fragrant pictures . . . where there is no sug-gestion of crowd or noise, no woman or girl who is not comely, the girls, in fact, all appealingly pretty, and even the men having a tendency to good looks . . ." (Salaman 252). Stripped of any suggestion of squalor, crime or pain, Wheatley's *Cries* pointedly elicit such emotional re-sponses to the poor and so impede any critical move to register their suffering or account for their poverty.

The most extreme solution to the problem of the representation of poverty may be found in the picturesque injunctions to strictly regu-late the kinds of poor to be included in painting, or, as in Humphry Repton's "View from my own Cottage, in Essex" before and after "pic-turesque improvement" (Plates 3 and 4), to banish it altogether. Notice again how the ruralization, that is, the picturesque improvement, of the landscape here imposes a safe distance between the spectator's vantage point and the bustle of the village street. Although the other figures remain in the "improved" version of the picture, the beggar—most likely a wounded soldier or sailor given his wooden leg and the patch over his eye—does not appear at all. Repton's picturesque improvement amounts to a kind of willful denial: where poverty cannot be seen it must not be. While the picturesque presents a special case, which I will dis-cuss at length in Chapter Two, Repton's radical proposal to contain the spectator in a prettified landscape that serves to remove him or her from the embarrassment of beggars and the ugliness of poverty is the logical conclusion of the move to beautify the poor. Absence, in this case, is the ultimate beauty—the most picturesque of all treatments of poverty.

As John Barrell, Ann Bermingham, Carol Fabricant and Alan Liu have shown, the naturalization of poverty in picturesque or rustic scenes constitutes a "politics of landscape," part of which involves the agrarian idyll with its call to beautify poverty and distance the reader and spectator from the actual poor by means of banishing poverty alto-gether, obscuring poverty beneath a Claudean veneer of sentimental scenery, or, as I will discuss below, affiliating poverty with labor.[4] With these strategies, or any combination of them, these cultural works substi-tute a second order of poor—a simulated spectacle of poverty—for any actual encounter with the poor. The aggregate simulacra that constitute this spectacle bear the values that those who are not poor themselves impose upon the poor. Hence the "deserving poor" as represented in art and literature become the heroes and heroines of the sentimental novel,

Plate 3: "View from my own Cottage, before Picturesque Improvement." Humphry Repton, *Fragments on the Theory and Practice of Landscape Gardening.* By permission from The Huntington Library, San Marino, California.

Plate 4: "View from my own Cottage, after Picturesque Improvement." Humphry Repton, *Fragments on the Theory and Practice of Landscape Gardening*. By permission from The Huntington Library, San Marino, California.

the noble cottagers in the paintings of Gainsborough and Wheatley, and, as we will see, the happy laborers in the poetry of Cowper, Gray and Crabbe.[5] The "undeserving poor" become the beggars, the gypsies and the idle clowns. In these figures we see the prototypes for the vagrant and industrious poor in Wordsworth's poetry, though as I hope to show, Wordsworth's representation of the poor sometimes disrupts the comfortable position of the reader or spectator of poverty. Even as it invokes many strategies of the agrarian idyll, Wordsworth's poetry often moves up close to the poor, leaving behind a troubling sense that this visit to the Other enacts a return of the repressed—a confrontation with more than just a spectacle of poverty, but with an empowered pauper who holds a mirror up to the reader's own impoverishment.

III

While the agrarian idyll distances the spectator or reader from the place of poverty, substituting for actual social conditions a composite image of rural England as a place of social harmony, fulfilling labor and blissful simplicity, it simultaneously confers an ontological value upon the idealized inhabitants of that indigenous Eden. More broadly, the agrarian idyll serves as one of the primary topoi of the broader movement of romantic anti-capitalism sweeping Europe in the early nineteenth century. As it transforms the working subject into a mythic and transcendental subject, and as it naturalizes the relations of production in the countryside as timeless and essential processes of nature, the agrarian idyll confers upon the rural poor a sense of human dignity and registers its disenchantment with the burgeoning commodity culture invading its rustic sanctuary. In its most conservative forms, the agrarian idyll serves the interests of the past, inventing a golden or green age of England against which to try what it posits as the disjunctions and alienation taking place in the present. In its more utopian forms, the agrarian idyll anticipates the liberation of the agricultural laborer from the aristocratic gaze that denies his or her right to self-determination and bars his or her access to political power.[6] Thus, the agrarian idyll, however fraught with ideological contradictions that temper and even threaten to disable its potential, actively criticizes (and even exaggerates) the forces of depopulation, industrialization and alienation as it sometimes moves toward the recognition of agricultural laborers and farmers as people with real political as well as human rights, as people whose histories and stories are worthy of attention and respect.

As the social value of the epithets "honest poverty" and "industrious poor" began to decline within the practical discourse of the industrializing political economy, their nostalgic and critical value began to increase.[7] In the cultural productions of the late eighteenth century the moral economy of pre-industrial England gained force as a critique, however contradictory it may be, of industrialization. Indeed, the structural economic changes that disturb the tacit assumptions of social place and the legitimations of hierarchy affect the way in which what were once perceived as politically neutral cultural formations—e.g., the pastoral—are read. Barrell, for example, has discussed the way that the agrarian idealism in Goldsmith's *The Deserted Village* became increasingly less acceptable (more threatening) to its English readers among the polite classes, especially after the 1790s, when the English poor were seen as a potentially radical body. In the 1790s, as Barrell suggests, the "pastoral vision of society"—an egalitarian image of agricultural rest or rustic ease—was increasingly incompatible with the polite classes' need to put all of England to work. In discussing the few proposals for the redistribution of land along egalitarian lines—Robert Wallace's *A Dissertation on the Numbers of Mankind*, (1753), William Ogilvie's *The Right of Property in Land* (1781), and William Godwin's *Political Justice* (1793)—Barrell writes:

> It seems in fact that the polite classes in the eighteenth century had no fear of such notions making much headway among the poor until the 1790s; that to write approvingly of them in the polite literature—where an agrarian egalitarianism appears either as an imagined original, as in Goldsmith's poem, or as a theoretical or remote ideal—was more or less acceptable till then; and that only from about the 1790s could *The Deserted Village* be read as a radical poem which pointed (by implication) to the future as well as to the past. (*Dark Side* 82)

Because the pastoral vision was perceived as a threat and because it could be "appropriated as a radical ideology" (*Dark Side* 81), increasingly it was displaced by a more politically acceptable georgic (or Georgian) vision of agricultural labor.

One can speak, then, at least after 1790, of a critical nostalgia, a possible revisionist reading and a new writing of pastoral and georgic that redeploys their conventional epithets and ideologemes—"cheerful toil," "rustic simplicity," the "Noble Savage"—as a vision of not just social harmony, but social equality and political justice. This critical nostalgia is placed into the service of works largely critical of the industrial transformation of English society, such as Goldsmith's *The Deserted Village* and Wordsworth's *The Ruined Cottage* and *Home at Grasmere*. Rather like a melodic line played against a harmonic background that has shifted from, say, the major Ionian mode to a minor mode like the Dorian, these pastoral epithets or ideologemes evoke a more foreboding atmosphere and suggest far different ideas than formerly. From ringing in the dominant ideology of a natural aristocracy, these terms now sound the contradictions and displacements of a culture whose socio-economic and cultural grounds are radically disjointed. While such epithets may be—and are—criticized for pointing backward to a golden age of benevolent paternalism that never existed, the critically constructive and utopic function of such epithets and motifs should not, as they have largely been, simply impugned or ignored. Indeed, the latent content of a golden or green England, while a nostalgic vision of a mythic and invented past, enables but does not necessitate a utopic vision of the future.

In *Ideology and Utopia*, Karl Mannheim suggests that utopian constructs may call attention to what he calls the "discrepancy . . . between the traditional mode of thought and the novel objects of experience" in a society undergoing change (101). While we cannot ignore that it was often used, as in Goldsmith's *Deserted Village*, by Tory writers whose primary concern was the incursion of new money into the reserved spaces formerly held fast by a relatively fixed landed aristocracy, in its stark antipathy to and reaction against the industrial transformation of England, the agrarian idyll of late eighteenth-century pastoral/georgic at least points to the harmful effects of capitalist expansion, both in the country and in the city, even as it often fails to posit a viable alternative.[8]

Although the idealized pauper or laborer may have been to some readers a sentimental repository of affective power or a sign of the laboring class under the control of an idealized natural aristocracy, this same pauper or laborer embodied those virtues and values that in fact enabled the working poor to form a political consciousness of self-worth and to achieve some portion, however small, of effective power. While the sentimental portrayals of rural simplicity in Gainsborough, Goldsmith, Cowper, Pratt, Wordsworth and even "peasant poets" like Collier, Clare, Bloomfield and Yearsley, may have blinded some readers to the problems of rural poverty or reinforced for others an ideology of labor, these portrayals encouraged some readers to acknowledge the human worth of the rural poor, to recognize the suffering and hardship they endured as a result of socio-economic practices, and perhaps even to act in behalf of the poor to protect their human rights and sense of dignity. In particular, in the works of William Wordsworth, the agrarian idyll posits a romantic alternative to the capitalization of agriculture which challenges the assumptions of industrial ideology and the new habits of work discipline even as it reinforces some of industrialism's basic, and we might add, bourgeois, values.

If Wordsworth's work does not present an exhaustive analysis of the industrial practices that threatened to value human beings as commodities for exchange in a marketplace of labor, we might remember that the conditions for a materialist critique of the new industrial relations were hardly in place in time for Goldsmith, Crabbe and

Wordsworth, among others, to achieve the kind of rigorous and dialectical awareness that we associate with economic and sociological analysis. At least since Friedrich Engels's *Anti Dühring* and the 1880 pamphlet derived from that work, *Socialism: Utopian and Scientific*, cultural critics have recognized that certain economic conditions and the visible class struggles of the 1830s in England and France were necessary to move socialist critique from its early phase of utopian longing to its later phase of materialist critique.[9] To ask for more is to engage in a kind of romantic ideology and an ahistoricism: to ask the poet to be a prophetic visionary who not only escapes wholly the ideological limitations of her or his time, but basks in the sun of the postmodernist present to return as a revisionary priestess or priest to illuminate the caves of a pre-Marxist moment.

Rather than a prolepsis of a poststructuralist or postmodernist critique (with all the advantages of hindsight) of the turbulent socioeconomic changes taking place in the moment of its production, what we might expect from late eighteenth- and early nineteenth-century poetry may be something more like the *presentiment* of what Bloch dubs the "utopian function." Chastened, if not restrained, by the concrete material conditions of its historical moment, the anticipatory gaze of poets must grasp the actual potentials of the contingent material conditions in which they are placed. A poetry of hope, not fantasy, in other words, must embrace the limits, as well as the imaginable horizons, of possibility. The "positive utopian function," in Bloch's terms, is the *active* substance of a desire for transcendence whose wings are kept trimmed by a conscious embracing of its *historical* substance— "human culture referred to its concrete utopian horizon" (*Principle of Hope* 1: 146). While Bloch argues that the positive utopian function emerges from the dialectical interplay of subjective and objective factors within a particular nineteenth-century discourse, we can adapt Bloch's and Mannheim's concepts here to ascertain the degree to which Goldsmith, Crabbe and Wordsworth embrace their own historicity as they construct, by positive construction or negative critique, their own utopian imaginings. We may ask, do these poets deploy a critique of industrialization that is merely fanciful and nostalgic, a kind of empty supplement or atavistic excess, or do they indeed anticipate in their work a potential transformation latent in the aggregate materiality of their own historical moment? In their romantic turn toward the past, what latent utopian possibilities remain as an unconscious, unrealized surplus? As I will argue, despite the historical displacement of Wordsworth's work so well demonstrated by Levinson, Liu, McGann and Simpson, among others, some of Wordsworth's poems clearly engage their history and allow later readers—even working-class readers—to appropriate their utopian potentials and romantic anti-capitalism in the interests of progressive change.

IV

As Hugh Sykes Davies believes, there is much, even in the so-called "experiment" of the *Lyrical Ballads*, in Wordsworth's poetry "which belonged, with some characteristic but minor differences, to the traditional modes of poetry of the eighteenth century . . ." (193). As we have seen and as Barrell discusses at length in *The Dark Side of the Landscape*, two of those traditional modes of poetry in particular, the pastoral and the georgic, governed the representation of the rural poor in poetry, just as the conventions of landscape and genre painting determined the appropriate use of rustic figures in painting. The social and juridical categories that distinguished the poor into two basic groups—the industrious and the idle—infiltrate the eighteenth-century pastoral and georgic loco-descriptive poem or painting to become determinate features of the industrious laborer, the beggar, vagrant, gypsy or bandit. In many ways, the silent vagrants of Wordsworth's *Lyrical Ballads*, the beggars, pedlars and discharged soldiers, with their "artless tales" and measured speech, serve as paradigmatic examples of those indigent deemed worthy of charity according to the principles set down by Steele, Smith, Townsend and others, who wanted the poor to be industrious, frugal, deferent and independent of charity. Thus, to treat Wordsworth's representations of the poor, his appropriation of rustic language, imagery, incidents and settings for his poetry, without showing their role and relative position within the broad network of representations of the poor in the theoretical, political and cultural works of the late eighteenth century would be to ignore the role of his poetry to modify, as well as to reproduce, features of the discourse on poverty, and to negotiate, rather than simply represent, relationships between the poor and those who are not poor.

Like many of the writers I discuss in the course of this book, within certain ideological limitations, Wordsworth sympathizes with the poor, criticizes the inadequate systems of poor relief that often exposed them to abuse and contempt, and in general attempts to lead the reader's understanding of the poor, especially the rural poor, beyond the constitutive polarities of the discourse on poverty. Wordsworth's representations of the poor in his early poetry rely on different narrative and rhetorical strategies from those of his immediate predecessors and his contemporaries. Pratt's poetry and Wheatley's paintings, for example, displace the problems of urban poverty into a rustic setting that naturalizes indigence and allows the spectator to forget—at least for a moment—the harsh edges of urban indigence. Crabbe's *The Village* and *The Parish Register* rely primarily upon a Hogarthian progress narrative and the medium of metonymy to call attention to the "disgusting" moral and physical conditions of the laboring poor (as I discuss in Chapter Three). The representations of the poor in Wordsworth's *Salisbury Plain*, *Lyrical Ballads*, *The*

Ruined Cottage, "Resolution and Independence," "The Old Cumberland Beggar," among others, like Thomas Bewick's engravings of the poor in his "tailpieces" to *History of Quadrupeds* (1790) and *History of British Birds* (1787–1804), rely primarily upon a stark detailism and a narrative, as Glen has shown, that subvert neat moral closure. Glen cogently argues that the poems of *Lyrical Ballads* deny the reader the traditional stance of either protest or pity toward the vagrants and solitaries. As she explains, the poems "refuse to offer a clear-cut moral directive to the reader" (244). Consequently, the poems "question the unarticulated moral assumptions of the polite reader; most centrally, that paternalistic diminution of the other which insidiously structured late eighteenth-century social thinking, even in its conspicuously radical manifestation" (245).[10]

While the harsher aspects of indigence are sometimes offset by framing Wordsworth's vagrant portraits within a sanguine landscape of moral sympathy and affective intensity,[11] often his poetry sets its vagrants in a severe landscape of scarcity. That is, while Wordsworth's poetry certainly heightens the affective sympathy for the rustic poor in order to attenuate the shock of a vampire nature, it does *not* erase that shock altogether; nor does it always successfully conceal the violence of the social *and* the natural world beneath a pastoral veneer. Unlike the rustic figures of the pastoral or georgic poets, Wordsworth's rustic figures do not simply appear as types and emblems of an idealized rustic poverty in antique garb upon a harmonious, if not idyllic, scene; rather, they appear as unique individuals with private histories, and they inhabit an austere landscape marked with social turbulence, economic deprivation and personal degradation. While Wordsworth's poetry obviously does not escape completely from the commonplace idealization and sentimentalization of the poor, it does mark a radical intervention into the nitty-gritty world of its production. If Wordsworth's poetry may swerve from history, it does not deny it altogether.

In its conflicted engagement with the historical, Wordsworth's poetry demands a different way of reading, a different way of seeing and engaging the working poor. In dispensing with personification and poetic diction, eschewing conventional ideologemes such as "happy swain" and "lubbard Labor," Wordsworth's representations of the poor brought his contemporaries into an uncomfortable proximity to poverty, while striking a balance between totally offending and totally placating their sensibilities and expectations. In terms suggested by Barbauld's "An Inquiry into Those Kinds of Distress which Excite Agreeable Sensations," Wordsworth's representations of the laboring poor mix "grace and dignity" with suffering, maintaining a fine balance between features that might be met with disgust and those that might arouse sympathy. We see in the stoic fortitude of Simon Lee, Michael or Ruth, examples of that virtue tempered by "something of helplessness and imperfection, with an excessive sensibility, or a simplicity bordering upon weakness" that Barbauld recommends for a writer who would have us "feel a strong degree of compassion" (224).

The attempt to create sympathy for the poor while trespassing conventional poetic propriety and transgressing boundaries of the discourse on poverty, however, creates a double bind for the poet. In order to gain the reader's sympathy for his rustic characters, Wordsworth ultimately must rely upon the very conventions governing the definition of the "good" and the "bad" poor that his poetry challenges. At best it seems that he can only resituate the reader in relation to those conventions, so that the arbitrariness and the inflexibility of the conventions become apparent. At its most subversive, Wordsworth's poetry, while it depends upon the normative conventions of the discourse on poverty to elicit a sympathetic response from the reader, alerts the reader to the questionable value and the artificiality (i.e., the social origin) of those conventions which have through habitual use in discourse attained the status of *a priori* or ontological truths. Thus, while the discourse on poverty and its binary system of morality haunt the rustic demesnes of Wordsworth's poetry, the poetry threatens to expose them as artificial constructs, if not to exorcise them altogether. In the chapters that follow, I hope to show that Wordsworth's poetry engages but does not affirm the conventional assumptions about poverty, that it deploys those assumptions in a poetic discourse that challenges and questions them.

2

Spec(tac)ular Reversals: The Politics of the Sublime and Wordsworth's Transfiguration of the Rustic Poor

The spectacle is not a collection of images, but a social relation among people, mediated by images.
          Guy Debord, Society of the Spectacle

In *The Theory of Moral Sentiments* (1759), Adam Smith describes the governance of the self as a kind of theatrical self-projection in which the subject assumes the gaze of the Other—in this case the gaze of the collectivity—and places himself or herself under the disciplinary surveillance of that gaze. As Smith puts it: "We can never survey our own sentiments and motives, we can never form any judgment concerning them; unless we remove ourselves, as it were, from our own natural station, and endeavour to view them as at a certain distance from us" (110). Smith imagines the subject's entrance into social life as a splitting of the self into an "impartial spectator" and a spectacle—the first, a simulated, composite self made up of the subject's anticipation of how other people would view his or her actions; the second, in his words, "the person whom I properly call myself" (113).[1] This second self—an internalized and inverted panopticon from whose center the collective gaze of society surveys the outward behavior of the subject—also functions as a mirror. As Smith writes, "to suppose ourselves the spectators of our own behaviour" provides us with "the only looking-glass by which we can, in some measure, with the eyes of other people, scrutinize the propriety of our own conduct" (112).

Smith's mixing of metaphors—the second self is impartial spectator *and* speculum—subjects "the I which is myself" to a public gaze and simultaneously reflects "the I which is myself"; indeed, it suggests the "subtle system of feints" that Foucault analyzes in Velazquez's "Las Meninas." Here, too, as in "Las Meninas," "the observer and the observed take part in a ceaseless exchange," an infinitely protracted reversal between public and private roles, between judge and judged, beholder and beheld (4).[2] In contrast to "Las Meninas," however, from the mirror of this spectacle no reflection of king and queen peers forth to establish a center of power around which the other figures in the painting, the painter and the spectator devolve. Rather, in Smith's canvas of moral perspective, the center is always absent—somewhere between the imaginary public gaze and the reflected image of "the I which is myself." Locating the subject in society somewhere between spectator and spectacle, speculum and spectacle, Smith's mixed metaphor suggests the arbitrary nature of social identity and the dialectical construction of the self in a world where the sovereign gaze of the monarch no longer offers an established center from which to accept one's role as "subject."

I invoke Smith's metaphor to begin this chapter on Wordsworth's transfiguration of the poor because, as I will show, in contrast to Cowper's poetry—in which the "sovereign gaze" that brings order to the collective dissolves into the privileged gaze of Burke's natural aristocrat—Wordsworth's poetry further redistributes that gaze into the collective itself. Especially with regard to the place of the poor in a poetry, like Cowper's, encumbered with an "aristocratic ethic," compared to a poetry, like Wordsworth's, identified with (in its early moments) the politics of reform, we can identify a change from a perspective that stands above the poor in a hierarchy of vertical relations to a radical reversal of that perspective in a world where the position of the subject along any axis seems to be uncertain. This distinction between Cowper and Wordsworth results in part from the destabilization of the fixed place of the observer in relation to the observed in Wordsworth's poetry, a destabilization that is entangled in the economic insecurity and consequent social precariousness of the middle-class subject in a society teetering off balance even in an advanced stage of the breakdown of an ordered and comfortably predictable system of social stratification. While Cowper and his relatively secure and comfortable reading audience could (and in the case of Cowper did) rely upon the security of independent fortunes, family connections or generous friends to keep them from misfortune, Wordsworth and his self-mirroring implied reader were less certain of such support (though indeed Wordsworth did in the last instance rely upon legacies from friends and family for his means of living). It is clear from the very subject matter of Wordsworth's poetry that he was aware of the fragility of social position among the middle and lower classes. Mimicking Smith's confusion of spectator and speculum, Wordsworth's poetry places the middle-class subject before the gaze of the Other, while at the same time holding up a mirror that reflects the precarious and arbitrary nature of the self in a society that exposes individuals to political, economic and social flux.

I

Humphry Repton's *Enquiry into the Changes of Taste in Landscape Gardening* (1806) records his impression of the social transformations taking place after about 1760:

> Within the last forty years the property and even the char-
> acters of individuals have undergone more change than in any
> period of the English history: we daily see wealth acquired by
> industry, or by fortunate speculations, succeeding to the heredi-
> tary estates of the most ancient families; and we see the descen-
> dants of these families reduced, by the vain attempt to vie in
> expence with the successful sons of commerce. . . . (65)

These transformations were accompanied by what Martin Price calls a
"reordering of the field of aesthetic experience" occurring precisely at the
point when the picturesque moment—"that phase of speculation . . .
where the aesthetic categories are self-sufficient"—collapses into the contingency of "moral and religious grounds" (262). Once moral considerations perforate the formal boundaries of the picturesque object, "the
picturesque moves toward the sublime" (262). Because the picturesque
suspends the tension between "an appeal to unlimited complexity against
limited canons of beauty," between order and disorder, and between "the
centrifugal forces of dissolution and the centripetal pull of form," the
picturesque tends to draw the spectator's attention away "from the work
of art as we traditionally conceive it to the larger sphere in which it plays
its role" (276–77). That larger sphere, of course, involves moral, religious
and social considerations so that, as Liu has recently shown, the picturesque moment of a purely formal interest remains always on the horizon
of desire and is never realized in practice.[3]

This tendency of the picturesque to give way to moral grounds is
nowhere more evident than in picturesque theory's discussion of human
figures in the landscape. Price suggests that the appeal of human figures,
especially those which outside of the confines of the picturesque would
either be called ugly or be dismissed altogether, depends upon some
"mixture of the picturesque with either the beautiful or the sublime";
"the merely picturesque gypsies and beggars," he adds, "make little
direct appeal to sympathy" (282). But sympathy for the vagrant inhabitants of the picturesque landscape was not an object for picturesque
theorists. The sublimity of marginals—that is, their moral interest—lies
entirely in that appeal to the "larger sphere" in which they play a role.

As Malcolm Andrews, Ann Bermingham and Alan Liu have
recently shown, the attempt on the part of the picturesque theorists to
sustain a purely formalist interest in the landscape fails on many
grounds, but on none more profoundly than when it argues in favor of
representing the lower orders in positions of repose and idleness, qualities reserved absolutely for the privileged aristocracy and which, when
applied to the poor, amount to nothing less than turning the social
pyramid upside down.[4] In *The Search for the Picturesque*, Andrews
notes that representations of poverty and ruin in the picturesque participate in "a value-laden system of imagery" (60–61). As he explains:

" 'Sensibility,' 'soft' primitivism, the rise of evangelicism—these and other pressures manipulated the images of the rural poor and their environment, and endowed them with complex moral and political associations. The trouble is that the Picturesque enterprise in its later stages, with its almost exclusive emphasis on visual appreciation entailed a suppression of the spectator's moral response to those very subjects which it could least hope to divest of moral significance—the ruin, the hovel and rural poverty" (59). Yet in its attempt to treat the indigent poor as merely formal objects, picturesque theory called further attention to the questions of idleness, profligacy and immorality that were said to cause vagrancy and begging, punishable crimes against society. Thus, Andrews is right to conclude that "pure formalism" with regard to the representation of the lower orders "could not be sustained" in the picturesque (61). Similarly, Bermingham's *Landscape and Ideology* shows how the picturesque unwittingly "endorsed the results of agricultural industrialization" in its "distancing of the spectator from the picturesque object, and the aestheticization of rural poverty" (75).

In this moral question about the status of the poor raised by the picturesque, we can assemble a kind of Claude-glass through which to view the transformation in perspective between the poetry of William Cowper and that of William Wordsworth, a transformation that registers certain changes in the economic status of the English subject in an increasingly fluid social system where neither status nor security could be guaranteed by birth, connections, talents or industry. In showing how Wordsworth's representations of the poor distinctively transform the spectator's relationship to poverty or the poor as represented in Cowper's poetry, I hope to further elaborate what Price noted as the pivotal importance of Wordsworth's poetry in registering this change in perspective—both aesthetic and social—as it is linked to the awareness that one's place in the social structure was subject to the sudden, sometimes accidental, reverses to which Repton alludes (287). For Cowper, poverty appears to the spectator (by which term I mean to conflate writer-narrator-reader) as a distant spectacle; as is typical of eighteenth-century loco-descriptive poetry, Cowper's poetry places the spectator above the scene of poverty so that the poor appear as part of a panorama of rural society subject to the spectator's privileged gaze. In Wordsworth's poetry, on the other hand, this spectacle of poverty gives way to a speculum of poverty—a mirror, like Adam Smith's, that disciplines the "person whom I properly call myself" and subverts the spectator's customary privilege of looking down at the rural poor. As in a convex carnival mirror that exaggerates the body's proportions, in Wordsworth's poetry of sublime vagrancy the spectator shrinks before the gargantuan spectre of poverty with a human face—potentially construed to be the spectator's own.

While both Cowper and Wordsworth produce idealized representations of the working and vagrant poor, Cowper's poetry presents the laboring poor as generalized aesthetic objects figurally distanced from the spectator by personification, periphrasis and conventional epithets. These figures mediate a polite distance between the spectator and those objects that might offend and produce what Catherine Belsey in *Critical Practice* calls a "hierarchy of discourses" within a text that addresses the reader as a privileged subject (70). Indeed, to paraphrase Belsey, Cowper's *The Task* (1785) interpellates the spectator as a unified subject from whose center the text becomes intelligible and whose social position is naturalized as a fixed and stable identity (70). Therefore the spectator readily identifies with the narrator's natural superiority over the poor, whom the poem objectifies as the excluded Other. Cowper's "aesthetic objects," then, are not so in a Kantian sense, for their position in the text is already political, structured in the social ideals of "order, degree, and subordination" touted by the English landed gentry and aristocracy in the late eighteenth century (Clark 93).

Wordsworth's representations of the laboring poor, on the other hand, displace what we might call—invoking an apt metaphor from Roger Sales's *Pastoral and Politics* (15)—Cowper's picturesque "long shot" with a potentially disturbing "close up" shot. Wordsworth's poetry substitutes for the panoramic distance a disturbing proximity, where the spectator comes face to face with, if not "squalor and dirt," at least the "squalid appearance" and "mean employments" of the poor that Anna Barbauld cautioned writers to avoid. In "An Enquiry into those Kinds of Distress which Excite Agreeable Sensations" (1775), Barbauld warns: "Poverty, if truly represented, shocks our nicer feelings; therefore, whenever it is made use of to awaken our compassion, the rags and dirt, the squalid appearance and mean employments incident to that state, must be kept out of sight . . ." (*Works* 2: 222). Wordsworth's poetry casts Barbauld's caveat aside as it portrays characters like Simon Lee, Goody Blake, the Discharged Soldier and the old Waggoner with sometimes laughable realism. In a passage from an early draft of the *Prelude,* Wordsworth describes the subjective mechanism of this refigurative move as an "optic tube of thought" by which his mind's eye zooms up close to the object of his gaze, even as it internalizes and universalizes that object:

> Without the glass of Galileo [the poet] sees
> What Galileo saw, and, as it were,
> Resolving into one great faculty
> Of being bodily eye and spiritualneed,
> The converse which he holds is limitless—
> Nor only with the firmament of [thought]
> But nearer home he looks with the same eye
> Through the entire abyss of things." (148–58; MS Y)

Through Wordsworth's "telescopic imagination," the smooth surface of Cowper's picturesque spectacle of poverty gives way to a speculum rifted with the subjective evils of pain and suffering and—despite all industrious efforts to make ends meet—the objective evil of indigence.

In *The Search for the Picturesque* Andrews demonstrates that picturesque theory, developing roughly at the same time Cowper was working on *The Task*, moves the spectator from a high to a low station. As I will show, the change in perspective on the poor between Cowper and Wordsworth involves a similar descent from the high position of the loco-descriptive to the low of the picturesque—from the noble stations atop a promontory to what Andrews calls the "humble stations" below and in front of such promontories (56). This descent is both a topographical and an ideological move, for the view from the promontory correlates with the privileged gaze of what Burke terms the "natural aristocrat," while the view from the valley correlates with the less privileged vantage point of the middling and lower classes.[5]

In discussing the works of James Thomson and John Dyer, Barrell has ably shown that the "view from the top" was a familiar topos in eighteenth-century loco-descriptive poetry and landscape painting. This "prospect of Britain," as Barrell calls it, involved a generalization of the social and topographical landscape below and a kind of self-aggrandizement of the spectator (*Equal, Wide Survey* 56). Joshua Reynolds formalized for painting the first aspect of this trope in the third *Discourse*, where he claims that "the whole beauty and grandeur of the art consists . . . in being able to get above all singular forms, local customs, particularities, and details of every kind" (44). Burke formalized the pleasures of the privileged spectator's self-aggrandizement in a rather less likely place, his *An Appeal from the New to the Old Whigs*. Here Burke politicizes the aesthetic stance of the privileged spectator as he considers the "elevated ground" from which the natural aristocrat oversees his (and I use this pronoun advisedly here) world. From this "elevated ground," the natural aristocrat attains a comprehensive and unifying perspective on the expansive and diverse social life below: "To stand upon such elevated grounds [is] to be enabled to take a large view of the wide-spread and infinitely diversified combinations of men and affairs in a large society" (130).

In *Observations on the River Wye* (1782), William Gilpin at first appears to offer an alternative to the grand prospect recommended by Reynolds and Burke. Because nature works on a grand scale beyond human comprehension, Gilpin believes, neither the picturesque traveller nor the picturesque artist can discern the harmony of nature's vast schemes. In order to confine his or her landscapes "to a span," as Gilpin advises, the picturesque artist "lays down his little rules . . . which he calls the principles of picturesque beauty, merely to adapt such diminutive parts of nature's surfaces to his own eye, as come within its scope" (18). Nonetheless, in the *Observations, Relative Chiefly to Picturesque Beauty* (1786), Gilpin extols the "beautiful distance" by which it is possible to observe objects without seeing their "awkwardnesses": "The obscurity, occasioned by the intervening medium, softens each line, or tint, that is harsh, or discordant" (1: xxvi). Despite the prominent place of the foreground in picturesque theory, picturesque travelers and artists alike must exercise a fine selectivity both in choosing the station from which they observe a landscape and in culling natural scenes for their most picturesque parts, otherwise the objects in the landscape might be disgusting: "as the landscape advances on the eye, the deformity grows more apparent, and on the foreground, objects are so magnified, that it is very rare indeed, if they do not in some part, offend. Their features become so strong, that if they be not beautiful, they are disgusting" (*Picturesque Beauty* 1: xxvi). Hedges, for example, up close may be "disgusting in a high degree," but "when all these regular forms are softened by distance—when hedge-row trees begin to unite, and lengthen into streaks along the horizon—when farm houses, and ordinary buildings lose all their vulgarity of shape, and are scattered about, in formless spots, through the several parts of a distance—it is inconceivable what richness, and beauty, this mass of deformity, when melted together, adds to landscape" (1: 7–8). Wordsworth's hedge-rows of "Tintern Abbey"—"hardly hedge-rows, little lines / Of sportive wood run wild" (lines 15–16)—exemplify what Gilpin calls this "rich distance" that blurs fine distinctions; as he puts it, "pictures are not designed to be seen through a microscope," and so the picturesque painter would waste time trying to achieve any high finish of detail (*Picturesque Beauty* 2: 14).

Among the objects whose identity must be blurred both Gilpin and Uvedale Price include human beings, especially the banditti and vagrants who are the bona fide human configurations of the picturesque. Gilpin and Price both describe human figures in the landscape as objects, like trees or rocks or mountains, to be apprehended by the picturesque painter only as the sum total of extrinsic, empirical and, above all, generalized features, so that such figures would not suggest any particular expression that might invest them with moral or individual (one might add, historical) human qualities. A typical sentiment comes from Gilpin's *Observations, Relative to Picturesque Beauty*: "In the human figure we contemplate neither exactness of form; nor expression, any farther than it is shown in action: we merely consider general shapes, dresses, groups, and occupations; which we find casually in greater variety, and beauty, than any relation can procure" (2: 44-45). The objects associated with picturesque human figures receive primary value, and even their presence dissolves in a metonymic displacement. "The fisherman," Gilpin writes, ." . . may follow his calling upon the lake: but he is indebted for this privilege, not to his art; but to the picturesque apparatus of it—his boat, and his nets, which qualify his art. They are the objects: he is but an appendage . . ." (2: 45).

Similarly, Price's *Essay on the Picturesque* (1796) objectifies marginal human beings as objects in a pleasing spectacle. Commenting on a sudden encounter with a band of gypsies, Hamilton, a character in Price's fictional dialogue, instructs his auditors that "the set of objects [including the gypsies] we have been looking at, struck you with their singularity; but instead of thinking them beautiful, you were disposed to call them ugly: now, I should neither call them beautiful, nor ugly, but picturesque; for they have qualities highly suited to the painter and his art, but which are, in general, less attractive to the bulk of mankind; whereas the qualities of beauty, are universally pleasing and alluring to all observers" (1: 116–17). For Price, as for Gilpin, gypsies, itinerant vagrants and banditti arouse interest only as objects fixed in a stabilizing aesthetic classification. Any non-aesthetic grasp or apprehension of the gypsies would disgust, or would involve the viewer in a face-to-face encounter that would quickly turn the pleasing, picturesque experience into a moment of fear that might anticipate the sublime.

A scene from Ann Radcliffe's *Mysteries of Udolpho* shows that when gypsies escape the picturesque freeze-frame, a sublime, not a picturesque, encounter ensues: "Emily looked with some degree of terror on the savage countenances of these people, shown by the fire, which heightened the romantic effect of the scenery as it threw a red dusky glare upon the rocks and foliage of the trees, leaving heavy masses of shade and regions of obscurity, which the eye feared to penetrate" (40). Contained within the frames of a Salvator Rosa, the gypsy vagrants appear at an aesthetic distance that is palatable and safe, but confronted in actuality the gypsies arouse such terror that the spectator's eye itself is arrested. Thus, although the picturesque stations the spectator on a plane of topographical equivalence with the lowest orders of society, it insists upon maintaining a polite distance from whatever rude and irregular objects, including human figures, it would incorporate into the body of the painting. Gilpin's "rich distance" is so in a double sense, then, for the picturesque eye absorbs abundant riches from the landscape, while it entertains the point of view once exclusive to the aristocracy and gentry. That is, the spectator maintains a privileged position even from a "low" point of observation; distance now measured along a horizontal topographical axis, but which preserves the vertical distinctions of social station, affirms the spectator's superiority over the vagrants, idlers and gypsies who are allowed to remain as humble spectacles within the highly regulated territory of the picturesque.[6] Since the picturesque traveler may not be absolutely free from the necessity of labor, to remove all traces of labor and leave behind only the indigent ensures a kind of economic and social station above those who have fallen through the cracks or slipped to the margins of social value. Moreover, the picturesque traveler, as we have seen, maintains a spatial distance from those otherwise threatening banditti and gypsies, though that distance may now be measured horizontally rather than vertically.

Cowper's *The Task* also places the spectator on a high road above the naturalized landscape below. Like Burke's "natural aristocrat," Cowper's spectator surveys the scene from a vantage point that constitutes the perceiving subject as autonomous and outside of ideology. Positing itself as the powerful originating center of all meaning, knowledge and value, the spectator constructs the inhabitants of the landscape below as a containable Other—as empirical objects for analysis and aesthesis. In Cowper's rural scenes, for example, the agricultural laborers appear as mere objects among a variety of other objects presented to keep the spectator's eye, always grounded in its supervisory power, sweeping across the scene. The spectator may derive pleasure from such a view, especially when the laborers appear in homely scenes which assure the spectator that the lower classes are frugal, obedient, industrious and humble.

One typical source of pleasure for the Burkean spectator was the spectacle of agricultural labor from afar. In a scene from "The Sofa" section of *The Task*, for example, with "admiration feeding at the eye, / And still unsated," the narrator and his walking companion pause to view a sight of ongoing labor in the distant field:

> with what pleasure have we just discern'd
> The distant plough slow moving, and beside
> His labouring team, that swerv'd not from the track,
> The sturdy swain diminished to a boy. (*Task* 1.159–62)

Here spatial distance supplies the buffer necessary for the spectator's repose. The spectator does not engage in a direct face-to-face encounter with the laborer; instead, metonymy initially negotiates a safe distance between them—"the distant plough slow moving" and "his labouring team"—before the the laborer appears directly. Even then, he appears so far in the distance that he looks like a "boy"; the laborer has been transformed into a non-threatening child. To further screen the spectator from a direct confrontation with the laborer, Cowper uses the pastoral term "swain" and so invokes historical and formal, as well as topographical, distance. Because the team "swerv'd not from the track," this scene affirms that all is well with the world below: no errant laborer here deviates from the straight and narrow way.

Cowper uses linguistic and rhetorical as well as visual techniques of distancing in his poem. As noted, the pastoral epithet "sturdy swain" in the passage cited above displaces the scene from the historical present to a mythic but conventionally proscribed agrarian past in which the laborer's otherness is objectified and contained in a familiar and pleasing linguistic construct. To invoke conventional pastoral is to conjure up visions of a world at rest, in which agricultural labor—if it intervenes at all into the topical otium of the green world—appears as "blissful toil," a balancing of effort and ease according to the natural rhythms of the day and season. Even blissful toil, however, threatens the pastoral with an invasion of georgic; thus Cowper keeps labor in the spatial and historical distance so as not to disturb the spectator's comfortable idyll and to affirm the spectator's social status. Such distancing points forward to William Gilpin's absolute banishment of labor and objects of utility from the picturesque, even though Cowper's poetry does not aspire to the complete bracketing of aesthetic experience from social utility.

To dissociate the aesthetic and moral spheres, picturesque theory attempts to erase all signs of utility and labor from its painterly spaces. In his *Observations, Relative Chiefly to Picturesque Beauty*, for example, Gilpin notes that "moral and picturesque ideas do not always coincide" (2: 44). Any figures or objects in the landscape suggestive of power, productivity, liberty, or other useful qualities or ideas would invoke the moral idea, which belongs to the georgic. Therefore Gilpin advises: "In a moral light, cultivation, in all its parts, is pleasing; the hedge, and the furrow; the waving corn field, and the ripened sheaf. But upon all these the picturesque eye, in quest of scenes of grandeur, and beauty, looks with disgust. It ranges after nature, untamed by art, and bursting wildly into all its irregular forms" (2: 44). Since labor is a primary sign of commerce and utility, Gilpin throughout his work banishes labor from the picturesque, as in his verse essay, "On Landscape Painting," included in his *Three Essays on Picturesque Beauty* (20–21):

> The spade,
> The plough, the patient angler with his rod,
> Be banish'd thence, for other guests invite
> Wild as those scenes themselves, bandittie fierce
> And gipsy-tribes, not merely to adorn,
> But to impress that sentiment more strong,
> Awak'd already by the savage scene.
> (lines 574–80; *Three Essays* 20–21)

Although in the later *Observations on the Western Parts of England* (1798), Gilpin permits the use of "manufactured scenes"—that is, scenes of land under cultivation—in poetry, he insists that painting can never tolerate such scenes: "[H]owever pleasing all this may be in poetry, on canvas, hedge-row elms, furrowed lands, meadows adorned with milkmaids, and hayfields adorned with mowers, have a bad effect" (329). Similarly, as Bermingham has shown, Price objects to the gardens of Capability Brown and other "improvers" because of their association with commerce and mechanization. For Price, as Bermingham claims, "[t]he picturesque landscape was precisely the opposite of the landscape produced by the agricultural revolution, and therein lay a primary aspect of its value" (66).

Indeed, Gilpin's own work contradicts his attempt to separate the aesthetic from the moral spheres, as is evident in *Observations on the River Wye* (1782), where he praises the imperceptible regularity of nature's great design, and in *Observations on the Western Parts of England* (1798), where he politicizes the landscape by arguing that the beauty of the whole legitimates what we perceive as inequalities in nature. Distance and magnitude of the scene, he says, obscure these inequalities: "If a comprehensive eye, placed at a distance from the surface of the earth, were capable of viewing a whole hemisphere together, all its inequalities, great as we make them . . . would be compressed, like the view before us; and the whole would appear perfectly smooth. To us, a bowling green is a level plain; but a minute insect finds it full of inequalities" (*Western Parts of England* 246). Because the spectator's view is necessarily limited, Gilpin argues, what the eye perceives as irregularities are actually constituent parts of a uniform whole. Gilpin's appeal to a comprehensive view beyond the ken of ordinary human beings serves, as it does in Alexander Pope and William Paley, to vindicate inequalities in landscape and in society. What aesthetic distance can do for the privileged spectator, religion, in Paley's view, must do for those who otherwise would have reason for discontent. As Paley put it: "Religion smooths all inequalities, because it unfolds a prospect which makes all earthly distinctions nothing" (*Reasons for Contentment* 422). The banishment of labor from the poem or the canvas that Gilpin recommends helps to smooth all inequalities, for it unfolds a prospect from which any reminders of earthly economic distinctions have been carefully excised.

I should pause a moment to explain a difference between Cowper's objectification of the poor and the objectification theorized by Gilpin and Price. As Malcolm Andrews notes, the picturesque station moves from the high promontory down into the field, from "palace to ruin to hovel," so long as that field is depopulated in the ways outlined by Price and Gilpin in the citations above (61). Andrews links this descent to the increasingly formalist interest in landscape, as the picturesque rejects the *paysage moralise* more typical of the loco-descriptive. Thus, picturesque theory goes much further than Cowper's pastoral-georgic poetry to remove the spectator to a station at a topographical level equivalent to that occupied by pedlars, beggars and other persons of middle to low status. Nonetheless, picturesque theory, as we have seen, is no more successful at achieving a socially egalitarian perspective on the vagrants and gypsies left behind in those depopulated fields than it is at fully ejecting moral and ethical questions from its canvases.

Despite using Burkean panorama to distance the spectator from the commons below, Cowper does admit labor and laborers into his work. Nonetheless, as Gilpin would recommend, Cowper does not recognize the agricultural workers as persons with distinctive physical features, character or personal histories. In the scene from "The Sofa," the reader first notices the "distant plough" and the "labouring team" of the swain, to which the miniaturized "swain" becomes, as in Gilpin, a picturesque appendage: not the essential focus of the scene, but a mere adornment to the objects of his labor. The gypsies the spectator later encounters appear only metonymically, their presence signaled by a column of smoke, "A kettle flung / Between two poles upon a stick transverse," their "flutt'ring rags" and "tawny skin" observed from a safe remove (*Task* 1.560–61, 568).

Another trope Cowper uses to negotiate distance between spectator and the rural laborer is personification. In "The Garden," for example, we find the narrator remarking how important it is to exercise a supervisory gaze over his workers:

> conscious how much the hand
> Of lubbard Labour needs his watchful eye,
> Oft loit'ring lazily, if not o'erseen
> Or misapplying his unskilful strength. (*Task* 3.399–402)

The personification abstracts the laborers and underscores the categorical difference of kind between the narrator and those he observes.

In *Personification and the Sublime: Milton to Coleridge*, Stephen Knapp notes that a "paradoxical desire for safe participation in ideal or fixated modes of agency accounts for the special relation of personification to the sublime." For Knapp, "sublime personification uniquely balances the conflicting criteria of power and distance required by the Enlightened stance of urbane admiration" (82–83). Cowper's "lubbard Labour" invokes the distance of such personifications, but because the trope reminds the spectator of his or her power over laborers, the admiration falls reflexively upon the spectator. If we consider Clifford Siskin's observation that eighteenth-century personification offers the reader a "metonymic affirmation of community" in which, in this case, "lubbard Labour" signifies the distinction between those who labor and those who manage labor, we can see that Cowper's personification serves to reinforce the moral and social distinctions within a relatively stable social hierarchy (69).[7]

As overseer, the spectator's pleasure in *The Task* derives from his vicarious participation in the power over labor. This power appears in the narrator's patronizing of his servants, who appear to be little more than instruments of his superior ingenuity and will. Indeed, Cow-

per assigns the division between mental and manual labor to geneal-
ogy, thereby affirming for the "natural aristocrat" his rightful duty to
direct the hands in his service. To the landlord, Cowper's narrator
advises,

> No works, indeed,
> That ask robust tough sinews, bred to toil,
> Servile employ; but such as may amuse,
> Not tire, demarking rather skill than force. (3.404–7)

Unbred to toil, the landlord (or landlord's guest, as in this case) takes up
imaginative activity as his pleasurable task, appropriating for mental
labor the topos of "cheerful toil." Meanwhile the less palatable task of
manual labor is clearly set apart as the province of the Other.

By means of metonymy and personification, then, Cowper's
poetry allows the spectator to oversee —in both a visual and proprietary
sense—these scenes of property, the propertiless, and labor in such a
way as to "overlook" any particular features or qualities that would
individualize the gypsies or laborers and trouble him or her with the
equivalent of a face-to-face encounter.[8] Cowper does not, however, go
so far as to banish all questions of ethos from his text, for the poem
makes explicit that the landlord's role as overseer is natural and inevitable. In separating spectator from agricultural laborer as a kind of rural
spectacle of the means of production, Cowper avoids any possibility of a
literary identification between the spectator and the laborer. Whatever
generalized unity exists among the various "tasks" of the landlord, poet,
worker, domestic animal and implements of labor must appeal to a
transcendental purposiveness of nature that palls beneath the very precise distinctions Cowper's poem maintains between the various sectors
of work and the gap between mental and manual labor.

To recall Adam Smith's *Theory of Moral Sentiments*, with
which I began this excursion into Cowper's poetry, it is now clear that
Cowper's narrator always remains a spectator of poverty, the spectacle.
In Cowper's poetry we find no uneasy confusion of spectator and spectacle, no moment when the spectacle becomes speculum, when in the
face of the indigent Other (which never comes into focus) the narrator
sees the outlines of his own possible impoverishment. Any approxima-
tion to sympathetic identification remains a possibility over which the
narrator reserves complete control, as when he pauses at a low-roofed
cottage, a "peasant's nest," to entertain fantasies about becoming a
hermit poet. Once he realizes that "the dweller in that still retreat /
Dearly obtains the refuge it affords" (*Task* 1.237–38), the narrator cuts
short his imagined occupation of the peasant's hovel. Unwilling to
embrace an abject poverty too harsh for the narrator's delicate taste,

he quickly bids adieu to his momentary envy of the humble abode of the cottagers:

> If solitude makes scant the means of life,
> Society for me! Thou, seeming sweet,
> Be still a pleasing object in my view,
> My visit still, but never mine abode. (*Task* 1.248–51)

Better to view such humble abodes in the distance than to entertain the thought of taking up one's dwelling therein. Again Cowper seems to have anticipated Gilpin's *Observations on the River Wye* where Gilpin observes that "little cottages, and farms, faintly traced along their shadowy sides" at an appropriate distance, "rather varied, and inriched [*sic*] the scenes than impressed it with any regular, and unpleasing shapes"— he might have added, or ideas of actually serving as places of residence (50). What is disturbing to the moral sense may still be pleasing to the aesthetic, and in an evasion of the sublime questions of self-preservation that Wordsworth will confront in such encounters, Cowper's narrator moves the reader on to another, more comforting, scene.

Invoking conventions of pastoral steeped in the idealized doctrines of primitivism and simplicity that engaged the eighteenth-century imagination, Cowper's laborers confirm a landlord's pleasure in his servants' happy toil and the moral integrity of humble dwellers in the rural "cot." Since the 1780s were a time of displacement and dispossession for many such laborers, Cowper's representations seem particularly remote from the historical processes of land accumulation, enclosure and social displacement taking place in the countryside. Certainly his representations of the poor, as Richard Feingold notes in *Nature and Society*, do not suggest a critique of social injustices. In Feingold's view, the laborers and the industrious poor in Book Four of *The Task* "do not come into focus as subjects of the poet's attention when it is turned towards the criticism of society: the laborer, like the postboy, represents that order of life which is committed neither to active involvement nor retirement, but connected to nature in the simplest of ways . . . " (138). As such, Cowper's poetry upholds the conventional moral views of the gentry upon whom he depended, and which gave his poetry, as Marilyn Butler observes, its "strong appeal to the conservative, traditionally Christian strain in the gentry and the prosperous middle class, which . . . sought a spiritual regeneration within individuals rather than by disturbing the present hierarchical order of things" (36). Thus, in treating the reader to a spectacle of rustic poverty as viewed from a proprietary gaze, Cowper's *The Task* naturalizes the hegemony of the aristocracy, or, in the words of Burke's *Appeal from the New to the Old Whigs*, it affirms that "the state of civil society, which necessarily generates this [natural] aristocracy, is a state of nature . . . " (130).[9] Certainly, as Butler concludes, "his kind of concern with the simple and humble of the earth, the bless-edly meek, need not be in the least politically inflammatory" (36).[10]

II

In contrast to the naturalized social relations displayed in Cowper's poetry, Wordsworth's poetry of 1798 to 1802 removes the poor into a marginal space, outside the conventional relations of production and into a sphere of relative indeterminacy. If we follow Victor Turner's analysis of the ritual process of liminality, this move invests the laborer or vagrant with a certain, if ambiguously realized, power that turns the tables on the spectator by transforming the marginal figure into that impartial spectator/speculum which, in Adam Smith, subjects "the person whom I properly call myself" to a disciplinary redoubling of the self. In *The Ritual Process*, Turner describes the liminal as a phase of transition in which the subject (in his examples usually a neophyte in some rite of passage) enters a state of ambiguity outside the normative conventions and values of the society. During this phase, the subject "passes through a cultural realm that has few or none of the attributes of the past or coming state" (94). In some situations, the liminal person becomes a kind of blank slate upon which are inscribed the intrinsic values of the community. As the carrier of such values, often sacred and mystical, the liminal person—usually a person of low status—assumes special powers and authority during the ritual phase of transition. As Turner puts it: "[I]n liminality, the underling [be]comes uppermost"; the weak is invested with the powers and values of the entire community so that his or her speech or behavior is "not merely communication but also power and wisdom" (102–3). In particular cases, the phase of liminality involves a ritual reversal of status within the community; the usual figure of authority becomes subject to the liminal person, who may chastise, mock, scorn or otherwise order and abuse the political ruler of the community. It is this latter function of the liminal that Wordsworth's marginals in the poetry of 1798 to 1802 seem most to embody.

The power of the marginals in Wordsworth's poetry derives partly from the telephoto lens of his poetic camera that brings the itinerants close to the spectator. However distorted and sometimes blurry the resultant picture may appear to the modern reader, Wordsworth's contemporaries' reactions to his depictions of the rural poor—disbelief, mockery and scorn—indicate that his audience was not fully prepared to grant the marginals and outcasts of their society a sense of character and history, a knowing and knowable self, and a place within the privileged space of the lyric poem. Further confounding Wordsworth's early readers, these poems turn the voyeuristic mode of the loco-descriptive and picturesque upside down, positioning the spectator not just on equal ground with, but sometimes beneath, the gaze of the rustic poor. Arrested by the policing gaze of the Ancient Mariner-like marginals with their tales to tell, the spectator comes under the sway of their pardigmatic display of virtue and moral strength, as in the case of the leech gatherer or old Simon Lee, who brings the narrator to tears. Thus Hazlitt's comment that Wordsworth's Muse was "a levelling one" may not have gone far enough, for in some cases this muse is an inverting one.[11]

In particular, the old laborer of "Point Rash-Judgment," the leech gatherer and the discharged soldier visit the spectator as apparitions from the marginal spaces of society. In the poetry these figures of a society out of balance acquire a liminal power that is at once affective and sublime as the spectator falls before the shadow of the solitaries' stoic fortitude, their relentless industry, their resolution and independence, and perhaps above all their spectral poverty. In these figures Wordsworth's reader looks into a mirror of his or her own repressed Otherness and his or her own potential privation. The spectacle of another's poverty comprehended from a safe distance has given way to a speculum of the middle-class subject's own possible pauperization; the stable footing of the privileged spectator in Cowper gives way to the precarious balance at the edge of what Bentham called the "abyss of indigence" for the person of the middling ranks now subject to social fluidity in a society open to talents and hence to the possibility of "miserable reverses" (*Theory of Legislation* 127–28).

Let me turn here to Burke's *Philosophical Enquiry into the Origin of Our Ideas of the Sublime and the Beautiful* (1758) to show how the status reversal involved in this presentation of the powers of the weak can be construed in terms of eighteenth-century conceptions of the sublime and beautiful. In his *Enquiry* Burke affiliates the sublime with forms of power, especially those governing the relations of production in an agrarian society ruled by a landed aristocracy and gentry. When Burke illustrates his thesis that power is a constituent feature of the sublime, he turns to agriculture for examples of animals that do (the bull) and do not (the ox and the horse) elicit the sublime. Since for Burke that which effects the sublime must be accompanied by terror, the spectator must be threatened by a superior, possibly destructive power in order to feel the sublime. Power under domination, however, strength or force harnessed or domesticated for production, does not produce the sublime, for "whenever strength is only useful, and employed for our benefit or our pleasure, then it is never sublime; for nothing can act agreeably to us, that does not act in conformity to our will; but to act agreeably to our will, it must be subject to us; and therefore can never be the cause of a grand and commanding conception" (66). Such non-threatening forms of power may even cause contempt. Though Burke elsewhere in the treatise says that "we love what submits to us," he reminds his readers that "love approaches much nearer to contempt than is commonly imagined" (113, 167). Sorting out love from contempt, as the vexed contemporary reception of Wordsworth's representations of the poor illustrates, presented a major problem for writers whose sympathies for the agricultural laborer led them to depict rustic characters realistically.

The politics of the sublime enables in part the transference of power between spectator and spectacle as the relationship changes between Cowper and Wordsworth. This contrast becomes clear in comparing Cowper's rural spectacle to an apparently similar situation from Book 8 of *The Prelude* in which Wordsworth appears to be invoking a Cowperian distance between the spectator and the Hawkshead shepherds. Here Wordsworth comments on his youthful encounters with shepherds who appeared in the mountain mists as gigantic forms, as "solitary object[s] and sublime" (8.407). Such encounters presented to Wordsworth a transcendent spectacle of humanity stripped of the contradictory particulars of human beings acting and being acted upon in the world. For receiving such "appearances" of shepherds, the poet gives thanks:

> blessed be the God
> Of Nature and of man that this was so,
> That men did at the first present themselves
> Before my untaught eyes thus purified,
> Removed, and at a distance that was fit. (8.436–40)

In *The Dark Side of the Landscape,* Barrell cites this passage to gloss the ideological position of John Constable's representation of laborers in his paintings. For Barrell, "only by being kept at 'a distance that was fit' can Wordsworth's shepherds be acceptable as representative of what is noble and most to be loved in Man. Men as they are, as Wordsworth clearly says, are too impure, the actuality of their appearance too much in contrast with the ideal of the human, for them to invite us to move beyond our merely selfish and familial concerns to a concern for general humanity" (139). Yet a signal difference of tone and perspective obtains between Wordsworth's objectification of the shepherds as giant humans and the objectification of gypsies and vagrants as human miniatures in Cowper, Gilpin and Price. In his *Enquiry* Burke distinguishes between the spectator's experience of being subjected to power beyond his or her control— the sublime—and the spectator's experience of exercising his or her power over an object (or person) that submits to him or to her—the beautiful. In Cowper's encounter with the "swain" the potential power of the laborer is diminished in the distancing strategy of the panorama. Cowper's "sturdy swain diminished to a boy" presents a spectacle of domesticated power, which in the picturesque frame of the spectator's eye becomes even further subdued. The labor power of the swain, summarily deposed in the disempowering gaze of the "man of taste," is re-valued in Cowper's scene as an object of aesthetic pleasure—"a pleasing object in my view" (*Task* 1.250). In Wordsworth's poem, however, the inversion of this relationship between spectator and spectacle invests the apparently powerless with an alarming power. In the encounter with the giant shepherd figures the boy stands in awe of their spectral sublimity. Unlike Cowper's narrator, the boy cannot contain the shepherd as an object of his cognitive grasp. Escaping the boy's powers of naming, the shepherd appears rather as an object to which the boy submits in a moment of cognitive erasure. The boy can feel, but cannot know the shepherd's power:

> A rambling schoolboy, thus
> Have I beheld him; without knowing why,
> Have felt his presence in his own domain
> As of a lord and master, or a power
> Or genius, under Nature, under God,
> Presiding— and severest solitude
> Seemed more commanding oft when he was there.
>
> (8.390–96)

Gilpin's "Essay on Picturesque Travel" describes a similar moment when the natural sublime immobilizes the spectator's "scientifical employment" of the mind, leaving only the ability to experience deep feeling:

> We are most delighted, when some grand scene, tho perhaps of incorrect composition, rising before the eye, strikes us beyond the power of thought . . . and every mental operation is suspended. In this pause of intellect; this deliquium of the soul, an enthusiastic sensation of pleasure overspreads it, previous to any examination by the rules of art. The general idea of the scene makes an impression, before any appeal is made to the judgment. We rather feel, than survey it. (*Three Essays* 49–50)

In contrast to Cowper's spectator who surveys the scene, Wordsworth's spectator becomes the object of the shepherd's surveying eye.[12]
   Whereas Cowper in assigning the laborer a conventional name, "swain," subjects that laborer to an official category that he controls, the boy in Wordsworth's poem has crossed into the very domain of the shepherd, "a lord and master" over his own terrain, a *terra incognita* to the boy, who cannot presume any certain knowledge of the shepherd.[13] However exalted or universalized, the shepherd remains a mystery to the spectator, who is here inspired to "an unconscious love and reverence / Of human nature" (*Prelude* 8.414–15). The shepherd's commanding presence interpellates the subject as an invading Other, trespassing

upon his familiar territory. The encounter with the shepherd awakens in the spectator, the rambling schoolboy, a sense of his own Otherness, then, a sense of self-alienation that the sentimental poet must return to recover.

Wordsworth's encounter, typical of other encounters in his poetry with itinerant vagrants and laborers, places the spectator in a realm of uncertainty and doubt, a Burkean state of "obscurity," in which the spectator, in Burke's terms, is vulgarized—that is, "diminished to a boy" before an object or idea that he (in this case) cannot comprehend. Here is Burke's formulation from Part 2, Section 4 of his *Enquiry into . . . the Sublime and the Beautiful*: "It is our ignorance of things that causes all our admiration, and chiefly excites our passions. Knowledge and acquaintance make the most striking causes affect but little. It is thus with the vulgar, and all men are as the vulgar in what they do not understand" (61). Wordsworth's encounter, then, involves a kind of ritual of status reversal in which the spectator trades places with the indigent to whose gaze he or she is now subject. But in order to accomplish this reversal, the traces of utility in these figures must be erased and their subordination in the social hierarchy, which would negate their sublimity, must be decentered. Were the figures useful, in Burke's aesthetic, they could not be sublime. Strategically set at the margins of society, in an economic border realm in which material deprivation is offset by moral surplus, the socio-economic boundaries of the vagrants and indigents in Wordsworth's poetry appear sufficiently blurred to invest privation and obscurity with the power of the sublime. "To see an object distinctly, and to perceive its bounds, is one and the same thing," claims Burke (*Enquiry* 63); and as Adam Phillips observes in his recent edition of Burke's treatise, the breaking of boundaries characteristic of the Burkean sublime anticipates the power to disrupt the order of experience and tradition that Burke identifies with the "spirit of liberty" in the *Reflections* (*Enquiry* xv). Thus, the very liminal character of Wordsworth's indigent laborers and itinerant poor, their economic deprivation combined with their refusal to conform to the juridical categories the Poor Laws inscribe upon them, vests them with a certain affective sublimity and subversive liminality. In a Kantian sense, Wordsworth's poor are purposive without purpose; or, to transfer Kant's terms, powerful without power—powerful precisely because they appear to be powerless.

III

Destabilizing the conventional relationship between spectator and spectacle, Wordsworth's itinerants leave inconclusive the spectator's own social and subjective boundaries. While the industriousness of the old man in "Point Rash-Judgment," for example, or the determination of the leech gatherer in "Resolution and Independence" may reflect the spectator's desire for virtue, the indigence of these sublime vagrants figures the spectator's own fear of poverty from which industriousness and resolution won't necessarily protect him or her. These figures, therefore, present the spectator with a mirror image of the precariousness of his or her economic, social and psychological identity, at a time when socio-economic transformations introduced an alarming fluidity—up and down—into a once fixed social hierarchy. This uneasiness on the part of the spectator may well explain the negative reactions to Wordsworth's poems, especially those of Francis Jeffrey and Coleridge, for, as Turner notes, "from the perspectival viewpoint of those concerned with the maintainance of 'structure,' all sustained manifestations of communitas must appear as dangerous and anarchical, and have to be hedged around with prescriptions, prohibitions, and conditions" (109).

These moments of encounter between the spectator and the spectral vagrants, however, also open a space outside of structure and the boundaries of discursive time, a moment in which the vulnerability of the subject and the arbitrariness of the relations of production suggest the possibility to escape the conventional relations of power; hence, the encounter offers at least a transitory glimpse at a utopian horizon. In "Resolution and Independence," for example, the encounter with the leech gatherer leaves the spectator in a state of confusion in which the articulated words of the leech gatherer's discourse fuse together into a stream of sound: "The Old Man still stood talking by my side; / But now his voice to me was like a stream / Scarce heard; nor word from word could I divide . . ." (113–15; *Poems* 128). Similarly in "Point Rash-Judgment," the narrator, chastised by the old man's gaunt figure, loses focus on the man as a whole and fixes his eyes upon the old man's legs: ." . . for my single self I looked at them, / Forgetful of the body they sustained" (61–62; *PW* 2: 117). Confronted with the sublime language of the Other, whether it be the spoken word or the articulate body marked with a sublime indigence, the narrator is suspended momentarily in the synchronic moment of liminality. In this sublime moment, the narrator's own history dissolves and the diachronic structure on which his own sense of identity is fixed breaks down.

Cut loose from the narrative that defines social structure, the spectator loses the grounds of his or her own social status and identity. This moment of liminal instability that subverts structure amounts to the suspension of cognitive understanding and experience that constitutes the Kantian sublime; it offers, therefore, an erasure of that empirical, surveying power of the mind that the "civilizing" eye of the loco-descriptive and picturesque assumes on the part of the unself-conscious spectator. "Liminal entities are neither here nor there; they are betwixt and between the positions assigned and arrayed by law, custom, convention, and ceremonial"; and, as Turner might have added, language assigns those positions (including subject positions) (95). The encounters with the spectral shepherds, the old man of "Point Rash-Judgment" or the leech gatherer throw the spectator into a moment when he or she cannot presume to know the object of his or her gaze, when the socially constructed and hence arbitrary rules for judgment collapse. The apparition of the boundary-lessness of the old men, equivalent to the "boundlessness" of Kant's "formless object" of the sublime, perforates the naturalized boundaries of social class and places the spectator in a field of indeterminacy which, for Lyotard, makes possible the idea of community.[14]

In Turner's terms, the spectator here experiences the potentials of an egalitarian communitas, which may or may not be reaggregated into the normative social structure. Thus, the liminal moment, the "spot of time," opens to the potentials of political change and transformation as it frees itself from what Shelley in *A Defence of Poetry* calls the story—"a catalogue of detached facts, which have no other bond of connexion than time, place, circumstance, cause and effect"—which in socio-political terms constitutes ideology. In its place the liminal moment unfolds into what Shelley calls the poem—a "creation of actions" outside of time that "contains within itself the germ of a relation to whatever motives or actions have place in the possible varieties of human nature" (281). When the hierarchical gaze constructed in Cowper for the reader as spectator gives way in Wordsworth to a specular encounter with the poor, the distinctions of kind and class are shown for what they are—artificial and social, not decreed by any necessity or natural law, the aristocratic claim, nor secured by personal qualities like industriousness, the bourgeois claim. The sublime moment of this specular encounter, then, exposes the spectator's (subject) position in the social order as similarly arbitrary, unstable, and subject to reverses and multiplicity—somewhere betwixt and between the public self of Smith's "impartial spectator" and its double, the speculum of "the person whom I properly call myself."

If the representations of the poor in Cowper's poetry show us how poetry can "aestheticize" a predetermined political-historical idea of community, perhaps Wordsworth's poetry shows how the "aesthetic" becomes repoliticized as it disturbs the distance between the middle-class subject and the subjected classes. The relationship between Wordsworth's spectator and the specular solitary may indeed be considered a figure of the relationship between the social and the aesthetic sphere as the two act and re-act in a mutually interdependent but perhaps not overdetermined fashion. Wordsworth's specular figures, unlike the sublime objects of the Kantian aesthetic as described by Terry Eagleton in *The Ideology of the Aesthetic*, decenter the human subject as they discipline and chastise it from a position of marginal, but sublime, power.[15]

In "Resolution and Independence," to which I will return in Chapter Four, Wordsworth puts it this way:

> the whole Body of the man did seem
> Like one whom I had met with in a dream;
> Or like a Man from some far region sent,
> To give me human strength, and strong admonishment.
>
> (116–19; Poems 128)

That strength derives in part, I believe, from the recognition of the arbitrariness of power, which requires the spectator to abandon—if only for an ideal moment—the bounded forms of social practice and engage what Lyotard calls the "sorrow of the spectators in this end of the twentieth century": the obligation to embrace a troubling but potentially liberating heterogeneity that defies final solutions and totalizing theories of the subject, the political and the aesthetic.[16] Thus, Wordsworth's transfiguration of the spectacle of poverty opens a liminal moment of utopian potentiality that may, however, be claimed by both reactionary and radical interests, as I will discuss in the last section of this book.

3

The Silence of the Looms: Industry, Idleness and Ideology in Crabbe's *The Village* and Wordsworth's *Salisbury Plain*

> *Alas! in rural life, where youthful dreams*
> *See the Arcadia that Romance describes,*
> *Not even Content resides!*
> Charlotte Smith, The Emigrants

As I have noted in the first two chapters, industry and industriousness received a premium value from writers in the late eighteenth century. Indeed, the industrious laborer, servant or cottager is one of the most—may well be the most—ubiquitous literary types in late eighteenth-century narrative, figuring not only in poems like Langhorne's *The Country Justice* (1774–77), Cowper's *The Task* (1785), and Southey's *Botany-Bay Eclogues*; but in novels like Goldsmith's *The Vicar of Wakefield* (1766), Burney's *Cecilia* (1782), and Inchbald's *Nature and Art* (1796); in collected tales for children and young adults, like Wollstonecraft's *Original Stories from Real Life* (1788), Barbauld and Aikin's *Evenings at Home* (1792-96), and Charlotte Smith's *Rural Walks*; in addition to the hundreds of tracts and pamphlets containing stories about the virtues of industry, the pitfalls of idleness, mass-produced by the Evangelical, Sunday School and Philanthropic societies. In these works and in the pamphlets and treatises cast into the debate over reform and the Poor Laws the industrious poor appear as mythic, even chthonic, laborers whose lives illustrate the virtues of industry, patience and suffering. As objects of pity and sympathy, these industrious poor offer up a spectacle of poverty that invites middle-class readers to compare their own good fortune with that of the benighted paupers and meditate upon their duties to the poor, their sensibility and their compassion, often measured in the obligatory shedding of a tear.[1] Perhaps most importantly, the spectacle of poverty served as a scene of moral instruction. Inviting its middle-class readers to reflect upon their advantages over, and their social responsibilities toward, the poor, Smith's "The Sick Cottager" from *Rural Walks* typically poses the moral to which such works point:

"Are not sickness and poverty real evils? And do not such spectacles teach us the wickedness and folly of that discontent we are apt to indulge, if we are not exactly in the place we prefer, or with the people who amuse us?" (15). In the preface, Smith explains that her work is concerned with *"les petites morales."* In particular, "to repress discontent; to inculcate the necessity of submitting cheerfully to such situations as fortune may throw them into; to check that flippancy of remark, so frequently disgusting in girls of twelve or thirteen; and to correct the errors that young people often fall into in conversation, as well as to give them a taste for the pure pleasures of retirement, and the sublime beauties of Nature; has been my intention" (iii–iv). Thus the spectacle of poverty—whether urban or rural—intends to reinforce rather than challenge the social relations of the late eighteenth century; so long as the industrious poor appear to be the objects of charity and pity, as they do even in Wollstonecraft's *Original Stories*, the social structure itself remains unchallenged.

Nonetheless, as Janet Todd has explained in *Sensibility*, in the politically charged atmosphere of the 1790s, the cult of sensibility, despite its complicity in maintaining the status quo, was synonymous with radicalism from the point of view of many contemporaries, and especially as perceived through the reactionary lens of *The Anti-Jacobin* (130–32). Conservative propagandists like William Canning, James Gillray and Arthur Young campaigned vigorously to show that sensibility and the idea of universal benevolence (associated in particular with Price, Priestley and Godwin) were linked to principles dangerously revolutionary and unacceptably French. Drawing upon, even as it withdraws from, the conventions and political implications of sensibility, Wordsworth's poetry represents a direct intervention into this highly politicized arena as it moves the reader toward a more intense, if ambiguous, identification and solidarity with the laboring poor. As Todd notes, both "Blake and Wordsworth share many of the anti-rational, experiential assumptions of sensibility, but they both flee from its moral instructional aim. The stock characters of sentiment become enigmatic in Wordsworth's *Lyrical Ballads* and the sentimental situations of victim and abandoned woman refuse to yield clear moral generalizations" (143). In this refusal to draw moral conclusions, Wordsworth's poetry presents the reader with the possibility for an engagement with the laboring poor as subjects, rather than as objects, a possibility that disconcerted many of his early readers, most notably Francis Jeffrey. Here I want to show how far Wordsworth's spectacle of poverty subverts, even as it appeals to, the expectations of readers steeped in the conventions of sensibility and the discourse on poverty.

Wordsworth's poetry certainly imports features from the discourse on poverty that link his figurations of the laboring poor with the agrarian idyll of the eighteenth century—a kind of pastoral-georgic in which rustic *labor* is valorized at the same time that the rustic *laborer* is distanced from the reader or spectator. Nevertheless, the way in which his work assimilates those features in the industrious laborer represents a change in kind, to invoke Siskin's phrase—a change in tone, means of figuration and political resonance—from what Robert Mayo calls the "stereotyped pathos and generalized poverty, hardship, and old age" typical of the late eighteenth century (505).[2] While the works of writers like Pratt—and one might add the poems and stories by Barbauld, More and the magazine poets—sustain the reader's aloofness from the object of pity, Wordsworth's early work negotiates a more genuine, if unsettled and sometimes unsettling, familiarity with and sensitivity to the concerns of the poor. Moreover, although the silent vagrants of Wordsworth's *Lyrical Ballads*—the beggars, pedlars and discharged soldiers, with their "artless tales" and measured speech—serve as paradigmatic examples of those indigent deemed worthy of charity according to the discourse on poverty, their very presence—more immediate and palpable than in the conventional poems about the agricultural poor—suggests an implicit critique of the distancing conventions of the pastoral. Like Crabbe, as I will discuss below, Wordsworth uses these figures to criticize rather than confirm the reader's complacency in the face of a growing rural poverty. While Crabbe and Wordsworth draw upon a fund of "official" discourse that leaves intact and reinforces the value of a person's "industry" as a determinant of his or her moral worth, they criticize specific injustices built into both the language and the practice of Poor Law administration and the inchoate welfare system of their time. Thus, their entanglement with the structural polarities of the discourse on poverty must be examined in light of their poetry's implicit critique of the tacit assumptions of that discourse. By comparing their work to the sentimental depictions of the poor found in the poetry of Pratt, the powers and the limits—the utopian and reactionary potentials—of their critique of the discourse on poverty become evident.

I

Both Crabbe and Wordsworth present the poor with greater descriptive detail and precision than more popular poets, including Samuel Jackson Pratt, known to many by his pseudonymn Courtney Melmouth. Like his painterly counterpart Francis Wheatley, Pratt celebrated honest poverty and the industrious poor in best-selling volumes titled *Bread, or the Poor* (1801) and *John and Dane, or the Loyal Cottagers* (1803). Pratt's poetry represents the poor in a state of the post-industrial fall, stripped from the paternal care of benevolent landlords and subject to the hazards of a market economy disturbed by a centralized welfare policy. In his nostalgia for the happy laborer, Pratt apparently captivated the popular imagination, for his *Bread* went through three editions in just three years. The generic sentimentalism of Pratt's verse—the very stuff that Crabbe criticized and Wordsworth hoped to dignify—may seem simplistic, yet the signs of industriousness and thrift that it presents amply served its readers' taste for a picture-perfect agrarian poverty.

Echoing the pastoral-georgic models from which his work derives, Pratt indulges in a kind of gratuitous sentimentality in his depiction of rural poverty, and his poetry invokes the conventional epithets and subvening ideology of the agrarian idyll. In *Bread,* Pratt describes agricultural laborers as though they occupied an English paradise lost—a "blithsome band / A ruddy reckless, merry hearted crew," whose present hardship contrasts starkly with their former bliss:

> Illustrious swain! 'twas thine, from youth to age
> In hard, yet wholesome labour to engage;
> With spirit ready, and with patient hand,
> To raise an Eden on a nook of land,
> A flowery nook, with nature's bounty grac'd,
> Meed of thy toil, and rescued from the waste.
>
> (Part 1, p. 12)

Pratt outlines a scene of rural comfort and abundance. Here, as is typical of the agrarian idyll Bakhtin describes in *The Dialogic Imagination*, the cottagers' ale links them to the cycles and produce of nature. The cottager himself appears a kind of mythic "man of the people," to use Bakhtin's phrase, who represents "eternal productive labor" (236). Yet, Pratt's ideal worker in agriculture—a kind of eighteenth-century incarnation of Piers Plowman—blurs with the ideal worker in industry, for both are valued primarily because of their productivity:

> Hail, venerable cottager! and hail,
> Thy labour-cheering draughts of vigorous ale;
> Hail too, the secret cause of all thy wealth
> The constant toil that brought thee constant health.
>
> (1.12)

The discourse on poverty, with its emphasis upon industry, governs Pratt's lines. In its pastoral figures (swain) and pastoral-georgic ideologemes (healthful toil, rural paradise), Pratt's poetry maintains an absolute distance from the poor who inhabited the streets of London or the stubble fields of Suffolk.

From this doctrinal spectacle of rural poverty not even Charlotte Smith was immune, as we can see in a conversation between Mrs. Woodhouse and her daughters in *Rambles Farther: A Continuation of Rural Walks* (1796). Despite her sympathies for the revolution in

France, Smith reproduces the precious commonplace that the industrious poor enjoy a luxury and freedom that the affluent will never know. Observing a group of rural children decked in garlands on their way to a May Day festival—"a group that Gainsborough himself would have chosen" for figures in his landscapes—Mrs. Woodhouse expostulates: these children are the "happy heirs of laborious poverty; who, obtaining a very scanty subsistence, want no more, and find amidst the fields and coppices their slender *desert*" [*sic*] . . . (118). Like forest creatures released from their winter hiding places, these children celebrate in May their escape from "dark and dirty cottages" and their newfound "liberty to enjoy the only luxury they know, that of wondering among the meadows and woods, which offers these simple children of nature so many charms; and though certainly incapable of describing, or perhaps incapable of discriminating what they feel, yet it is theirs, more free from care and from restraint than the favourites of affluence, to enjoy what some poet . . . so well describes: By vale or brook to loiter; not displeas'd / Hear the streams pebbled roar, and the sweet bee / Humming his fairy tunes in praise of flowers" (118–20) Indeed, Pratt and Smith build their vision of rustic bliss on the same fantastical foundations Goldsmith used to construct his Auburn, an imaginary village "Where health and plenty cheered the labouring swain" (*Deserted Village* 2). Pratt's depiction of "rustic industry" combines the celebration of work in Morland's genre pieces with the domestic simplicity of one of Gainsborough's cottage scenes:

> The rich man's pastimes, are the poor man's wealth,
> And yield him plenty, happiness, and health,
> The fattening porket, and prolific sow,
> The brooding hen, and balmy-breathing cow . . .
> These fill'd the home-stall spare, with life and glee
> These gave enough—enough's prosperity! (1.6)

Pratt's vision of poverty here, like Smith's, is steeped in the doctrines of William Paley's *Reasons for Contentment*, in which Paley takes pains to show that the carefree lot of the poor was to be envied when contrasted to the burdens involved in the busy life of the rich. Paley actually accuses the poor of being "irreligious" and irrational when they complain of their lot, since such complaint indicates that they do not accept Providence and do not understand the supposed advantages of poverty: "I contend, that the man who murmurs and repines, when he has nothing to murmur and repine about, but the mere want of independent property, is not only irreligious, but unreasonable in his complaint; and that he would find, did he know the truth, and consider his case fairly, that a life of labour, such, I mean as is led by the labouring part of mankind in this country, has advantages in it which compensate all its inconveniencies" (*Works* 4: 422). The advantages Paley attributes to the poor are those we see repeated in Cowper and Pratt: steady employment and activity, better health, ease of mind, freedom from anxiety and—perhaps most preposterous of all—"constant cheerfulness and serenity of temper" (423). Pratt's eminently derivative *Liberal Opinions, upon Animals, Man, and Providence* (1775), which appeared only five years after Goldsmith's *Deserted Village*, gave vent early to the commonplace attacks upon indiscriminate charity, the corruption of luxury, and the carefree bliss of the peasantry. At one point Pratt writes: "Congratulate . . . the labourer, upon the bread that is to be earned only by the sweat of his brow: from his wants arise at once his virtues and his joys" (5: 117). From the joys of poverty comes "health, who diets upon the ears of the sheaf, that he may snore at night upon the stalks, formed without difficulty into a bed of tranquility." While conceding that rural labor does indeed involve toil, Pratt claims that the poor man is *"sea-soned"* to it; while he may " 'sweat . . . in the eye of Phoebus, he stoops to the exercise of the sickle, whistles cheerily in his progress, and tells blithly [*sic*] to his companion the story of his last frolic" (5: 117–18).

A standard feature of Pratt's rural world is the caring paternal lord, whose diligent observance of his duties to his family of laborers cemented the tripartite social structure—the domestic affections in Wordsworth's phrase—of rural England, and whose generosity led to the simple abundance that "rais'd the hind, and lifted him to man" (1.13):

> And FAIRFAX hail to thee, whose gen'rous mind,
> At little cost, thus rais'd th'industrious hind.
> Ah were the rich, like thee, their aid to lend,
> The weak to strengthen, and the poor befriend,
> Like him thy own swain the peasantry might live,
> And liberal share the comforts which they give;
> Like him, his cot might build, his garden dress,
> His patron honour, and his offspring bless;
> Like him, might look with pride on his retreat,
> And the hut flourish near the rich man's gate. (1.13)

Here Fairfax and his estate serve as a metonymy for the ideal social hierarchy in which each recognizes his or her place and in which rural workers exchange gratitude and "cheerful toil" for the customary tokens of paternal care from their generous lords. Blaming the consolidation of lands and the monopolization of farms for the presence of starving bands in the country, Pratt looks back with nostalgia to the generosity of land-owners who granted customary rights to their laborers: "Blest who like thee, O CARRINGTON, afford, / The plots that make the peasant *love* their lord" (1.14). Thus, Pratt's poem celebrates that chain of subordination so highly praised in Edmund Burke's *Thoughts and Details on Scarcity*:

"in all things whatever, the mind is most valuable and the most important; and in this scale the whole of agriculture is in a natural and just order; the beast is as an informing principle to the plough and cart; the labourer is as reason to the beast; and the farmer is as a thinking and presiding principle to the labourer" (10). The guiding light above them all, of course, is the natural aristocrat, signified in Pratt's poem by the benevolent Carrington.

Pratt takes up his position as spectator of a social drama, the conflicts from which he seems pleasantly immune, though even he presents a picture of the desperate conditions in rural England at the turn of the century. Indeed, from rural ease Pratt's poem introduces a kind of *schadenfreude* when the narrator visits the "wretched paupers of the PRESENT HOUR" (Part 1, p. 14). Deprived of their harvest home and their rural sports by greedy and upstart landlords, these present-day Hobbinols have been reduced to "spectres thin of hollow penury" (1.14). After a decade of poor harvests and bread riots, the sentimentalism of Pratt's golden age of paternalism is tempered by the intrusion of present social conditions of the rural poor, viewed from a careful distance—perhaps a reason for Pratt's wide acclaim.[3] The popularity of his poetry shows a persistent taste for the formulaic features of the pastoral-georgic idyll of agrarian poverty, even after Crabbe's thrashing of such features in *The Village*.

As portrayed in the guise of the industrious rural laborer, Pratt's and Smith's representations of the poor typify the contradictions inherent in the agrarian idyll. The "man of the people," though often deployed in a narrative critical of the ill-treatment of the poor, finally serves to naturalize the relations of production within the transforming political economy and so to qualify, if not completely neutralize, the critique of the industrial transformation of English agricultural society and the rural poor implicit in these works. Pratt's invocation of a golden age of social relations in the English countryside hearkens back to Goldsmith's *The Deserted Village* and its "bold peasantry, their country's pride" (55; Lonsdale, 678), but Pratt's poem lacks the meditative engagement with loss that blends public and private suffering in Goldsmith's. Unlike the progressive vision of the agrarian radicals, such as Joseph Spence or even William Cobbett (who was just beginning to reappear on the scene as an advocate for the rights of rural laborers), Pratt's Eden looks backward to a ready-made idyll of benevolent paternalism that could stifle any critical efforts to analyze and resolve the problems of rural poverty.

II

If Pratt's poetry invokes the discourse on poverty to set up a spectacle of blissful poverty contrasted to present decay, Crabbe's poetry deploys that discourse as a means to infiltrate the private space of the cottage and tenement to place the poor under surveillance. In order to point up the absurdity of using pastoral conventions to describe the English rural scene, Crabbe in *The Village* (1783) displays before his polite readers parallel series of both the misery and the vice thought to attend upon poverty. While eschewing the pastoral conventions and misleading georgic idealizations of rural poverty and labor, Crabbe, a self-described "realist" when it comes to describing the laboring poor, does not escape the stereotypes and categories framed within the discourse on poverty. Crabbe describes his project as an attempt to "paint the cot, / As truth will paint it, and as bards will not" (*Village* 1.53–54), and he condemns the pastoral conventions governing the representation of the poor. His attack on treating the poor as spectacle, as mere objects of pity, provided a necessary relief and contrast to the bathos of poetry like Pratt's. Yet even his own work imports features of the discourse on poverty, especially the binary categories of industry and idleness, in such a way as sometimes to undermine the reader's sympathy for the deserving poor by raising his or her contempt for them.

Crabbe attacked the idea of "wholesome labour," a familiar conceit of the agrarian idyll, and he recognized that the aged laborer received "aches and anguish," trembling knees and beating temples, rather than Pratt's constant health (*Village* 1.149).[4] Even the proud young laborers, attempting to outdo their mentors, can hope for small rewards other than pain for their efforts, and their actual pay gives them barely enough for subsistence:

> There may you see the youth of slender frame
> Contend with weakness, weariness, and shame;
> Yet urg'd along, and proudly loth to yield,
> He strives to join his fellows of the field;
> Till long contending nature droops at last,
> Declining health rejects his poor repast
> His cheerless spouse the coming danger sees,
> And mutual murmurs urge the slow disease.
> (*Village* 1.156-63)

Furthermore, Crabbe completely rejected the often touted qualities of "vigorous ale" and the frugal diet. In his view, ale offered nothing more than short-lived cheer, and the sparing meal promoted nothing like the health or longevity poets attributed to it. Crabbe is indignant with those like Pratt who praise what Crabbe mockingly calls "homely, healthy fare" (1.166), for he recognizes the hypocrisy involved in recommending diets for others that urban-dwelling writers of pastoral would reject for themselves. The presentation of such fare amounts to a trope, a pleasant spectacle from which the poets keep a proper, aesthetic distance in their own lives. Thus Crabbe points out "the misery of a stinted meal; / Homely not wholesome, plain not plenteous, such / As you who praise would never deign to touch" (1.169–71).

With the introduction of the aged swain in *The Village*, Crabbe's poem turns from a criticism of the agrarian idyll to a trenchant attack upon the system of parish poor relief—especially indoor relief. Crabbe creates a scene of desperate alienation in his depiction of the parish workhouse. The Poor Laws, in Crabbe's view, compel orphans, abandoned wives, the elderly, the mad and the infirm to huddle together:

> There children dwell who know no parents' care,
> Parents, who know no children's love, dwell there;
> Heart-broken matrons on their joyless bed,
> Forsaken wives and mothers never wed;
> Dejected widows with unheeded tears,
> And crippled age with more than childhood-fears;
> The lame, the blind, and, far the happiest they!
> The moping idiot and the madman gay. (1.232–39);

Ronald Hatch rightly portrays Crabbe's description of the workhouse in *The Village* as "the decrepit asylum of all society's undesirables" (21), and as if to emphasize the moral undesirability of such intermingling, Crabbe again uses metonymic devices to conjure up images of sexual license and unhealthy contagion, thereby anticipating later mid-Victorian objections to the depraved atmosphere of the workhouse. Only "one rude beam divides" the great room of the particular house that Crabbe imagines; its sides are formed with "naked rafters"; and "vile bands" hold together the thatch of the thin roof (1.262–64). Within the confines of the "dismal walls" among "putrid vapours" a more dismal mixing takes place: "loud groans from some sad chamber flow, / Mixt with the clamours of the croud below" (1.301, 230, 242–43).

Hatch reminds us that Burke and Knox reprinted Crabbe's description of the workhouse in *The Annual Register* and the *Elegant Extracts*, respectively (21, 23). Once again, we see, poverty was put on display in this mediated form, and readers of Crabbe's verse who would never set foot in a workhouse to observe the conditions there could count upon their memory of these lines to substitute for any immediate encounter with those confined within the workhouses they might pass by. Jeffrey's comment on Crabbe's readers is telling. He knew, Jeffrey writes in the *Edinburgh Review* 12 (1808), "more than one of our unpoetical acquaintances who declared they could never *pass by* a parish workhouse, without thinking of the description of it they had read at school in the Poetical Extracts" (131; qtd. in Hatch 22; my italics). He did not know, or at least does not mention, any unpoetical acquaintance who *walked into* a parish workhouse.

In his description in *The Village* of the aged laborer Crabbe also attacks those who impugn the poor without investigating the particulars of each case. This laborer, Crabbe's equivalent of Wordsworth's Simon Lee, "once was chief in all the rustic trade" (1.188). Though he had won many prizes for his skill at the plough, the old swain is unable to work any longer and so faces pain, disease and the parish workhouse, because the rich landlords who formerly employed him now scorn him as one of the "lazy poor" (1.199). Crabbe condemns those taskmasters who single out the feeble efforts of the aged laborer who "when his age attempts its task in vain / With ruthless taunts of lazy poor complain" (1.198-99). Like Wordsworth's Simon Lee, similarly abandoned by all but his wife, the old man is meant to throw the unfairness of such categories in the face of the reader and to point out the "cold charities of man to man" (1.245) that have replaced a paternal, but purportedly more personal and hence more sympathetic, system of relief. That Crabbe can point out the unfairness of the epithet "lazy poor" in the individual case of the old laborer, but reproduce that very category in his overall description of the poor, points to the ideological power of discursive frames to delimit generalizations about poverty; it equally shows the power of the particular to fracture the discursive frames that govern the general.

The power of descriptive accuracy to throw off the prescriptive and totalizing ideologemes of the discourse on poverty in part vindicates Hatch's general assessment that "the picture of the poor at the opening of 'The Parish Register' is so obviously naive and so obviously out of keeping with the complexity of the picture presented in *The Village*, that it should arouse suspicions as to whether it is Crabbe's complete view" (54). The complete view, Hatch believes, can be seen only by "tak[ing] into account the many individualized character sketches . . . depicting the complicated processes by which individuals participate in social situations" (54). Yet, as in Wordsworth's "Simon Lee," *The Ruined Cottage* or "Point Rash-Judgment," in *The Village* the aged swain's former industry redeems him from the narrator's censure in the present. Thus even as it criticizes this particular use of the common epithet "lazy poor," Crabbe's poem draws upon and underscores the idleness/industry opposition as determinate in the last instance of the old swain's worth.

Crabbe's *The Village*, then, deploys the determinate categories of the discourse on poverty even as it deplores their use. The poem objects to the indiscriminate and universal assocation of idleness with the poor. Such automatic labeling of the poor, which was accelerated by the bureaucratization of Poor Law administration, obliterates what Crabbe and Wordsworth perceive and insist upon reaffirming: the individual characteristics and particular histories of those who find themselves dependent upon parish relief. Nonetheless, both Crabbe and Wordsworth must invoke a generic construct—industry—as a means to invite sympathy, if not respect, for their poverty-stricken heroes. As in

"Point Rash-Judgment," in *The Village* the old man deserves the reader's sympathy because we learn that he has been industrious; his present or apparent idleness can be justified by his infirmity and age, for which the Elizabethan Poor Law made provision.

Of course, along with Crabbe's criticism of the alienating effects of bureaucratic management of the poor comes a nostalgia for private charity and a celebration of those few propertied individuals who purportedly realize the ideal of *noblesse oblige*. After censuring the rich in Book 1 for ignoring rural laborers' hardships and poverty, Crabbe presents in Book 2 a checkered scene of promiscuity, intoxication, riot and domestic violence. Despite its intention to "show the great, those mightier sons of Pride / How near in vice the lowest are allied" (2.89–90), Book 2 effectively relapses into a catalogue of familiar charges against the poor. To compare the poor with the aristocracy is at best a backhanded slap in the face. The concluding encomium to the Duke of Rutland for his charity and benevolence adds insult to injury, as the poem enjoins the poor to revere their patron and forget their own troubles in the contemplation of his.:

> Oh! if in life one noble chief appears,
> Great in his name, while blooming in his years;
> Born to enjoy whate'er delights mankind,
> And yet to all you feel or fear resign'd;
> Who gave up joys and hopes to you unknown,
> For pains and dangers greater than your own
> If such there be, then let your murmurs cease,
> Think, think of him, and take your lot in peace. (2.107–14)

Crabbe seems to acknowledge the bias of *The Village* when, in his Preface to *Poems* (1807), he notes that those who write about rustic life tend to exaggerate either the idyllic or the vicious aspects of the countryside. In the Preface to *The Parish Register* (1807), Crabbe explains that he will "endeavour once more to describe Village-Manners, not by adopting the notion of pastoral simplicity or assuming ideas of rustic barbarity, but by more natural views of the peasantry, considered as a mixed body of persons sober or profligate, and from hence, in a great measure, contented or miserable" (*CPW* 1: 207). Even in this statement, however, we can see the binary moral structure of the discourse on poverty construct the either/or: the industrious and idle, the sober and profligate, the content and miserable, the rural and urban. Thus, despite Crabbe's intentions to transcend the discourse on poverty, the representation of the poor in *The Parish Register* poem operates on the very binary system constructed in that discourse.

The Hogarthian narrator of *The Parish Register*, for example, announces his project as the comparison of the "State of the Peasantry as meliorated by Frugality and Industry" with the "State of the Poor, when improvident and vicious" (*CPW* 1: 212). The narrator furthermore claims that the industrious poor appear to be far fewer in number than the vicious: "Toil, care, and patience bless th'abstemious few, / Fear, shame, and want the thoughtless herd pursue" (*PR* 1.29–30). Moreover, like most middle-class writers on the poor, Crabbe aligns the virtuous and vicious poor with the country and the city, respectively.

Typical of such oppositions is John Aikin's contrast of agricultural to industrial laborers in his "Description of the Country from Thirty to Forty Miles Round Manchester" (1795), in which he finds "neatness, cleanliness, and comfort" among the families of "labourers in husbandry," but "filth, rags, and poverty" among the "families of manufactures in general"—though the wages of the industrial worker, he notes, are nearly twice those of the agricultural laborer (220). This familiar opposition between town and country, factory and field, shapes Crabbe's description of the rural cottage, inhabited by the industrious poor who adorn their walls with signs of religious devotion and patriotism. In contrast, Crabbe describes those who live in the urban tenement on the city's "infected Row" as a "disputacious crew" (*PR* 1.169, 170). Unlike the orderly rural families, these urban dwellers live in the kind of semiotic riot that Wordsworth describes in Book 7 of *The Prelude*. When Crabbe's narrator pans from the hard-working inhabitants of the "Fair scenes of peace" to the hovel of the urban poor, "offence / Invades all eyes and strikes on every sense" (*PR* 1.166, 188–89). Instead of the "industrious Swain," we meet "the Sot, the Cheat, the Shrew" (*PR* 1.31, 171); instead of prints of goodly kings and heroic scenes from history, sensational and indecent ballads line the walls; and instead of the signs of industry so abundant in the rustic domesticity of the Cot, signs of wasted time and idle play abound in the promiscuous riot of the city:

> Here are no Wheels for either Wool or Flax
> But packs of Cards—made up of sundry packs;
> Here is no Clock, nor will they turn the glass
> And see how swift the important moments pass. . . .
> (*PR* 1.230–33)

Thieves, beggars, smugglers, fortune tellers, hungry children, cursing mothers and neglected infants strain to burst the order of the rhymed couplets in a phantasmagoria of profligacy better suited to the blank verse of Wordsworth's similar scene of chaos in Book 7 of *The Prelude*. Indeed, in that poem Wordsworth too associates the "throng" of the city with "files of ballads [dangling] from dead walls" (*Prelude* 7.209).

As is evident, Crabbe's poem uses metonymy to evoke guilt or virtue by association with value-laden objects. Indeed, Crabbe constructs a picture of the good and the bad poor by means of the same narrative strategies that William Hogarth uses, perhaps with most striking similarity in the famous *Industry and Idleness* series of 1747.[5] Hogarth's Francis Goodchild and Tom Idle, of course, embody the binary value system of the discourse on poverty. Hogarth's method of constructing character by associative display of external effects allows him to construct the apprentices' résumés as a series of parallels and contrasts. The copious array of objects associated with each apprentice functions as a visual objective correlative by which Hogarth represents the simple moral character of the industrious and the idle apprentice. While *The Parish Register*, unlike Hogarth's series of prints, does not show the successive stages of rise and decline among the parish poor,[6] the poem follows fundamentally Hogarthian techniques in its binary development of morally antipathetic characters associated with external objects steeped in conventional values. Whereas Hogarth neatly hangs the ballads of *Dick Whittington* and *The London Prentice* behind Francis Goodchild's workplace in the Spitalfields' shop, Crabbe neatly places prints of good kings on the walls of his cottage dwellers. Whereas Goodchild's well-thumbed but well cared-for copy of *The Prentice's Guide* lay by his side, the "pious works for Sunday's use"—*Pilgrim's Progress* and the Bible, "bought by sixpence weekly saved"—rest neatly in place among Crabbe's cottagers (*PR* 1.81, 83). Even the narrator's intrusion into the poem seems strikingly similar to the captions of Hogarth's prints.

In Crabbe's poem, to the narrator's inevitable question "whence all these woes," comes the predictable response: "From want of virtuous will / Of honest shame" and "From want of care to employ the vacant hour" (*PR* 1.226–29). The narrator's direct—and hardly necessary—intervention into the poem establishes a bond between the narrator and reader, serving much the same function as the mostly biblical proverbs attached to the plates of Hogarth's prints: to appeal to an authority outside the scene as a means of tacitly recognizing the reader's position of moral superiority over the subjects of the work. Through this moral identity, Crabbe's tale establishes a kind of consensus—even complicity—between the narrator and the reader, as it confirms their social and moral superiority to the paupers and working poor.

The contrast between virtuous industry and profligate idleness well set and the relationship between reader and writer firmly established, Crabbe concludes this sequence of scenes from the poor thus:

> Such are our Peasants, those to whom we yield
> Praise with relief, the Fathers of the Field
> And these who take from our reluctant hands,
> What Burn advises or the Bench commands. (*PR* 1.269–72)

Despite declaring in the preface that he will avoid the bipolar structure of *The Village*, Crabbe once again divides the peasantry into a contrastive pair. The industrious and deserving of the countryside receive both praise and relief, while those who are unwilling to be regulated by the workplace clock (or the natural clock that regulates agrarian labor) must pilfer the pool of parish funds collected from reluctant hands. By placing both deserving and undeserving peasants as the objects of relief, Crabbe further strengthens the implicit compact between reader and narrator, both of whom are presumed to be the potential benefactors of the poor.

While Hatch would like us to dismiss this "so obviously naive and so obviously out of keeping" picture of the poor in *The Parish Register*, on the grounds that the individual characters in the rest of the poem are more complex, I believe we must rather consider how the larger, and perhaps overly simplistic, moral system governing the opening generalizations of the poem also grounds the affective value of those individualized portraits (54). No matter what contributions Crabbe may have made in his later works to a narrative description that allows for nuances in character, the binary terms that he uses to weigh the moral worth of his characters come ready-made from the mainstream discourse on poverty. As Peter New has observed: "In [Crabbe's] world it is excessively easy to distinguish good from evil," a failure of understanding that "deprives him of the possibility of writing some of the higher forms of tragedy" in which moral choice is confused by multiple, competing options for right or wrong action (11). With regard to the moral value of the poor, Crabbe's work does not escape the disciplinary mechanisms of the discourse on poverty, in which "industry" and "idleness" attain the status of *a priori* truths—apparently natural and unquestionable categories that frame the possibilities for describing and perceiving the poor.

To the degree that Crabbe's work relies on the binary oppositions governing the representations of the poor, it does not engage in the kind of realism that critics from Francis Jeffrey to Jerome McGann have claimed for it.[7] His praise for the industrious and contempt for the idle derive not from a close, hard look at the plight and condition of the poor; rather, Crabbe's characterizations are framed within the conventional wisdom regarding the poor. Nonetheless, in his attack on the demoralizing and dehumanizing conditions of "pauper palaces," Crabbe explores some of the possible causes of poverty and, like Wordsworth, at least attempts to move his middle-class readers to sympathize with the poor and recognize their own complicity in creating the conditions that give rise to poverty.

III

Steeped in controversies over the rights of men and women, the administration of the Poor Laws, and the obligations of those who were not poor to support, educate or simply ignore those who were, Wordsworth and his contemporaries would have heard the rustle of protest in the female vagrant's plaintive tale in *Salisbury Plain* or on the other side of Margaret's silence in *The Ruined Cottage*. Only when we similarly immerse ourselves in the controversies of the mid-1790s can we too hear that rustle of protest that disturbs, if it does not subvert, the normative schema of idleness and industry on which the sympathetic mechanisms of the poetry depend—not only in *Salisbury Plain* and *The Ruined Cottage*, but in poems included in *Lyrical Ballads*, such as "The Female Vagrant" and "The Last of the Flock," perhaps the poems most specifically targeted at the Poor Law reformers.

As Mary Jacobus observes in *Tradition and Experiment in Wordsworth's Lyrical Ballads*, during the crisis years of the 1790s, Wordsworth "turned to narrative poetry to express his indignation at the plight of the poor, the dispossessed, and the casualties of war" (142). Jacobus notes too that Wordsworth spoke out directly—though one should add not publicly—against policies that led to an inordinate amount of suffering among the poor in the unpublished *Letter to the Bishop of Llandaff* (1793), in which he notes the gap between the accumulated wealth of the higher echelons and the abject poverty among the laboring poor: "Even from the astonishing amount of the sums raised for the support of one description of the poor may be concluded the extent and greatness of that oppression, whose effects have rendered it possible for the few to afford so much, and have shewn us that such a multitude of our brothers exist in even helpless indigence" (*PrW* 1: 43).

Of all the *Lyrical Ballads* perhaps none more directly engages the social crises of the 1790s than "The Female Vagrant." Wordsworth's revisions to this poem reveal the degree to which he later muted his radical critique as he became more reserved in his political opinions. Originally written as a sequence in *Salisbury Plain* in 1793 and 1794, the poem uses the poverty and destitution of the female vagrant to criticize Pitt's war against France and the Pitt administration's failure to provide for the destitute, the numbers of whom were visibly growing in the mid-1790s. From the earliest commentators to more recent critics such as Mary Jacobus, Nicholas Roe and John Williams, many have rightly pinned the motivations for *Salisbury Plain* upon the political and social crisis in which it is implicated. A review of the poem in the *British Critic* for October 1799 well expresses the politically unacceptable position Wordsworth's contemporaries found in the poem. I will quote at length here to show the reviewer's praise of the aesthetics, but distaste for the politics, of the poem:

> "The Female Vagrant" is a composition of exquisite beauty, nor is the combination of events, related in it, out of the compass of possibility; yet we perceive, with regret, the drift of the author

in composing it; which is to show the worst side of civilized society, and thus to form a satire against it. But let fanciful men rail as
they will at evils which no care can always prevent, they can have
no dream more wild than the supposition, that any human wisdom can possibily exclude all evils from a state which divine
Providence has decreed, for reasons the most wise, to be a state
of suffering and trial. (366–67)

This review, which brings Providence to bear as a witness against the
political import of the poem, readily affirms that Wordsworth's poem
cut against the grain of the *status quo*.

Jacobus is certainly right, then, to claim that "it is anti-war
protest, as well as the more general humanitarian protest of the period,
that provides the chief impulse behind *Salisbury Plain*" (143).[8] Indeed,
as the female vagrant, narrating her own historically displaced story,
laments, " 'Twas a hard change, an evil time was come; / We had no
hope, and no relief could gain" (91–92). In the chronological displacement of the poem, that "evil time" would suggest the years 1794 to 1797,
a time of grain shortages and the consequent inflation of prices due to
poor harvests in 1794 and 1795; an increasingly costly war against France
in the West Indies and on the continent; an escalation of alarm over the
possibility of popular revolt or revolution in England and Ireland; and
restrictions on commerce as a result of that war.

In mentioning the 1795 revisions he made to *Salisbury Plain*,
Wordsworth told Francis Wrangham that he wrote the poem "partly to
expose the vices of the penal law and the calamities of war as they affect
individuals" (*EY* 159). Wordsworth here reveals his endorsement of the
popular and radical view that the high cost of bread could be directly
traced to the war. As revised between 1795 and 1799 under the title
Adventures on Salisbury Plain (*ASP*), the poem strategically deploys
poverty as the basis of a Godwinian critique of the way social injustice
and poverty foster criminal behavior. Moreover, it plainly tells of the
despair to which the loss of property due to enclosure and consolidation
of property drove many tenant farmers and small holders, making them
easy game for the press gangs and recruiting parties taking advantage of
the desperate. Like *Caleb Williams*, the poem also shows the degree of
harassment that a landlord could bring to bear upon his tenants if the
latter stood in the way of the economically adventurous enterprise of the
former. Thus, the poem turns on its head the familiar propensity to
blame indigence upon the laziness and profligacy of the poor; it points
instead to social, political and economic conditions beyond the control
of the laboring poor as the cause of their destitution.[9]

Attributing the female vagrant's poverty to what was widely
considered to be an unjust military action, Wordsworth places himself
squarely among the radicals and reformers, from Paine to Fox, who

vehemently attacked Pitt for the war with France. Moreover, as Roe reminds us in *Wordsworth and Coleridge: The Radical Years*, the revisions to *Salisbury Plain* stemmed directly from Wordsworth's reading of Godwin's *Political Justice* and *Caleb Williams* in 1794–95 (132). While Williams rightly argues that Wordsworth in *Salisbury Plain* sets himself apart from Paine's revolutionism, he perhaps goes too far to discountenance, because of the traces of pastoral in the poem, Wordsworth's own version of radicalism. Williams concedes "that Wordsworth was no lover of his country's Government," but denies the radical implications of Wordsworth's opposition; in his view, Wordsworth looks backward— unlike Paine and the French—to "an earlier, purer social order (associated aesthetically with pastoral imagery) [that] had been corrupted and destroyed by an increasingly materialistic establishment . . ." (75). However much the pastoral may loom in the background of the poem, Wordsworth's Salisbury Plain is no Auburn. As I have already suggested, nostalgia does not always serve the interests of the *status quo*, for it may be deployed as a critique of the present. Moreover, in 1795 Wordsworth's censure of war would sound a distinctively Jacobin reverberation to the contemporary ear; in Marilyn Butler's words, "[w]hen literature dwells on the sufferings of war's English victims, it inevitably sounds like opposition to authority, or perhaps literally Opposition to Government" (*Romantics* 31).

In *Rights of Man*, Paine had attacked war in general as a means by which an imperious government could extort money from its citizens— especially from those who could least afford it:

> The inhabitants of every country, under the civilization of laws, easily civilize together, but governments being yet in an uncivilized state, and almost continually at war, they pervert the abundance which civilized life produced to carry on the uncivilized part to a greater extent. By thus engrafting the barbarism of government upon the internal civilization of a country, it draws from the latter, and more especially from the poor, a great portion of those earnings, which should be applied to their own subsistence and comfort. (233)

For Paine, European states, including England, had discovered a "pecuniary advantage . . . in keeping up this state of uncivilization," drawing from war both power and revenue, thereby strategically using declarations of war to legitimate massive and extortive schemes of taxation which benefitted those in power. In *Political Justice*, Godwin showed that "[w]ar has . . . been found the inseparable ally of political institution" (84). The result and sign of the corruption and perversion of human reason, moral purpose and ingenuity—themselves caused by political injustice and despotism—war *and* poverty for Godwin devolve from the same perversions of justice which had made plunder and murder a kind of business:

> Because individuals were liable to error, and suffered their apprehensions of justice to be perverted by a bias in favour of themselves, government was instituted. . . . Men were induced deliberately to seek each other's lives, and to adjudge the controversies between them, not according to the dictates of reason and justice, but as either should prove most successful in devastation and murder. This was no doubt in the first instance the extremity of exasperation and rage. But it has since been converted into a trade. One part of the nation pays another part, to murder and be murdered in their stead; and the most trivial causes . . . have sufficed to deluge provinces with blood. (510)

To inflame his reader's imagination, Godwin paints a grim picture of the battlefield, observing that "the plain is strewed with death in all its forms" (510).

Wordsworth's Salisbury Plain, we may remember, is also a "plain strewed with death [and violence] in all its forms"—from the early sacrifices of the Druids to the most recent victims of the trade in death; from the peasant who abuses his child to the discharged sailor whose abject poverty has led him to murder for money; from the gibbet that reminds the sailor of his guilt and the capital punishment he will face to the final scene where the political system that used him as an instrument of its unjust war hangs him from the gibbet, in the poem's ultimate social irony:

> They left him hung on high in iron case,
> And dissolute men, unthinking and untaught
> Planted their festive booths beneath his face. . . .
>
> (*ASP* 820–22)

Not until Thomas Hardy's *Tess of the D'Urbervilles* will we again see this powerful use of tragic sympathy for a character to vilify a social and political system that has alienated and dehumanized its most humble citizenry. Indeed, the poem repeatedly points out that the political system that executes the destitute sailor is the same system that started the war in which he fought, denied him the pension he deserved, and thereby led him toward the very crime for which it hypocritically condemns him to death.

John Williams claims that the emphasis upon the sailor's and the female vagrant's individuality in the 1795 revision shows "their alienation from any kind of existing social or political context—radical or otherwise. Their only hope for survival lies in their inherent virtues of love and sympathy . . . which must come from them in isolation or not at all" (77). Williams's point here is that Wordsworth's poem undermines the possibility of working-class consciousness and collective dissent by throwing responsibility for justice and social change onto individuals destined to remain powerless without the benefit of radical organization. Yet the poem has taken pains to show that these outcasts' attempts to form a viable alternative community have failed precisely because unjust laws and unjust wars have driven them into exile and criminality.

Adventures on Salisbury Plain (*ASP*) explicitly delineates the social causes of the female vagrant's poverty. In the early version of the poem, abstraction and the passive voice conveniently leave ambiguous the reasons why the female vagrant's father loses his property: "Oppression trampled on his tresses grey . . . / His all was seized" (*SP* 257, 260). In the *Adventures*, however, his loss clearly arises from the excessive ambitions of a landlord who has trampled upon the hereditary rights of his tenants in order to increase his commercial profit: "Then rose a mansion proud our woods among / And cottage after cottage owned its sway" (*ASP* 300–301). Wordsworth's 1841 reworkings of these lines indicate that the "lost leader," more interested in psychological motives and effects than in social or political causes, found these lines too politically volatile to risk publishing; thus in *Guilt and Sorrow* the reasons for the old man's demise are all but obliterated in revisionary mystifications: "through severe mischance and cruel wrong, / My father's substance fell into decay" (228–29; *SPP* 243). What remains common to all three versions of the poem, however, is that when the old man falls into poverty, his misfortune sets off a chain of events that lead to the further demise of his family. Even in the least critical version, the poem cuts through the veneer of rustic simplicity to show a poverty that destroys the simple virtues of the countryside; moreover, the poem affiliates the rural world with the political and social bustle of London and its less than glorious machinations.

It is important to remember that the first published version of the female vagrant's story, which appeared in *Lyrical Ballads*, was based upon the *Adventures* revisions, so that as late as 1798 and 1800 Wordsworth was willing to leave intact the political and social critique that her story explicitly entails. Indeed, "The Female Vagrant" contains direct allusions to Godwin's *Caleb Williams* and *Political Justice*. Like Hawkins, the tenant farmer brought to ruin by ruthless Mr. Tyrrel in *Caleb Williams*, the female vagrant's father puts up certain resistance to the landlord's designs to remove him from his "old hereditary nook" (44):

> when he had refused the proffered gold,
> To cruel injuries he became a prey,
> Sore-traversed in whate'er he bought and sold:
> His troubles grew upon him day by day,

Till all his substance fell into decay.
His little range of water was denied;
All but the bed where his old body lay,
All, all was seized, and weeping, side by side,
We sought a home where we uninjured might abide.
(46–54; *SPP* 133–34)

Hawkins had been a small freeholder, ousted from his first farm by one Mr. Underwood, who wanted to punish Hawkins for voting contrary to his landlord's desires. Tyrrel, who ironically rescues Hawkins from Underwood in an action "contrary to the understood conventions of the country gentleman" (71), subjects Hawkins to even worse punishment for refusing to sign his seventeen-year-old son into Tyrrel's service. Hawkins vows to Tyrrel, "I will lose all that I have, and go to day-labour, and my son too, if needs must; but I will not make a gentleman's servant of him" (74). To crush Hawkins's will, Tyrrel's stooges flood the Hawkins's land and loose cattle to destroy their few crops. Eventually Tyrrel invokes the hated Black Act to bring charges of poaching against the youngest Hawkins, Leonard. As readers of the novel will recall, Leonard and his father, who "had trusted to persevering industry and skill to save the wreck of his little property from the vulgar spite of his landlord" (78) are eventually sentenced for the murder of Tyrrel and are executed.

I recall this scene from *Caleb Williams* to remark the similarity in circumstances between Hawkins and the female vagrant's father and the discharged sailor in the *Adventures* version of the poem. Caleb, who narrates the Hawkins's tale, comments that the elder Hawkins deserves our pity "since his being finally urged to desperation, and brought, together with his son, to an ignominious fate, was originally owing to the sturdiness of his virtue and independence" (108). Wordsworth, too, takes pains to establish the virtue and independence of the female vagrant's father—"My father was a good and pious man, / An honest man by honest parents bred" (10–11; *SPP* 131)—and the honesty and virtue of the sailor through his acts of charity and kindness to those in distress. While not so clearly specified as in *Caleb Williams*, the female vagrant's father meets with "cruel injuries" as he resists the attempts to deprive him of his hereditary rights. The extortion of his land sets in motion a chain of worsening conditions that ends ultimately in the absolute alienation and exile of the female vagrant that brings her to this plain of sorrows.

As if to fulfill the fears Hawkins had for himself and Leonard, the old man becomes dependent upon his soon-to-be son-in-law's alienated day labor for support. Moreover, despite their "constant toil and constant prayer" (83; *SPP* 135), the female vagrant and her husband are driven to desperate measures:

'Twas a hard change, an evil time was come;
We had no hope, and no relief could gain.
But soon, with proud parade, the noisy drum
Beat round, to sweep the streets of want and pain.
(91–94; *SPP* 136)

As David Simpson reminds us in *Wordsworth's Historical Imagination*, "relief" for Wordsworth's contemporaries was "a very important word, for in contemporary discourse it was the one always used to describe the general, public enterprise of assisting the poor" (179). Unable to gain poor relief, the husband is forced to enlist in the army, whose unscrupulous recruiters and crimpers always lay in wait for those who had exhausted their last resources. Thus, Wordsworth's poem points directly to the inadequacy of the Poor Laws to remediate the sufferings of the poor. More importantly, however, he criticizes the insidious complicity between poverty and war, in that the enlistment of the female vagrant's husband, like Robert's in *The Ruined Cottage*, results not from an act of patriotism but from a desperate attempt to survive. The original lines of *Salisbury Plain* make clear that the "spirit of independence"—the husband's refusal to rely upon parish relief or private charity—leads him to enlist, for like the widowed female vagrant upon her return from America, "[h]e could not beg" (*SP* 304). Striking this line, which, like one of Crabbe's progress poems, emphasizes the moral choice of the female vagrant's husband, Wordsworth stresses the social determinism of this incident and thereby strengthens his critique of the way that Pitt's war machine benefited from the hopelessness of the poor during the war years.

This critique becomes all the more important when we remember that in 1794, the year before Wordsworth began his revisions to *Salisbury Plain*, individuals with no military experience were authorized to raise—by whatever means at their disposal—companies of men who would then be absorbed into existing battalions. As Clive Emsley explains, these "recruiters," who received commissions based on the number of recruits they raised, often did not even go into service with their companies, though they could sometimes get a lifetime pension for reaching their quotas (36). The less scrupulous resorted to extortion, bribes, false promises and even crimping—the kidnapping of recruits—which was so extensive that in the summers of 1794 and 1795 riots against crimping broke out in London and elsewhere. In April 1795, about seven months before Wordsworth began his revisions to *Salisbury Plain*, Parliament passed an act (35 Geo.III.34) that allowed magistrates to send able-bodied idlers or petty criminals directly to the navy. The sense of outrage at these acts of crimping and bribery readily impresses itself in "An Address to the Nation from the London Corresponding

Society" (1793), drafted at the Crown and Anchor Tavern by Maurice Margarot and Thomas Hardy, who were later tried for and acquitted of treason in the famous trials of 1794:

> [F]or fresh supplies of blood the Liberties of our Country are invaded! the Seaman is forcibly torn from his family! the Peasant kidnapped from the plough! and the starving Labourer is compelled to sell his Life and his Liberty for Bread—If such, O much oppressed Britons! are the effects of a Four months' War, what are you to expect when it shall have lasted as many years! (qtd. in Cole and Filson 45)

If Wordsworth enters directly into the debates over the treatment of recruits in "The Female Vagrant," his poem also suggests that he was aware that living conditions for English soldiers, sailors and their families, especially in the beginning years of the war, were wretched and dehumanizing. Indeed, preferring the indigence from which her husband has fled, the female vagrant nearly loses her sense of humanity as she follows the mercenary and misfit band of soldiers:

> better far
> In Want's most lonely cave till death to pine
> Unseen, unheard, unwatched by any star;
> Or in the streets and walks where proud men are,
> Better our dying bodies to obtrude,
> Than dog-like, wading at the heels of war,
> Protract a curst existence, with the brood
> That lap (their very nourishment!) their brother's blood
> (119-26; *SPP* 137)

What follows this life of "[d]isease and famine, agony and fear" (128; *SPP* 137), as she laments, is the very want the soldier's occupation was to prevent. As the chain of disasters unreels, the female vagrant loses her children and her husband to war and then returns to England a penniless vagabond in her own land.

Here again Wordsworth directs his satiric pen at an issue with some immediacy for his contemporaries, for the conditions of soldiers, especially in the early campaigns at Flanders and in the West Indies, were appalling. The historical displacement of "The Female Vagrant" is thinly veiled, so that though her story ostensibly takes place during the American wars, readers in 1798 would be thinking of current poor harvests and the war with France that had begun in February of 1793. Thus when the female vagrant announces with sufficient ambiguity that finally "[w]e reached the western world, a poor, devoted crew"

(117), Wordsworth's readers would be thinking perhaps particularly o General Grey's campaign to weaken French imperialism in the Wes Indies, in hopes thereby, in the words of Henry Dundas, secretary o state for war operations, of "enlarging our national wealth and secu rity" (qtd. in Christie, *Wars and Revolutions* 231). The West Indie: campaign, especially in the early years of 1794 and 1795, was notori ous for the "pains and plagues," "disease and famine, agony and fear" that rained down upon the inexperienced and ill-equipped English soldiers, many of whom were drawn from the ranks of the indigent. Emsley notes that the shortage of shoes among English troops in the West Indies led to crippling maladies; many of the troops contracted yellow fever or other tropical diseases, and between thirty-five and forty thousand soldiers and sailors died there between 1793 and 1796 (37–38, 51).

In light of the often abject condition of returning soldiers, their accompanying families or those left behind in England, it was necessary to pass measures to provide assistance and distribute money to the military and their families. Emsley points out that the hesitation on the part of many men to volunteer was due to inadequate compensation for their services, and some were still waiting for the government to come through with entitlements due them from the American wars (34). Emsley cites a telling petition to Lord Dundas, which suggests that Wordsworth's discharged sailor in *Adventures on Salisbury Plain*, who received no separation pay or pension to support his family, was based on living prototypes:

> Your Humble Petitioners Formaley Belong to Lood Hood Fleet in the West Indies Captured two-hundred Vesels likewise three Million of Money at the Iland of Saint Eustatia and Never received one Farthing your Humble petitioners Haveing wifes and Famileys and not willing to leave them in Distress Prays to have one Paymentes as soon as Possable as we are all willing to Enter into his Majestys Royal Navey. (qtd. in Emsley 34)

In 1795 and 1796 acts were passed to rectify such oversights for the families of seamen and marines, who could now allocate some of their wages to their families. Parish officers were to distribute the pay- ments to families, who previous to such arrangements had been depen- dent upon parish relief if they did not have sufficient means to provide a living.[10] Because troops living in lodgings with their families had to provide for themselves out of meager pay, however, they were not pro- tected from the rise in prices during the mid-1790s; thus the female vagrant's description of the miserable conditions she and her family experienced in the port town—"And now to the sea-coast, with number more, we drew" (99)— before shipping out:

> There foul neglect for months and months we bore,
> Nor yet the crowded fleet its anchor stirred.
> Green fields before us and our native shore,
> By fever, from polluted air incurred,
> Ravage was made, for which no knell was heard.
>
> (100-4; *SPP* 136)

Upon her return to England, her condition—alas—has only become worse, and in lines poignant even today, the female vagrant finds herself a helpless outcast in her native land: "homeless near a thousand homes I stood, / And near a thousand tables pined, and wanted food" (179–80; *SPP* 141). Wordsworth quoted these lines in his argument against the Poor Law Amendment Act of 1834, an amendment which in many ways brought into official practice what Wordsworth saw as the bureaucratic and dehumanizing reforms proposed in the 1790s.

The female vagrant does, in fact, depend upon the Poor Law administration for her initial recovery. Like her husband, she cannot bear to beg—"At morn my sick heart hunger scarcely stung, / Nor to the beggar's language could I frame my tongue" (188–89; *SPP* 142)—and so she languishes into unconsciousness from hunger, only to be revived in the nearby hospital. Once she regains her health, however, she still can find no relief, and turns to a band of gypsies, who take her in and offer her charity and companionship:

> The wild brood saw me weep, my fate enquired,
> And gave me food, and rest, more welcome, more
>   desired.
>
> My heart is touched to think that men like these,
> The rude earth's tenants, were my first relief . . . .
>
> (215–18; *SPP* 143)

Despite her moral objection to the vagrant economy of petty thievery and dissembling upon which the gypsies depend, the itinerant band offers her a kind of liminal community that represents a possible alternative to the cold comfort of the hospital. Though she ultimately rejects the gypsies' "vagrant ease," they offer her kindness and relief when she can find none from family, friends or the parish. In a poem so critical of the perversions of charity and government, the community of these "rude earth's tenants" opens a horizon of radical utopianism in the poem, for their society, however idealized, represents a kind of mutual responsibility within a community of equals:

How kindly did they paint their vagrant ease!
And their long holiday that feared not grief,
For all belonged to all, and each was chief.
No plough their sinews strained; on grating road
No wain they drove, and yet, the yellow sheaf
In every vale for their delight was stowed:
For them, in nature's meads, the milky udder flowed.
(219–25; *SPP* 143–44)

Even though the gypsies paint their own lives more favorably than Wordsworth finally does, in the gypsies we visit momentarily a life of apparent idleness rewarded with abundance and revelry that sharply contrasts with the female vagrant's life of industry rewarded only by hunger, suffering and unwanted solitude.

I depart here from John Williams, who believes that the gypsy scene in "The Female Vagrant" minimizes the critical protest of the poem by linking it to the idyllic world of the pastoral. Williams writes, "The gypsies' 'semblance' to the potters he had seen in the Lake Districts indicates that he sought a picturesque resolution to their otherwise disturbingly degrading condition, holding them in this respect as much at arm's length in *Salisbury Plain* as he had done in *An Evening Walk*" (24). First of all, gypsies are figures of the picturesque, not the pastoral landscape, and in the picturesque they serve alongside banditti to heighten the otherness of the scene. Their presence here, as in the picturesque, disturbs the pastoral idyll, for beneath the still surface of their "vagrant ease" moves the turbulent force of the illicit vagrant economy; behind the *semblance* of potter lurks the midnight thief. No Robin Hoods, the gypsies nonetheless suggest the presence of an underclass in a state of war against the property holders. In the Godwinian demesnes of the poem, they serve as a reminder of the possible consequences of the continued repression and neglect of the poor, about which Godwin, Paine and Wordsworth had warned. As Godwin bluntly stated: "The superiority of the rich, being . . . unmercifully exercised, must inevitably expose them to reprisals; and the poor man will be induced to regard the state of society as a state of war . . ." (*PJ* 90). Although Godwin had little faith in any concerted, politically organized means of the poor to retaliate against their oppressors, he believed that crime and vice, such as those Wordsworth associates here with the gypsies, were indeed weapons—albeit self-defeating ones—unwittingly wielded by the poor in their struggle against injustice.

Thus, the presence of the gypsies bolsters rather than undermines Wordsworth's protest in "The Female Vagrant," for their warmhearted charity offers a foil to the calculating niggardliness of the mainstream community, and their theft of food from the propertied similarly puts into relief the landowners' theft of property from the customary small-holders. Moreover, the gypsies remind the reader that subversion was indeed afoot in the English countryside—the paranoia of which Wordsworth's and Coleridge's scrape with a Home Office spy in 1796 attests—and crime would be the outcome of further oppression of the poor. That the female vagrant rejects the gypsy life only places Wordsworth's radicalism within the limits of Godwin's, Paine's and later Shelley's, for none of these writers advocated violent revolution and none of them could accept what Deleuze and Guattari in *A Thousand Plateaus* would call the "nomadism"—that is an absolute rejection of all structures (including mentalités) subsumed under the totality of the State—that the gypsy life signifies.[11] Godwin similarly rejects such nomadism when he makes Caleb Williams ultimately abandon Raymond and the bandit society.[12] While admiring the cheerfulness, energy, unbridled freedom and defiance of injustice among this "society of equals," Caleb rejects the bandits' lack of reason, their unwillingness to plan for the future, and their preying upon society to satisfy their own needs. The female vagrant rejects the gypsies for virtually the same reasons, and with her rejection of that tainted freedom, the poem, rather again like *Caleb Williams*, shifts its focus to the psychological nature of her suffering.

The sign of her suffering at the hands of social and political injustice is idleness. But in this case, the female vagrant's idleness results from a series of misfortunes whose origins are traceable to a corrupt government. She is not misfortunate, as would be assumed about the poor in general, because she has been idle. Thus, although in the *Salisbury Plain* poems the opposition between idleness and industry determines the very basis upon which to compare the happiness and fortune of the past felicity with the dejection and misfortune of the present, Wordsworth's handling of the opposition between idleness and industry so familiar to the discourse on poverty challenges the underlying assumption that the poor would be idle were it not for want to drive them to work.

It should be clear, however, that Wordsworth does not attempt by any means to deconstruct the oppositions between industry and idleness, nor does he escape from assigning the highest value to the industrious poor. To generalize a comment Liu makes about *The Ruined Cottage*, labor in Wordsworth's works serves as a "signifier of a value immanent in household economy: humanity" (34).[13] Indeed, Wordsworth often fixes upon a familiar implement in the household economy, the loom, as a symbol of industry. In *Salisbury Plain* and in *The Ruined Cottage*, the loom and spinning wheel, which by the 1790s had accrued a good deal of cultural exchange value, signify rustic industry and idleness. For the late eighteenth-century poet or painter, the busy hum of the wheel or loom signals cottage industry and the labor value of the poor. From the poets to the political economists, the busy wheel moreover symbolized a flourishing economy and a "bold peasantry." Concerned with putting the able-bodied to work, Frederick Morton Eden invoked the image of the elderly matron spinning almost ad perpetuam. "Any old woman that has the use of her hands," he writes, "can sit in an elbow chair, or on a low stool, may spin at the distaff; and accordingly we rarely meet with an old woman in the North of Scotland, that is not otherwise employed, but who has got a distaff stuck in her girdle, and a spindle in her hand" (*State of the Poor* 1: 559). To corroborate his claim that the elderly women of Scotland exhibit exemplary industry, Eden cites lines from Fergusson's "Farmer's Ingle" depicting woman's work in the blithest of terms:

> Still thrift, industrious, bides her latest days,
> Tho' age her fair dow'd front w' wrinkles wave,
> Still frae the russet lap the spindle plays,
> Her e'ening stent reels she as weel's the lave.
>
> (qtd. in Eden 1: 559)

Like Wordsworth's Goody Blake, Isabel or Ruth, the old woman of Eden's ideal community fills her vacant hours with unrelenting labor. In particular, women and especially poor women were expected to fill up their time with labor, so as not to have idle thoughts—a tradition that Elizabeth Barrett Browning will criticize in *Aurora Leigh*.[14] David Davies, often thought to be a friend to the agricultural laborer, praised women for "rear[ing] those hardy broods of children, which, besides supplying the country with the hands it wants, fill up voids which death is continually making in camps and cities" (2). Yet at the same time, Davies complained that knitting and spinning, tasks "well calculated to fill up spare time," were declining (61). While it is true that these were tasks performed by both men and women, Davies clarifies who he has in mind in particular by commenting: "If constant employment were found for the wives and children of labouring men, as well as for the men themselves, the benefit public and private thence resulting would be great" (61).

Bentham's *Observations on the Poor Bill*, written in 1797 but not published until 1838, further indicates the cultural value that looms and spinning wheels had for middle-class observers of the poor: "The resource presented by a loom is a permanent one: it may be rendered an unfluctuating one. A loom eats nothing; is not apt to be sick; does not sink in value by underfeeding; has no legs to be driven away upon; and is not exposed to sudden death. The working of one loom need not hinder the working of another" (*Works* 8: 449). Bentham made this rather short-sighted (in view of the crisis in the textile industry in the early nineteenth century) proposition to counter William Pitt's proposal to give each poor family a small bit of commons and a cow, in order to relieve some of the stress on the poor rates. For Bentham the loom signified a predictable productivity, because machines, at least in his view, required little or no maintenance when compared to that other source of income and stability, the cow. To provide each pauper family with a loom would eliminate the element of uncertainty in their economic future and deprive them of an excuse not to work. In this case, the poet's vision seems to be more accurate than the political economist's, for throughout England the looms of cottage weavers were silenced over the next decades, and their presence in literature and art functioned as a sign of loss rather than gain.[15]

In *Salisbury Plain* the loom is only one of a larger field of signs that establish a contrastive pattern of productivity and stagnation. In every aspect of the female vagrant's early life we see evidence of productivity and cheerful toil: the binary system of value in the discourse on poverty—its *langue*, if you will—is very much present in this poem; what has changed is the articulation—the *parole*. Her garden was "stored with peas and mint and thyme / And rose and lilly for the sabbath morn" (*SP* 236–37). The peas and spices suggest her responsibility for preparing meals; the rose and lily, her Sunday preparations. The cherished moments from the past are instances of intensive productivity, and are linked to the festivals and fairs of the customary rural economy, in which celebration and play were associated with harvest days and work fairs. She remembers "shearing time," "cowslip gathering," washing and spinning, and "[m]y snow kerchiefs on the hawthorn spread / My humming wheel and glittering table store" (*SP* 246–47). Whereas the "humming wheel" evokes a nostalgia for "healthful toil," the subsequent silence of the loom and wheel signifies the female vagrant's abject loss of human purposiveness and social interconnectedness: "the grave did hide / The empty loom, cold hearth and silent wheel" (*ASP* 349–50).[16] Thus, the female vagrant's loss of productivity suggests the lost state of that blissful toil found in the poetry of Dyer, Beattie, Cowper and more contemporaneously in Pratt and Bloomfield—an idealized, non-alienated labor.

This same nostalgia for an idyll of agrarian labor appears in *The Ruined Cottage*, and its moral structure too hangs upon the hinge of industry and idleness. Wordsworth began writing the story of Margaret in 1797 when he was at work with the *Lyrical Ballads*; indeed the earliest version of this poem was the first verse that he read to Coleridge on that June day in 1797 when Coleridge first visited him at Racedown.[17] In his introduction to the Cornell Wordsworth edition of the poem, Butler claims: "Although *The Ruined Cottage* is not a work of social protest, the story of failed harvests and high prices that caused Margaret's husband to enlist as a paid recruit does accurately reflect social conditions" (4). In *The Ruined Cottage*, the opposition between idleness and industry governs the tropological permutations that lead the reader to sympathize with the plight of Margaret, the abandoned heroine of the poem. In what Liu calls the "collage of disassociated souvenirs and bric-a-brac" that constitutes the imagery of the poem, a larger principle of organization which is not simply iconic, as he suggests, but ideological, assembles those fragments into fields of the productive and the nonproductive (*Wordsworth* 313). As in *Salisbury Plain*, the poem tropes the erosion of human spirit as first a decline and then a corruption of agricultural industry, indicated by the falling off of labor, the inertia of cast-off tools, and the silence of the loom and wheel.

When the pedlar tells of his first meeting with Margaret and Robert, we see them as independent agents shaping their history. Robert at his loom and Margaret in the garden busy themselves in productive activity. Their relationship to nature is reflexive—they cultivate the earth, transform its raw materials into use values. As their story proceeds, however, the poor harvest, the war and the collapse of the textiles market disrupt their relationship to nature. That is, within the historical displacement of the poem, political and economic transformations disturb and eventually disrupt the productive relationship between the human and the natural worlds—the getting and spending of the Pitt administration combined with the accidents of nature lay waste the powers of Margaret and Robert. Little by little Robert begins to daydream in despair, and his poverty, the cause of which lies outside his control—indeed outside his parish boundaries—brings on disaffection: "Poverty brought on a petted mood / And a sore temper: day by day he drooped" (ms. B 232–33). A metaphoric transference takes place here. Robert, like a wilting plant, droops as a consequence of the political recklessness of an administration bent on war. Once "an industrious man / Sober and steady," Robert becomes idle (ms. B 172–73). As in *Salisbury Plain*, the silent loom stands out in the poem as a constant reminder of the demise of labor: on his final visit before Margaret's death, Armytage again "saw the idle loom / Still in its place" (ms. B 431–32). "Still" here falls upon the ear with a heavy trochaic weight, emphasizing both the duration and the degree of the loom's stasis. Thus, the abandoned tools signify the inertia of those who once put them to use. As Liu observes, in the lost paradise of cottage life, humanity "communicated itself during most of each day in the cares of labor—in the relation of person to artifact, the hand to the universe of its tools, utensils, products, and domicile" (*Wordsworth* 319).

In a parallel "progress," Margaret follows the same downward spiral from industry to idleness, marked similarly by her abandonment of the tools of her trade and the neglect of her duties. Robert had once filled his hours with labor. Even though he was "up and busy at his loom / In summer ere the mower's scythe had swept / The dewy grass," passers-by in the evening still "Might hear his busy spade, which he would ply / After his daily work till the day-light / Was gone" (ms. B. 174–76, 179–80). Similarly, when Armytage visits just after Robert has abandoned her, Margaret had been "busy with her garden tools" (ms. B. 342). With each subsequent visit, however, the house begins to show increasing signs of neglect. At first, weeds and excess in the garden signal her carelessness. Where once Margaret's busy hand, like Eve's, had kept her "paths and bowers . . . from wilderness with ease" (*Paradise Lost* 9.244–45), now her abandon allows a wanton superfluity to overtake the walks:

> The honeysuckle crowded round the door
> And from the wall hung down in heavier tufts,
> And knots of worthless stone-crop started out
> Along the window's edge and grew like weeds
> Against the lower panes. I turned aside
> And strolled into her garden. It was changed:
> The unprofitable bindweed spread his bells
> From side to side, and with unwieldy wreaths
> Had dragged the rose from its sustaining wall
> And bowed it down to earth; the border tufts—
> Daisy, and thrift, and lowly camomile,
> And thyme—had straggled out into the paths
> Which they were used to deck. (ms. B 366–78)

Eventually, however, even "her house / Bespoke a sleepy hand of negligence" (ms. B 439–40), and the pedlar and the poem's narrator now find themselves visiting a sort of Gothic ruin—"Twas a spot! / The wandering gypsy in a stormy night / Would pass . . . to house / On the open plain . . ." (ms. B. 313–34)—completely overtaken by natural, but unprofitable, abundance. The pedlar points out to the narrator "a plot / Of garden-ground, now wild" (ms. B 116–17), and all the cottage, what's left of it, "is tricked / With weeds and the rank speargrass" (ms. B 161–62).

Margaret's and Robert's withdrawal from the productive forces of life and nature deepens so completely that we see—at different times—both of them gazing off into a space filled only with the creatures of their idle fancy, not their productive imagination. In a perverse parody of his former productivity, Robert gives himself over to carving "uncouth figures on the heads of sticks" (ms. B. 217). Moreover, his confused activity indicates that he no longer can distinguish between idleness and industry, nor can he coordinate his labors with the seasons: Robert

> idly sought about through every nook
> Of house or garden any casual task
> Of use or ornament, and with a strange
> Amusing but uneasy novelty
> He blended where he might the various tasks
> Of summer, autumn, winter, and of spring. (ms. B 218–23)

To recall in this context Wordsworth's letter to Wrangham of 5 June 1808, in which Wordsworth suggests that a "select library" could serve manufacturing laborers as a "public dial, keeping every Body's clock in some kind of order" (*MY* 249), we could say that Robert has fallen from both the self-regulating order of nature and the artificial order of the word. The "brotherhood" between human and natural history now severed, Robert's activities fall out of synchronization with the natural and the "public Dial." Robert's "Body's clock" no longer receives its cues from nature or from books . Indeed, he neglects the rhythms of the agricultural calendar and literally loses his place in natural time. Given the popularity of the agrarian idyll with its conventional mythic laborer linked cthonically to the rhythms of the soil, Robert's asynchrony marks a severe rupture of the pastoral-georgic convention. Similarly, Margaret, in a corruption of the pedlar's "busy eye" productive of sympathy, gives in to an anxious fancy which seems to cause disturbing hallucinations: "evermore her eye / Was busy in the distance, shaping things / Which made her heart beat quick" (ms. B 454–56). Unchecked by the mediation of natural lore, the fancy prevents Margaret from reading the signs of consolation that nature offers to the busy eye of the pedlar—an eye "So busy, that the things of which he spake / Seemed present" (ms. B 211–12).

Many readers have noted that the loss of their imaginative sympathy with nature ultimately destroys the spiritual integrity and mental health of both Margaret and Robert. The only signs of human presence at the place are the broken utensils—"the useless fragment of a wooden bowl" (ms. B 145); all other signs of human activity—the "chearful" order and arrangement of the flowers and garden—have been erased by the rank weeds and spear-grass. Liu suggests that this "strangely laborless trope of vegetation" replaces the original bonds of labor. "As divined in the leaves," he writes, "the relation between persons and artifacts must now be seen to be a bond of affiliative vision—of 'convenient' and sympathetic imagery—rather than labor in the first place" (319). His point, as I understand it, is that the tropes of vegetation indicate Wordsworth's anxiousness to transfer labor value onto visionary "dreamwork"—the work of the romantic, sympathetic imagination. Thus, the poet's production of imagery redeems Margaret's and Robert's loss of productivity; the poet's industry converts their idleness to a use value, much as the charitable actions of the villagers convert the Old Cumberland Beggar's material deprivation into affective plenitude, as I discuss in Chapter Five.

Leaving aside possible qualifications to this easy exchange of poetic for manual labor, the point I want to emphasize here is that the value system of *The Ruined Cottage* hinges upon that binary opposition between industry and idleness.[18] In drawing our sympathy to Robert and Margaret, Wordsworth, like Crabbe in Book I of *The Village*, takes pains to show that their idleness proceeds from their poverty, *not* vice versa as was so commonly thought. What redeems Margaret and Robert within the context of the poem is that they once were willingly industrious and productive; though they did not lose their physical ability to work, like Crabbe's aged swain, they lost their psychological ability to do so. Thus Wordsworth shows in his poem that industriousness is a psychological attribute of character which social, political and economic forces may in fact erode and alter. In contrast to the "idleness and industry" progress narratives of Hogarth and Crabbe, in which the rise or downfall of protagonists results from their moral choices, Wordsworth's sympathetic narrative shows these principal characters as victims of a social and economic system over which they have little or no control.

Perhaps the most marked difference between the pastoral-georgic tradition and Wordsworth's representation of the laboring poor is that industry for Wordsworth appears not as an extrinsic moral injunction that governs characters who metonymically suggest an abstract category of people—Labor—but as an intrinsic quality of character. In his poems the emphasis falls not upon *industry* as a sign of distinction between a polite, leisured class and a class inured to a life of labor; rather, it falls upon *industriousness* as a moral imperative that links the middle-class reader and writer to the poor. Industriousness, in Siskin's terms, is one of the "new forms of socioeconomic behavior" that in the romantic discourse of the developmental self "became innate characteristics of that self" (154). In this transformation of industry into industriousness, we see an example of what Siskin has described as a feature of romantic discourse: the elimination of kinds which "makes sympathetic identification possible . . ." (53). With this abolition of distinction in kind, the reader and the represented laborer now have something in common: they both share, though not to an equal degree, in a common morality.

In the industrious laborers of Wordsworth's poetry, his contemporaries encountered a mirror of themselves as subjects enjoined, if not inured, to labor. Hence the "troubling proximity" to these sympathetic figures that I will discuss at greater length in Chapter Four. The possibility of such sympathetic identification with a rustic figure again gives weight to Hazlitt's observation that Wordsworth's muse was "a levelling one" (132). It is also one of the means by which Wordsworth's figures achieved a higher degree of narrative authority than did their literary prototypes of the pastoral-georgic tradition, who were silenced by the overwhelming authority of a narrative voice which maintained a privileged difference of kind from the poor. By evaluating the industriousness in a person, the "quality," the "middling ranks," and the "labouring poor" were now subject to a common standard: the sign of industriousness. As I will show in the next chapter, under the pressures of that standard and the "spirit of independence," Wordsworth would not only identify the work of the poet with the work of the poor, but lay claim to their "artlessness" and indigence as signs of authenticity.

If industriousness and virtue, as Simpson suggests, were not for Wordsworth a litmus test for the actual practice of charity, they were nonetheless constituent features of the poet's aesthetic representations of the poor.[19] In Wordsworth, as in Crabbe, the critique of the Poor Laws as well as the social and political origins of poverty relies upon a discourse that nonetheless reproduces the normative moral codes to which the laboring poor were subject. Thus, Wordsworth does not altogether escape the binary oppositions set up in the discourse on poverty, for in these characters he reproduces the ideal diligent laborer valorized as the deserving pauper in earlier poetry and in the treatises on the Poor Laws. In addition, he equates labor with virtue, though not with happiness, as did the earlier poets.

While in the course of his growing conservativism Wordsworth may reduce the specificity of his criticism, as in the case of the revisions to *Salisbury Plain*, he at least does not fault the victims of social and economic injustice for bringing adversity upon themselves. In view of the prevailing assumptions about poverty, particularly that idleness and profligacy were the *causes* of poverty, Wordsworth's complicity in reproducing the discourse on poverty must be qualified. In drawing our attention and sympathy to the female vagrant and to Robert and Margaret, Wordsworth's *Salisbury Plain* and *The Ruined Cottage* reverse the stereotype by showing that disabling idleness may proceed from poverty, which itself may proceed from social, economic and even natural causes beyond the immediate control of the victims of these powerful, predatory forces. While it may be true that the industriousness of these marginalized cottagers stems from a middle-class ideology of labor and industry, what struck Wordsworth's contemporaries was his troubling attempt, however entangled in the limitations of its time, to dignify the poor and shift responsibility for their destitution onto external accident rather than some intrinsic defect of class, lack of moral integrity or absence of will. Thus, in direct confrontation to the more common assumption that poverty is a providential incentive to industry, Wordsworth shows, on the contrary, that by deteriorating the spiritual, mental and physical strength of its victims poverty renders them incapable of industry. The silence of the looms in *Salisbury Plain* and *The Ruined Cottage* subverts Benthamite confidence in the stability and predictability of a machine-based industrial economy *and* system of poor relief, and suggests an uncanny and unsettling resemblance between the lethal forces of political economy and rapacious nature. Even though Wordsworth reproduces the discourse on poverty as a means to set up the field of moral relations in which the narrative takes place, *Salisbury Plain* and *The Ruined Cottage* present a concerted and radical critique of the treatment of the poor and the social and economic consequences of Poor Law reforms, which in Wordsworth's view threatened to further aggravate the miserable condition of the poor.

4

Minstrels, Marginals and the Making of Poetic Value: Liminal Power and "The Spirit of Independence"

But, modest Sir, you challenge, to be sure,
The boastful need of genius, to be poor.
George Dyer, The Poet's Fate

As I have argued in previous chapters, the spectacle of poverty in the late eighteenth century reaffirms the privileged position of the spectator/reader and shores up the boundaries between the leisured class, the industrious middle classes and the laboring poor. Yet, because the markers of social position or signs of distinction separating the classes begin to overlap in the same period, conventional boundaries between social ranks in literature and art begin to blur. Thus, Cowper's poetry appropriates for a rising middle class and mercantile *nouveaux riches* a privileged gaze that had before been the exclusive property of the nobility and hereditary aristocracy. This appropriation, however, involves a certain contradiction that produces anxiety in the middle-class reader attempting to occupy such a position, for to identify with the leisured gaze is to occupy a station that middle-class morality, with its emphasis upon labor, condemns. A similar confusion exists at the other end of the social scale where industry, thrift and other so-called "middle-class values" begin to negotiate an uneasy identification between the middle-class reader and the poor, who increasingly in literature, social treatises and other works were enjoined to emulate and practice these virtues. The industrious laborer in what John Barrell calls the pastoral-georgic not only becomes a repository of middle-class values, but serves as a kind of double of the middle-class reader whose values are reflected in the literary figure.[1] In the sympathetic identification with these figures, the reader may consciously or unconsciously acknowledge the absence of a distinctive boundary between the laboring poor and the middle class. In Wordsworth's poetry, I believe, we can see a conflicted attempt to engage this contradiction squarely.

In contrast to the classical version of pastoral and the Cowperian version of pastoral-georgic, Wordsworth's poetry figures rural industry as a sign of inclusion—a self-reflexive projection of middle-class industriousness that reminded the bourgeois readers of their common ties to the laboring poor. An attribute of character from which the aristocracy was excluded, industriousness could not serve as a sign of distinction for middle-class readers or writers, who, like the working poor, were themselves obligated to labor as a sign of their own value. To elicit the reader's sympathy, Wordsworth places his laboring poor in a position of marginal power that destabilizes their conventional, subordinate position in the relations of production. Transforming the conventional character of industry as an extrinsic sign of social difference into an intrinsic moral quality that becomes a sign of similitude, Wordsworth's poetry disrupts the complacent sense of social superiority conferred upon the reader by the hierarchical text of the pastoral-georgic. By thus leaving inconclusive the social status of both vagrant and reader, Wordsworth's early poetry initiates for the reader a liminal space that emphasizes the relative instability of his or her own social position in a society open to talents and in which the boundaries between the "middling orders" and the poor were rapidly eroding. Wordsworth's own sympathetic identification with the poor, his "vagrant muse," enables a more immediate identification between the itinerant beggars, discharged soldiers and indigent laborers haunting his poetry and the polite reader who can project his or her own anxieties about social and economic stability upon these "border figures." Furthermore, in Wordsworth marginals often achieve a degree of narrative authority—and hence a dignity and power—that earlier poetic forms had denied them.

In evoking an uncanny sense of familiarity between the indigent and the bourgeois reader, Wordsworth's poetry opens itself to historical reading even as it partially conceals the historical traces of its moment of production. If his representations of the poor parade as spectacle the free-floating signifier of the virtuous poor, they do not constitute the benign, politically neutral and safe spectacle of the eighteenth-century pastoral-georgic. On the contrary, the liminality and ambiguity of Wordsworth's poor, their spectral trespassing of social boundaries, surrenders them to historical interpretation and appropriation. Wordsworth's representations of the poor, while constructed within the parameters of the conventional discourse on poverty, nonetheless have appeared radically challenging and even potentially revolutionary to some of Wordsworth's readers—from his contemporaries to ours. As I hope to show here and in the next two chapters, while couched in the class-bound ideology of its moment of production, Wordsworth's poetry of human dignity did not simply serve the interests of those in power; it also had a liberating effect upon at least some working-class readers who went on to challenge the systems of domination implicit in several of Wordsworth's poems.

From Adam Smith's *Theory of Moral Sentiments* to Mary Wollstonecraft's *Original Stories from Real Life*, middle-class writers in the eighteenth century continually claim for their class the virtue of industry as a sign of preeminent moral value. Both Smith and Wollstonecraft would agree with Oliver Goldsmith's vicar, who exclaims in *The Vicar of Wakefield* (1767): "In this middle order of mankind are generally to be found all the arts, wisdom, and virtues of society" (116). Though in *A Vindication of the Rights of Woman* (1792) Wollstonecraft disagrees with Smith that the anticipation of how others view us should be the foundation of moral sentiments, she reaffirms the high value of the middle class—"the one in which talents thrive best," as she puts it (126). She quotes at length from *A Theory of Moral Sentiments*, where Smith questions whether hereditary wealth can lead to anything but an effete and useless nobility, and insinuates the superiority of the middle class. In a catalogue of virtues attendant upon the necessity that motivates those in the middle rank to exercise their talents and reason, Smith asks: "By what important accomplishments is the young nobleman instructed to support the dignity of his rank, and to render himself worthy of that superiority over his fellow-citizens, to which the virtue of his ancestors had raised them? Is it by knowledge, by industry, by patience, by self-denial, or by virtue of any kind?" (qtd. in *Vindication* 102; *Moral Sentiments* 53). Wollstonecraft answers this question later in her treatise when she poses her own rhetorical question: "What but habitual idleness can hereditary wealth and titles produce?" (212). In his *Letter to the Bishop of Llandaff* (1793), Wordsworth echoes Wollstonecraft's intent when he attacks the inequalities that result from hereditary authority : "I have another strong objection to nobility which is that it has a necessary tendency to dishonour labour, a prejudice which extends far beyond its own circle; that it binds down whole ranks of men to idleness while it gives the enjoyment of a reward which exceeds the hopes of the most active exertions of human industry" (*PrW* 1: 45).

If Wordsworth's contempt for aristocratic idleness links him to a radical writer like Mary Wollstonecraft, it also links him to a reactionary writer like Hannah More. In *Thoughts on the Importance of the Manners of the Great*, Hannah More makes explicit what many middle-class writers only implied: the industry of the middle classes was a distinguishing feature that set them apart from the unprofitable idleness of both rich and poor. Indeed, the idleness of the rich was, for More, an obstacle to reforming the poor: "To expect to reform the poor, while the opulent are corrupt, is to throw odours into the stream while the springs are poisoned. If . . . the rich and great will not, from a liberal spirit of doing right, abstain from those offences for which the poor are to suffer fines and imprisonments, effectual good cannot be done" (70–71). From these remarks, one can confidently agree with Barrell's claim that by

1800 industriousness had become for the middle class "the chief, and often . . . the only virtue" (*Dark Side* 86). The middling order of society was where that virtue was thought to reign supreme.

If for Smith, Wollstonecraft and Wordsworth industry was an index of middle-class moral and civic virtue, when applied to the laboring poor it was a sign of productivity and an index of duty and social stability. In *Farmworkers in England and Wales*, Alan Armstrong presents evidence that eighteenth-century tenant farmers, the entrepreneurs within the tripartite structure of English agricultural society, took measures to "stiffen labour discipline, inculcate more regular patterns of work, and extend hours . . ." (29). In Wiltshire, for example, a group of farmers entered into a formal compact to increase and regulate the number of hours " 'Threshers, and other Daily Workmen and Servants' " would work within their community. Moreover, as Armstrong notes, Arthur Young noticed to his dismay the apparent indolence of farm laborers in Lanvachers, and so recommended that farmers use a bell to regulate their workers' hours and immediately dismiss those who gave poor service (29). Political as well as economic interests stood behind the recommendations for the farm laborer's industriousness. For the writer of a letter in the *Gentleman's Magazine* (October 1797), the exercise of industry also served to chasten the poor and keep them in their place: "Industry is the great principle of duty that ought to be inculcated on the lowest class of the people, as it is the best and most effectual barrier against vices of every kind; as it occupies the mind, and leaves no vacancy for licentious thoughts and mischievous projects" (820). In the wake of revolutionary fears in England and the poor harvests of 1795 it seems clear just what kind of mischievous projects the unidentified correspondent had in mind.

Given the value of industry for the middle class, it should surprise us little that when cultural production fell primarily into their hands, industriousness was no longer depicted as a spectacle of labor viewed from above but as a projection of middle-class interest in economic security and social mobility. A problem lurks here, however. Industry became the mark of middle-class distinction at the very time the middle classes were enjoining the poor to be industrious, yet few of the reformers who hoped to train up the poor in habits of industry were willing to give up their sense of moral superiority. So far as I know, none acknowledged the paradox that the premium accruing to "industry" as a sign of distinction would be diminished once industry spread among the lower classes. Its value, that is, as a sign of middle-class superiority would be reduced if not altogether erased. In what follows I want to examine the consequences of this deflation of the value of industry as a sign of distinction, especially for poets, and trace the accompanying inflation of the value of poverty as its troubled replacement.

I

As I have shown in Chapter Two, Cowper's representations of rustic labor involve his readers in a knot of contradiction. Invoking the "cheerful labor" and "blissful toil" of the agrarian idyll, Cowper applies these epithets to both the laboring poor and the leisured writer. Indeed, Cowper, who once feared that he appeared to his benefactors as a "mere Vagabond" (*Letters* 1: 138), attempts in *The Task* to equate mental with manual labor in order to legitimate and at the same time valorize his own "laborious ease." In a letter of 3 April 1767, Cowper admitted to Maria Madan Cowper that he was concerned the Unwins had reason to doubt the social standing of his family connections. Of William Unwin's visit to his cousin at Park House, Cowper writes:

> Though My Friend You may suppose, before I was admitted an Inmate here, was satisfied that I was not a mere Vagabond, and has since that time received more convincing Proof of my Sponsibility, yet I could not resist the Opportunity of furnishing him with Ocular Demonstration of it, by introducing him to one of my most splendid Connections: that when he hears me called *that Fellow Cowper*, which has happened heretofore, he may be able upon unquestionable Evidence, to assert my Gentlemanhood, and relieve me from the Weight of that opprobrious Appellation. (*Letters* 1: 162)

Moreover, Cowper identified himself specifically with a comfortable leisure, looking down with characteristic sympathy at the poor but regarding poverty with contempt. In a letter to Lady Hesketh of 27 May 1791, Cowper calmly observes, "I live, indeed, where leisure abounds . . ." (*Letters* 3: 517–18), while to Mrs. Throckmorton, he writes, "I esteem the want of money, commonly called poverty, the most indelicate thing in the world, and so did the antient [*sic*] Romans, who therefore always annex to the word *paupertas* an epithet expressing their contempt and abhorrence of it—such for instance as *squalida*, or *sordida*, or some such reproachful appellation" (3: 467). Obviously uncomfortable with his social status, Cowper uses the occasion of *The Task* to claim the moral value of industriousness for leisurely activities such as writing and reading poetry. His stated purpose in writing *The Task* was "to discountenance the modern enthusiasm after a London life, and to recommend rural ease and leisure, as friendly to the cause of piety and virtue." Yet in a letter to Thomas Park, 10 March 1792, Cowper questioned whether his own rural leisure would justify such a claim: "From thirty-three to sixty I have spent my time in the country, where my reading has been only an apology for idleness. . ." (*Letters* 4: 26).

Cowper's appropriation of "blissful toil" appears most clearly in "The Garden" section of *The Task*, where the narrator defends a "[d]omestic life in rural leisure pass'd" (3.293). The narrator shows that rural leisure only appears to be idleness, and that such leisure actually promotes industry as that course of life "friendly to the best pursuit of man, / Friendly to thought, to virtue and to peace" (*Task* 3.290–91). Given Cowper's promotion of a life "studious of laborious ease" for the gentleman whose leisure constitutes a "delightful industry enjoy'd at home," it is little wonder that, as Marilyn Butler reminds us, Cowper was a "favourite of Jane Austen's" (*Task* 3.361, 356; *Romantics* 36). Yet in "The Sofa" Cowper sets himself apart from "libertine excess" and the stigmatizing disease of those with "pamper'd appetites" (*Task* 1.106). In a passage that anticipates the vagrant musings of Wordsworth's early books of *The Prelude*, Cowper writes,

> The Sofa suits
> The gouty limb, 'tis true; but gouty limb
> Though on a SOFA, may I never feel:
> For I have loved the rural walk through lanes
> Of grassy swarth close cropt by nibbling sheep,
> And skirted thick with intertexture firm
> Of thorny boughs: have loved the rural walk,
> O'er hills, through valleys, and by rivers brink,
> E'er since a truant boy I pass'd my bounds
> T'enjoy a ramble on the banks of Thames.
> (*Task* 1.106–15)

Indeed, like Wordsworth in the 1850 *Prelude*, who rises from his "soft couch" to take up the road toward Grasmere "Keen as a Truant or a Fugitive" (1.86, 90), Cowper relishes in the memory of an illegitimate leisure—a truancy toward which he is drawn yet for which he must provide an apology. In that justification, Cowper catches himself in a sort of tautology, for his vindication of rural leisure hangs upon a "truant" ramble. Hence his language censures his act even as he attempts to vindicate himself from the charge of idleness by demonstrating his taste and love for nature. Wordsworth, similarly struggling with justifying what appears to be leisure, conflates his "truant" ramble with the purposeful image of the pilgrimage:

> Keen as a Truant or a Fugitive
> But as a Pilgrim resolute, I took,
> Even with the chance equipment of that hour,
> The road that pointed tow'rd the chosen Vale.
> (*Prelude* 1850 1.90–93)

Here Wordsworth has transformed the homeward-bound "peasant" (110) of the 1805 version of this passage into a "Home-bound Labourer" (1850 1.101), thereby fusing leisure and labor in the same unresolved tension of Cowper's "The Sofa" and demonstrating his own preoccupation with vindicating poetry from the charge of idleness.

In *The Task*, Cowper is similarly preoccupied with establishing the value of poetic labor, a feat charged with all the more anxiety as the poem condemns nonproductive idleness and glorifies productive labor as the very foundation of civilization. The monarch himself, Cowper's narrator claims, "Himself derives / . . . From strenuous toil his hours of sweetest ease" (*Task* 1.388). Those who choose luxury over labor are doomed to physical and moral atrophy:

> The sedentary stretch their lazy length
> When custom bids, but no refreshment find,
> For none they need: the languid eye, the cheek
> Deserted of its bloom, the flaccid, shrunk,
> And wither'd muscle, and the vapid soul,
> Reproach their owner with that love of rest
> To which he forfeits ev'n the rest he loves. (*Task* 1.389-95)

In condemning the excesses of luxury among the wealthy and the predilection to laziness among the poor, Cowper's position wavers between Edmund Burke's justification of leisure (though not its excess) as a necessary means to produce men of wisdom fit to rule the state and Thomas Paine's retaliatory claim that aristocratic leisure was simply a masquerade for dissolute idleness. In accusing the French Assembly of turning the world upside down "by setting up in the air what the solidity of the [social] structure requires be on the ground"—that is, by making tailors, tallow-chandlers, hairdressers and carpenters, among others, eligible for political office—Burke asserts that only men of property and distinction, in whom true virtue and wisdom lie, are fit to govern the state. In a telling footnote, Burke supports his claim that the French are "at war with nature" by citing Ecclesiastes 38:24-25: "The wisdom of a learned man cometh by opportunity of leisure: and he that hath little business shall become wise. / How can he get wisdom that holdeth the plough, and that glorieth in the goad; that driveth oxen; and is occupied in their labours; and whose talk is of bullocks?" (*Reflections* 138). In *Rights of Man*, Paine rebuts Burke's claim, declaring that the aristocracy "when compared with the active world are the drones, a seraglio of males, who neither collect the honey nor form the hive, but exist only for lazy enjoyment" (249). Compare with Burke's claim Cowper's similar point in *Table Talk*, published almost ten years before Burke's *Reflections*, in which he deprecates "th'unwashed artificer" who would "indulge his genius after long fatigue, / By diving into cabinet intrigue"

(153–54). Neither a leisured man of property nor an idle pauper, Cowper attempts to find a comfortable middle ground in his loco-descriptive survey of the great chain of subordination, censuring those above and below him for excessive idleness and thus identifying himself with the industrious members of the middle rank.

Like Cowper, as we have seen, Wordsworth shows a profound ambivalence about his position in the continuum between idleness and industry. The question of industriousness persists throughout the Wordsworth canon, but figures perhaps nowhere more importantly than in the poetry written before 1802, for reasons I will discuss below. Indeed, industriousness marks the rustic figures of these poems as an essential quality and sign of moral virtue. Goody Blake, for example, seems never to stop working: "All day she spun in her poor dwelling: / And then her three hours' work at night" (25–26; *PW* 4: 173). Similarly, Michael and Isabel personify unrelenting labor:

> I may truly say,
> That they were as a proverb in the vale
> For endless industry. When day was gone,
> And from their occupations out of doors
> The Son and Father were come home, even then,
> Their labor did not cease; . . . (93–98; *PW* 2: 83)

Simon Lee and his wife Ruth also struggle heroically against the worst of conditions and despite their weakness eke out a bare subsistence:

> Oft, working by her Husband's side
> Ruth does what Simon cannot do;
> For she, with scanty cause for pride,
> Is stouter of the two.
> And, though you with their utmost skill
> From labour could not wean them,
> 'Tis little, very little—all
> That they can do between them. (49–56; *PW* 4: 63)

Finally, the "hunger-bitten girl" of Book 9 in *The Prelude* earns the regard of Wordsworth and Beaupuy as "The industrious, the lowly, child of toil" (9.526). Perhaps nowhere, however, does industry become a more central concern for Wordsworth than in "Resolution and Independence," first drafted as "The Leech Gatherer" in the period before the Wordsworths settled their estate with the Lowther family. In this poem, as in *The Prelude*, the dialectic between idleness and industry, between an undeserving and deserving poverty, governs Wordsworth's self-analysis and the question of the legitimacy of writing poetry. The poem also introduces another constituent feature of the discourse on poverty—"the spirit of independence"—as it attempts to turn poverty itself into a sign of legitimacy. Before turning to independence, let me first address Wordsworth's attempt to find in poverty—the poverty of poets, a minstrel vagrancy—a sign of legitimacy and value.

II

Thomas Percy's "Essay on the Ancient Minstrels" (1765) is one of the founding texts in the invention of a tradition of British bards and minstrels, a tradition that involves the reification of "natural genius" as the sign of value by which to judge poets and poetry. In the work of Thomas Percy, Joseph Ritson, John Aikin and Sir Walter Scott, to name only a handful of the antiquarian *flaneurs* who collected "ancient" ballads and songs, the minstrel becomes a kind of artifact vested with traces of an idealized feudal antiquity, native genius, primitive simplicity, artlessness and the immediacy of an oral literary culture. As Susan Stewart discusses in "Scandals of the Ballad," the theory of minstrel origins establishes for the ballad "an authentic authorship" and designates it as "a legitimating point of origin for all consequent national literature" (138).

A constitutive feature of the theory of minstrel origins is the association of minstrels and bards with an authenticating and enabling poverty. These poet-musicians, singers of songs "of their own composing"—at least in Percy's view—anticipate in their marginal status the romantic cultivation of exile and difference as signs of distinction. For the eighteenth-century antiquarian (and poet) the poverty of bards or minstrels functioned as a sign of their relative freedom from material concerns. Thomas Blackwell's *An Enquiry into the Life and Writings of Homer* (1735), for example, celebrates Homer's poverty, which purportedly allowed him to take a *via media* between the public road and the private lane—to expose his imagination to diverse customs and dialects without binding him down to any of them in particular. A "strolling bard" (104), Homer was said to wander from city to city observing "all the various situations of the human race" (22); welcome at various courts, feasts and festivals, the strolling bard stayed only long enough to observe, not to assimilate the manners and customs of his hosts: he "neither led a Country nor a Town-life; and was in this respect truly a Citizen of the Universe" (115). Ironically for the poet who anchors the Western literary tradition, Homer's life was represented as nomadic, liminal. He was neither here nor there, but betwixt and between; occupying the periphery of society, he was bound to no center, and yet could visit any. Thus, his poverty was both enabling and ennobling, giving him the freedom to wander and to wonder—to look around and to "look within." In Blackwell's view, Homer "obtains ravishing Views of silent nature, and undisturbed contemplates her solitary Scenes. He often turns his attention upon himself, canvasses his own passions, and ascertains his Sentiments of Humanity" so as to "lay up store of such Images, as Experience told him wou'd have strong effect" (120–21).

Notably absent from Blackwell's account of Homer's poverty is that brutal indigence faced by Wordsworth's rustic contemporaries. Rather, for Blackwell, Homer's poverty constitutes an "easy, independant State, that is unawed by Laws, and the Regards that molest us in Communities; that knows no duties or Obligations but those of Hospitality and Humanity: that subjects the Mind to no Tincture of Discipline, but lays it open to all the natural Sensations, with which the various parts of the Universe affect a sagacious, perceptive, mimicking Creature" (113–14). George Dyer, who quotes from Blackwell's *Enquiry* in his *The Poet's Fate*, cautions that the claims for Homer's poverty would be difficult to prove, given that "Homer" is a term serving what Foucault calls the "author function"—a term, in this case, to unify a particular body of works and cover over the controversy concerning the authorship of the poems attributed to him. Nonetheless, Dyer toys with the idea of Homer's poverty in a poem inscribed to "The Society for the Establishment of A Literary Fund." Bemoaning the apparent lot of poets to be poor, Dyer too celebrates Homer's independence, remarking that the "*Aoidos*, the ancient strolling bard, both in Greece and Britain, was a respectable and independent character, though not decorated with titles, or overburthened with riches" (fn. 41–42). In the poem itself, he remarks more comically: "A bard, you know, of light camelion breed, / On nature's bounty is content to feed" (39). The stature of Homer's noble poverty, however, seems to be lost upon the impoverished poet-protagonist of the poem, who sees little to cherish and much to despair in his destitution:

> woe is me! to rove with empty purse;
> My wit a torment, and my rhymes a curse:
> To rove and rove, and keep on roving still,
> A mere knight-errant of the grey goose quill
> Now doom'd in penance, for my former crimes,
> To scribble mournful verse in starving times. . . . (24)

Apparently the modern poet lacks the wanderlust of the ancient bard, and no doubt reaps little of the recognition and welcome that such bards were thought to receive from the wealthy lords through whose domains they traveled.

In the extensive inquiries of Thomas Percy, David Herd, John Pinkerton and Joseph Ritson into the bardic-minstrel tradition of the British Isles, poverty again appears as an enabling condition for the poet, but not without some important qualifications. Percy, for example, distinguishes between the minstrel and the poet on the basis of their respective modes of production. Commenting on the professionalization of poetry, Percy notes that while poets after the fourteenth century or so began to flourish under a protected patronage, minstrels and bards became subject to the unpredictability and anonymity of an inchoate literary marketplace. The English and Scottish minstrels directed their "artless productions" at the common people, while the "poets of a higher class . . . who had all the advantages in the times in which they lived wrote for fame and for posterity" (9). Poets tended to be cloistered away from the people; they wrote in leisure and retirement from the monasteries or under noble patronage. The "strolling minstrels," on the other hand, "got their livelihood by singing verses to the harp at houses of the great" (347); they composed songs that had "a pleasing simplicity, and many artless graces, which . . . compensate for the want of higher beauties and, if they do not dazzle the imagination are frequently found to interest the heart" (8). The strolling minstrels, Percy writes, "composed their rhymes to be sung to their harps, and . . . looked no farther than for present applause, and present subsistence" (9). Thus, while the minstrels might have been carefree souls, they paid for their freedom with economic precariousness. Indeed, Percy takes pains to show that the late fifteenth-century decline in respect for and trust of the "strolling minstrels" and itinerant bards led to their juridical classification in the Elizabethan statutes among rogues, sturdy beggars and other vagabonds.

Herd, Pinkerton and Ritson refine Percy's early work and introduce more complex histories of the bards and minstrels as they stir up the debate over authenticity of ballads, but all mention the connection between these itinerant singer-poets and vagabonds. In "An Essay on the Origin of Scotish [*sic*] Poetry" (1786), for example, Pinkerton reminds his readers that in Scotland as early as 1458 the Scottish Acts of Parliament classify bards (in his view, those inferior singers who entertained the lower classes) in the same lot with gypsies, masterful beggars and feigned fools (1: lxxiii). Ritson's *Ancient Engleish Metrical Romanceës* [*sic*] (1802) relates the tale of a beggar, a "venerable old man, the melancholy representative of an ancient minstrel," who had formerly frequented the streets of London, chanting minstrel-ballads to the accompaniment of "a canaster and string, which he call'd a *humstrum* . . ." (1: cxcvi). Ritson quotes from Stubbs's *Anatomie of Abuses* (1583), in which minstrels are described as a "parcel of drunken sockets, and bandy parasites" who "raunge the countries, riming and singing of unclean, corrupt, and filthy songs in tavernes, alehouses, innes and other publick assemblies. . . ." (1: ccxvi). Thus, by the end of the eighteenth century, bards and minstrels were affiliated with a conflicted, paradoxical poverty, from which they could derive authenticity, on the one hand, but illegitimacy on the other.

For Percy and other commentators, the minstrel—as we will see in Wordsworth's poetry—was a kind of vagabond, a nomad traveling betwixt and between fixed communities (geographically and socially), eking out a meager subsistence with his songs. Combining the qualities of the wanderer and the local tiller of the soil that Walter Benjamin sees as prototypes for the authentic "storyteller" in his essay of that title, the strolling minstrels accrue a kind of cultural capital in their honest poverty and in their doubly marginal status as paid laborer and homeless vagabond (84).[2] As a result of this reification of the ballad (and the subsequent stabilization of an ephemeral "oral" form in the written collections of ballads, which were often subject to extensive editing and revision), the ballad as artifact became a kind of fetish object for an exclusively middle-class and aristocratic readership who could afford the expensive editions produced by Percy, Ritson, Scott and others. Thus, when Wordsworth adapts the narrative and metrical form of the ballad for the poems of *Lyrical Ballads*, he deliberately sets his work before an audience whose taste had been suckled on the antiquarian collections of ballads and whose pocketbooks contained sufficient funds to purchase the little volume that Wordsworth and Coleridge hoped would finance their trip to Goslar, Germany, in 1798–99.

Poets like Beattie, Gray, Burns and Wordsworth would deploy the honest poverty of the bard popularized in the minstrel tradition as a sign of poetic genius, simplicity and authenticity. The "artless tale" of the indigent poet became a guarantor of truth, one that prose writers like Mary Wollstonecraft would borrow to establish the verity of their own narratives. In *Rambler* 91, 29 January 1751, for example, Samuel Johnson praises the relative autonomy of the poet freed, like the minstrel, from the political and imaginative constraints of patronage; an honored poverty is the price the poet pays for such freedom: "The Sciences, after a thousand indignities, retired from the palace of Patronage, and having long wandered over the world in grief and distress, were led at last to the cottage of Independence, the daughter of Fortitude, where they were taught by Prudence and Parsimony to support themselves in dignity and quiet" (*Works* 4: 120). While Johnson's conception of a cottage of independence implies that rather comfortable and privileged poverty of Blackwell's Homer, in Johnson's figure we see the affiliation of poetic authenticity with poverty—here perceived as a separate, if not marginal, space relatively uncontaminated by a base economy.

Beattie's hermit of *The Minstrel* (1771) a prototypical Wordsworthian solitary, similarly praises the poverty that freed his imagination from the vanity of human wishes:

> Hail Poverty! If honour, wealth, and art
> If what the great pursue, and learned admire
> Thus dissipate and quench the soul's ethereal fire! (p. 22)

Scott's widely read *Lay of the Last Minstrel* (1805) riveted the image of the minstrel as a liminal character in the popular imagination. Like Wordsworth's poet-solitaries, Scott's minstrel is "infirm and old; / . . . A wandering Harper, scorn'd and poor, / He begg'd his bread from door to door" (1). Even in Shelley's qualified tribute "To Wordsworth," poverty marks a productive political independence and imaginative authenticity:

> In honoured poverty thy voice did weave
> Songs consecrate to truth and liberty,—
> Deserting these, thou leavest me to grieve,
> Thus having been, that thou shouldst cease to be. (11–14)

Finally, Thomas Carlyle identifies poverty as a sign of distinction for poets, a mark of their authenticity. In "The Hero as Man of Letters" (19 May 1840), Carlyle, who called Shakespeare "our poor Warwickshire Peasant," codifies poverty as the distinguishing feature of true genius: "there ought to be literary men poor—to show whether they are genuine or not" (*On Heroes* 166).

In these eighteenth- and nineteenth-century encomiums to ennobled poverty, then, antiquarian critics, collectors and poets cultivated a kind of simulated poverty—a second-order indigence—as a legitimating quality of the minstrel/bard. The poet became a kind of Homeric wanderer, a hermit sage whose poverty always seemed to be protected from indigence and insult. Given the increasing numbers of discharged soldiers and destitute beggars in the late eighteenth century, the cultural transformation of poverty into a sign of affective value raises certain problems and questions which at least one poet could not put to rest by naturalizing indigence into an agrarian idyll. Thus, in Wordsworth's poetry the ennobling poverty associated with minstrels as the founding native geniuses of tradition threatens to become the disabling indigence of those itinerant singers who had lost their social distinction and hence were considered to be vagabonds and rogues. In Wordsworth's oft-noted identification between the poet and the vagrants and rustics that inhabit—I'm tempted to say haunt—his poetry, he presents a conflicted sign of poetic authenticity that threatens to unmask, even deconstruct, the appropriation of poverty as a sign of poetic value.

III

In *The Prelude*, Wordsworth confronts with a certain ambivalence that freedom to wander and wonder that Blackwell posed as Homer's greatest enabling condition. David Simpson has noted Wordsworth's conflicted position on poetic industry, independence and idleness in his superb chapter on "Gipsies" in *Wordsworth's Historical Imagination*. As

Simpson comments, "the author of 'Gipsies' is a poet acutely anxious about his dependence upon others, and about the public status of his 'work' as a poet. This goes some way toward explaining the peculiar superimposition of over-confidence upon insecurity that a careful reading of the poem can support" (41). Wordsworth's fascination with the freedom of the gypsies and his contempt for them in "Gipsies" and in the gypsy scene from *Salisbury Plain*, as discussed in the previous chapter, operates along the same principles as the double perspective of "internal spectator" and sublime speculum that I describe in Chapter Two, but here in terms of the poet's anxieties about the value of poetic labor.

In identifying with vagrant and itinerant figures, Wordsworth's early work shows the poet's ambivalence about the value of poetic labor; it shows too his inability to ignore that poverty may well affect the imagination adversely. Let us return to Book 1 of *The Prelude*, where Wordsworth, for example, speaks of the "careless steps" with which he found his way to Grasmere, there to begin "some work / Of glory" (1.70; 86–87). In the 1805 version of the *Prelude*, Wordsworth explicitly compares himself to a peasant on a "pleasant loitering journey": "So, like a peasant I pursued my road" (1.114, 110). By the 1850 version of the poem, however, Wordsworth has transformed the peasant into "a home-bound labourer" (101), thereby muting the moral dilemma he had earlier faced and conferring with the new simile a greater degree of legitimacy upon his profession. In the 1805 *Prelude*, Wordsworth furthermore attributes his difficulty settling down to bookish studies at Cambridge to his fondness for "rambling like the wind / As [he] had done in daily intercourse / With those delicious rivers, solemn heights / And mountains" (3.359–62) as a child. Again in Book 3, he apologizes for a digression from his main theme, saying, "I play the loiterer" (3.615). Perhaps most importantly, in Book 7 he identifies his work as poet with a band of red-breasts, "minstrels from the distant woods / And dells" (7.25–26). Pledging to these figural minstrels that "ye and I will be / Brethren, and in the hearing of bleak winds / Will chaunt together" (7.35–37), the poet goes on to describe his return to Grasmere in terms of vagabondage:

> soon I bade
> Farewell for ever to the private bowers
> Of gowned students—quitted these, no more
> To enter them, and pitched my vagrant tent,
> A casual dweller and at large, among
> The unfenced regions of society. (7.57–62)

In these lines we see a kind of triumphant vagrancy—the freedom to wander associated with Homer, the ancient bards and the minstrels. Yet more often than not, Wordsworth's affiliation of poetic value with poverty dispels such complacency in a more vexing figure of vagrancy. The key poem to this ambivalent stance toward enabling poverty and the necessity of labor, as I have suggested, is "Resolution and Independence," wherein the leech gatherer, unenviable in his indigence, nonetheless takes on the attributes of the native genius—a poet whose artless tale comes from a very troubled source indeed.

As a reply to Coleridge's original draft of "Dejection," "Resolution and Independence" collapses Wordsworth's own doubts about writing poetry for a living with Coleridge's fear that his "genial spirits" had failed.[3] Critics from Mary Moorman to Kurt Heinzelman have agreed that the encounter between the narrator and the Crusoe-like leech gatherer in some way figures Wordsworth's ambivalence about his financial and poetic future. Moorman believes "Resolution and Independence" to be "the poem in which we see more of Wordsworth than in any other single poem," while Heinzelman reads in the obstinate questions to the leech gatherer a "challenge [Wordsworth] makes to himself."[4] Most recently, in "A Gift that Complicates Employ," Charles J. Rzepka returns us to what he calls Wordsworth's "Preoccupation with Occupation," which he neatly describes as a conflict between Wordsworth's "attitudes toward poetic marketing as, on the one hand, something necessary to subsistence and enabling to prophecy, and on the other, as a defilement of his poetic gift and a distraction from the greater task for which that gift was intended . . ." (243). To note the identification between Wordsworth and the leech gatherer, however, only partly explains the dynamics of the poem and its relation to history. Such readings stop short of linking Wordsworth's discourse with the larger field of social texts in which "Resolution and Independence" was produced. I will argue here that in appropriating the leech gatherer to figure the marginality of poets Wordsworth does not simply conflate mental with manual labor; nor does he simply project doubts about his profession onto a comfortably stable sign of some transcendent permanence. Rather, through "Resolution and Independence" Wordsworth inscribes a figure of the poet into a discourse on poverty that valorizes the independent subject as a site of productive industry and thereby makes of marginality an "ennobling" condition. Thus, the poem invests the marginal with symbolic power while at the same time producing an ethic of labor for the poor.

We have already seen that the discourse on poverty—produced variously in Goldsmith's *The Deserted Village* (1770) and Crabbe's *The Parish Register* (1807), together with Hannah More's "The Riot, or, Half a Loaf is Better than No Bread" (1795) and Samuel Jackson Pratt's *Bread, or the Poor* (1801)—articulated the virtues of the industrious poor, the vices of the profligate. As Irvin Ehrenpreis notes in "Poverty and Poetry: Representation of the Poor in Augustan Literature," within the discourse on poverty the figure of a model pauper was reconstructed from prototypes that go back as far in England to Piers Plowman; before Piers, to Eumaeus in *The Odyssey* (3–4). These earlier figures of industrious, grateful and obedient agrarian laborers constitute that mythic laborer of the agricultural idyll which, as discussed in Chapter Two, unites human life and natural life in a common language. Within the agricultural idyll, laborers and their work lose historical specificity and come to signify what Mikhail Bakhtin in *The Dialogic Imagination* calls "essential life *events*" whose mythic dimensions in the late eighteenth century were drawn from the conventions and motifs of the pastoral. Bakhtin explains that "agricultural labor transforms all the events of everyday life, stripping them of that private petty character obtaining when man is nothing but consumer; what happens rather is that they are turned into essential life *events*" (227). Another constitutive feature of the agricultural idyll in its late eighteenth-century form is independence, an ideologeme that links the virtuous poor with the celebrated tradition of English liberty. Within what Bakhtin would call the "ideological environment" of the 1790s, "independence" is not a neutral term denoting a positive freedom.[5] Indeed, the term "independence" crosses over into the discourse on poverty, where it signifies the refusal of able-bodied laborers to rely upon charity or poor relief. Within an economy faced with increasing difficulty in providing basic and essential provisions for a growing number of itinerant and parish poor, "independence" masks in this case a particular *laissez-faire* attitude toward and practice of poor relief under the banner of liberty. As J. R. Poynter explains in *Society and Pauperism*, the concept of independence was subject to "subtle shades": "with most it was an equivocal ideal, in which the poor were to be independent of charity and poor relief, but also duly mindful of their place in the social hierarchy" (xvii). That is, when applied to the poor, "independence" meant a cheerful self-reliance.

That "independence" was interfused with the cult of pastoral simplicity which mediated perceptions of the poor is evident in William Green's *Plans of Economy, or the Road to Ease and Independence* (1803). Green asks, for example: "Where is to be found that simplicity, that blooming industry and sincerity, which once enviably distinguished those who lived remote from the capital? Where is the cheerful toil, the frugality, and innocence for which they were so justly celebrated?" (13). According to Green, the Poor Laws, releasing the poor from their traditional habits of frugality and industry, had created a new class of "dependent" poor. By following his plans for economy, these dependent poor would regain the independence that once characterized England's "bold peasantry." Thus, "independence" in Green's picturesque sketch of the model pauper appears to be the natural consequence of that cheerful industry celebrated throughout late eighteenth-century culture, in poems from John Dyer's *The Fleece* (1757) to Robert Fergusson's "The Farmer's Ingle" (1773) and Cowper's *The Task* (1785).

Cheerful industry elides with independence in the commonplace phrase "spirit of independence" that Wordsworth invokes in the *Postscript*. In a letter dated 17 December 1798 to the *Monthly Magazine*, January 1799, an anonymous writer makes the ideological force of this phrase clear, praising that "spirit of independence to be found in the walks of humble life, which would rather submit to great difficulties than rely too much on the bounty of others" (27). Another letter in the 1 June 1800 issue of the *Monthly* similarly values "that honest spirit of conscious independence, which ought to spurn the idea of depending on others for what our own exertions can attain, and which ought to actuate the breast of every individual, who makes any pretence to principle or character" (422). As we can see, "the spirit of independence" here denotes a moral quality particularly recommended for the poor.

The social meaning invested in "independence" extends into treatises on political reform and political economy as well. In "Some Considerations on the State of the Poor in General" (1787), for example, Joseph Priestley hopes "that the industrious poor . . . will be roused to exert themselves to the utmost, and aspire to that comfortable independence of which, in the present state of things, they can have but little prospect" (*Works* 25: 317). Priestley goes on to advocate making such independence compulsory. Similarly, Thomas Malthus' *Essay on Population* praises the "spirit of independence [that] still remains among the peasantry" despite the Poor Laws, which "are strongly calculated to eradicate this spirit" (84–85). Malthus claims that the "love of independence is a sentiment that surely none would wish to be erased from the breast of man: though the parish law of England . . . is a system of all others the most calculated gradually to weaken this sentiment, and in the end, may eradicate it completely" (67–68). Thus, with the phrase "the spirit of independence" a group of people who are themselves not poor formulate their own social desideratum for the poor as a universal moral imperative.

As defined within these normative demesnes, "independence" recognizes the material contingency of freedom: that is, the necessity of having surplus wealth or the need to labor for a modicum, at least, of surplus income in order to enjoy some leisure. Poverty, of course, did not mean for Wordsworth's audience abject deprivation, any more than it does for us. As Georg Simmel pointed out in his seminal 1908 essay "The Poor," individual poverty is relative to the social expectations of the class, group or family in which a person moves. As I will discuss further in the next chapter, in Simmel's view, a person is poor, sociologically speaking, once he or she becomes the recipient of any kind of poor relief or assistance (175). In England during the late eighteenth and early nineteenth centuries, however, to be sociologically poor was understood as the necessity to work for a living, to exchange one's labor for one's subsistence. In *The Idea of Poverty*, Gertrude Himmelfarb notes that throughout the 1790s the terms "laborers" and "poor" "continued to be used interchangeably, and were often amalgamated in the term 'laboring poor' " (77). Patrick Colquhoun expressed the prevailing definition of poverty in his *Treatise on Indigence* (1806): "it is the state of every one who must labour for subsistence" (qtd. in Himmelfarb 78). Malthus too linked poverty and labor in his *On Population* (1798), claiming that "want" was the fundamental incentive to labor of any kind, including poetic labor: "Want has not unfrequently given wings to the imagination of the poet . . ." (358).

Hannah More explicitly connects "the spirit of independence" to the literary marketplace in her foreword to the four-volume *Works of Hannah More* (1803). She alludes to what she considers the destructive social dimension of independence—what Goldsmith in *The Traveller* calls "That independence Britons prize too high, / [that] Keeps man from man, and breaks the social tie" (339–40). Nevertheless, she praises the effects of independence on the politics of publishing:

> The spirit of independence . . . which has in many respects impressed so mischievous a stamp on the public character, has perhaps helped to correct the style of Prefaces and Dedications. Literary patronage is so much shorn of its beams, that it can no longer enlighten bodies which are in themselves opake [*sic*]; so much abridged of its power that it cannot force into notice a work which is unable to recommend itself. (*Works* 1: iii–iv)

For More, the "spirit of independence" frees the literary work from the political influence of its patrons, but releases it into an anonymous and unpredictable marketplace where the work must vouch for itself.

Recall again Samuel Johnson's somewhat quaint celebration, in *Rambler* 91, 29 January 1751, of the independence that follows from the demise of patronage: "The Sciences, after a thousand indignities, retired from the palace of Patronage, and having long wandered over the world in grief and distress, were led at last to the cottage of Independence, the daughter of Fortitude, where they were taught by Prudence and Parsimony to support themselves in dignity and quiet" (*Works* 4: 120). While Johnson's conception of a cottage of independence may imply a rather comfortable, even privileged sort of poetic marginality, his figure nevertheless affiliates an ennobling poverty with the countryside and thrift, both later associated with the agrarian, and usually deserving, poor. In Johnson's figure we see the displacement of poetic labor not only from the contamination of aristocratic patronage, but also from the "getting and spending" of the city. In his figure, then, if not in his conscious articulation of poetic independence, Johnson anticipates Wordsworth's later appropriation of more precarious spaces at society's periphery.

As *genius loci* of these marginal spaces, the "spirit of independence" invokes the liminal as a means to confer a kind of otherworldly power upon the effectively powerless—paupers and poets alike. The masquerade of secular weakness as sacred and moral power contributes to the construction of an idea of poverty that blunts the sharp edges of its misery and sets it in a palatable glow of transcendental value. According to Victor Turner in *The Ritual Process*, liminal personae, like Wordsworth's leech gatherer, distinguished by signs that mark their lack of status, rank and property, often display symbolic or sacred power. Their actions or speech are replete with sacred instruction (95). Moreover, as Turner points out, "[i]n closed or structured societies, it is the marginal or 'inferior' person or the outsider who often comes to symbolize . . . ' the sentiment of humanity' " (111). In other words, liminal personae, like the "unacknowledged legislators" variously defined by Wordsworth, Coleridge and Shelley, claim a marginal but affectively privileged position in relation to the prevailing social structure. From the position of liminality, poets were to elevate at least symbolically their role within society. Like the Saora shaman Turner describes, the liminal poet attains a "statusless status . . . which gives him [or her] the right to criticize all structure-bound personae in terms of a moral order binding on all . . ." (116).

In terms more familiar to romanticism, the outsider position assumed by the poet in his or her liminal guise invests the poet with an affective power that appears to transcend the social structure upon which it depends. In Wordsworth, this liminal guise is produced in what Geoffrey Hartman calls Wordsworth's "boundary images," where distinctions between the natural, the human and the supernatural blur—as in the figure of the leech gatherer (198). As Turner points out, the blurring of secular and sacred in the liminal invests marginal figures with a kind of extra-structural, symbolic power that paradoxically may confirm the values of the social structure it appears to defy. In blending "lowliness and sacredness" liminal personae display the "powers of the weak" and make visible the values, norms and sentiments that bind together the members of the community (96). Turner notes that as expressions of *communitas* the voices of liminal personae often reaffirm symbolically the existential bonds of human relations that social hierarchy in practice may obscure or obliterate (109).

In British culture in the late eighteenth century *communitas*, an undifferentiated community of equals who stand outside of political structure, resided in part with the idealized poor—Wordsworth's gypsies, Godwin's bandit society, and the idealized beggars and rustics of countless poems, prints and paintings. Among these idealized poor circulate the minstrels, vagrants, bards, discharged soldiers and widows whose "artless tales" make visible the normative values that temper the grim face of indigence. Many of these tales and their tellers elevate poverty to a transcendental status, finding in poverty a claim for authenticity. In turning now to "Resolution and Independence" itself, we can see how Wordsworth takes advantage of this idealized poverty in a poem about the possible pauperization of poets. "Resolution and Independence" invokes the discourse on poverty to enlarge the claims of the marginalized poet.

IV

Originally titled "The Leech Gatherer," the poem became "Resolution and Independence" in 1807 when Wordsworth prepared the much revised original manuscript for publication.[6] Wordsworth's new choice of title should provide us with clear evidence that in his view the poem brings into focus the economic concerns that many critics have subsequently neglected. Indeed, the "spirit of independence" presides as a *genius loci* over the poem. Given that it elides poverty and freedom, labor and liberty, the polyvalent term "independence" seems fitting when assigned to a poem in which Wordsworth attempts to allay or transcend certain doubts about a marginal profession. In contrast to critics like Geoffrey Hartman and Alan Grob, who see what Grob calls "the destructive powers and the processes of nature" at the center of the poem (96),[7] I believe "Resolution and Independence" centers upon the destructive powers and processes of society—particularly those processes that allow a man or woman to fall into the recesses of structure, to sink into the abyss of indigence that Jeremy Bentham raised as a spectre threatening those who relied upon their labor for their living:

> [Indigence] is the centre to which inertia alone, that force which acts without relaxation, makes the lot of every mortal gravitate. Not to be drawn into the abyss, it is necessary to mount up by continual effort; and we see by our side the most diligent and the most virtuous sometimes slipping by one false step, and sometimes thrown headlong by inevitable reverses. (*Theory of Legislation* 127–28)

Here we find that independence has a bleaker signification than often admitted into the new pastoral idyll of poverty: social independence under the new economic dispensation admits a precarious vulnerability to the marketplace—even the literary marketplace. Frederick Morton Eden, a social commentator and author of the three-volume *State of the Poor* (1797), addresses these fears directly: "Those who are left to shift for themselves must sometimes, either from misconduct or misfortune, be reduced to want" (1: 58).

For Eden, Bentham and others who debated the Poor Laws, labor is the only means for those without independent incomes to stave off poverty, the only safeguard against the abyss. Yet, as these comments make clear, even diligent labor could not guarantee complete security. Thus, the "spirit of independence" has its price, not the least of which is a persistent fear that little help will be available to those who do not help themselves. As the once happy narrator of "Resolution and Independence" puts it:

> how can He expect that others should
> Build for him, sow for him, and at his call
> Love him, who for himself will take no heed at all?
>
> (40–42; *Poems* 125)

We recall that Wordsworth told Sara Hutchinson on 14 June 1802 that "Resolution and Independence" describes "A young Poet in the midst of the happiness of Nature" who finally "is overwhelmed by the thought of miserable reverses which have befallen the happiest of all men, viz Poets" (*EY* 366). The "happy Child of earth" is disturbed with "fears, and fancies" of "Solitude, pain of heart, distress, and poverty" (31, 27, 35; *Poems* 124). The narrator wonders whether some munificent hand unbidden—a patron's?—might care for him who has the "genial faith, still rich in genial good" (39; *Poems* 124). Despite the comforting allusion to Matthew 6:25–36 in lines 40–42, these musings do not produce the concluding aphorism "Take therefore no thought for the morrow" (Matthew 6:34)—that lesson belongs to the discharged soldier.[8] Thus, the poem persists in doubt not only about the future, but about the immediate past that has set the poet-narrator outside the path of labor.[9]

In *Wordsworth's Historical Imagination*, Simpson sums up precisely the problematic relation of "Resolution and Independence" to Wordsworth's past:

> The poet has lived a life of "pleasant thought," as if "life's business were a summer mood," and as if "all needful things would come unsought" (124). Knowing what we know of his career up to this point, we can read into these lines the awkward awareness that others *have* built for him—Calvert, Beaumont and John Wordsworth. He lacks the independence without which true resolution may well be impossible. . . . (38)

Such dependence contradicts the "spirit of independence" celebrated in the poem; moreover, it opens the idle poet to criticisms that Paine and Godwin had raised less than a decade before.

Recall again that in *Rights of Man* Paine condemned the leisure of aristocrats on the grounds of their parasitic dependence upon others: "when compared with the active world [aristocrats] are the drones, a seraglio of males, who neither collect the honey nor form the hive, but exist only for lazy enjoyment" (249). In *Political Justice* Godwin had gone further, connecting poets and aristocratic indolence. As he puts it, in the just society "[t]here will be no rich man to recline in indolence, and fatten upon the labour of his fellows. . . . The mathematician, the poet, and the philosopher will derive a new stock of cheerfulness and energy from the recurring labour that makes them feel they are men" (745). Malthus also condemned the leisurely dependence of the aristocracy; in the *Essay on Population*, he writes: "Leisure is without doubt highly valuable to man, but taking man as he is, the probability seems to be that in the greater number of instances it will produce evil rather than good" (370). Wordsworth's own critique of leisure appears in *Letter to the Bishop of Llandaff* (1793), in which he objects to the institution of nobility partly because "it has a necessary tendency to dishonour labour, a prejudice which extends far beyond its own circle; that it binds down whole ranks of men to idleness while it gives the enjoyment of a reward which exceeds the hopes of the most active exertions of human industry" (*PrW* 1: 45). Though in "Resolution and Independence" the narrator's implied leisure is naturalized in the allusion to the transhistorical myth of Christian innocence and its appeal to the childhood world of play, the vision of "life's business" as leisure is nonetheless a reverie of the *rentier* poet. As the narrator ponders whether his own genius is a "good" that makes him "rich," he remembers Chatterton and Burns, poets whose lives were certainly no summer mood.

The allusion to Chatterton and Burns in "Resolution and Independence" underscores the question of the poet's economic position in society. Poets who began their work "in gladness" but came to end in "despondency and madness," Chatterton and Burns received little substantial financial compensation for their "genial good[s]." Burns—"who walk'd in glory and in joy / Behind his plough, upon the mountain-side" (45–46; *Poems* 125)—would have suggested to Wordsworth's contemporaries both native genius and poverty. As A. D. Harvey has noted in *English Poetry in a Changing Society*, Burns "in his own life as well as in his writings, engaged the public's sympathy for poor country folk" (79). Similarly, Chatterton—"The sleepless Soul that perish'd in his pride" (44)—symbolized unrewarded genius, the poet as marginal. In 1789, Chatterton's early biographer George Gregory succinctly summarized in his *Life of Chatterton* the young poet as a person whose life's journey began and ended "in indigence and misfortune" (3).

Wordsworth's strenuous effort to justify his choice of profession shows that even after 1800 he had, as he puts it in Book 3 of *The Prelude*, "some fears / About [his] future worldly maintenance" (77–78).[10] Michael Friedman rightly believes that "pauperization was a readily enough available social fact to become for Wordsworth the conscious symbol for an inner and personal terror" (41). These fears, both social and personal, led Wordsworth to find in the leech gatherer a means to project doubt about his own place within the relations of production. Burns and Chatterton were haunting portents of Wordsworth's own possible marginalization as a poet before a small and sometimes unsympathetic audience. Yet the partially successful ideological strategy of the poem valorizes Burns and Chatterton as figures of native genius and poetic power. If Burns and Chatterton signify poverty, they also represent the "dignity and quiet" that Samuel Johnson believed to have replaced the grief and distress found in the "palace of Patronage." This transformation depends upon the dialectic of liminality discussed above—the powers of the weak.

The ambiguous position of the leech gatherer—an admonitory figure whose very existence appears indeterminate—defines his liminality. Like the liminal personae Turner describes, the leech gatherer eludes "the network of classifications that normally locate states and positions in cultural space" (95). As Thomas McFarland notes in *Romanticism and the Forms of Ruin*, the leech gatherer "represents for Wordsworth a kind of existential boundary situation . . ." (159). Lacking wealth and status, the leech gatherer fits Turner's description of a marginal figure "betwixt and between the positions assigned by law, custom, convention and ceremonial" (95). As has often been observed, the leech gatherer's status is not only indeterminate in relation to the social structure, but within the phenomenological structure as well. He is betwixt and between the inanimate and animate, natural and human worlds:

> As a huge Stone is sometimes seen to lie
> Couch'd on the bald top of an eminence;
> Wonder to all who do the same espy
> By what means it could thither come, and whence;
> So that it seems a thing endued with sense:
> Like a Sea-beast crawl'd forth, which on a shelf
> Of rock or sand reposeth, there to sun itself.
>
> Such seem'd this Man, not all alive nor dead,
> Nor all asleep; . . . (64–72; *Poems* 126)

The multiplex, phylogenetic simile of stone, sea-beast and man suggests process, transience and uncertainty, all features of the liminal, which is often described in terms of a transitional state—being in the womb or at the threshold of death. Hartman rightly notes that the leech gatherer here appears to be amphibious, commuting "between natural and supernatural" (200). Yet Hartman exaggerates, I believe, the sanctuary of the "middle ground" the simile spans and the affirmation of faith in nature's permanence the leech gatherer's example may imply. The simile rather destabilizes the leech gatherer's ontological status; its indeterminacy disturbs the narrator, whose own perception already seems uncertain: "Such seem'd this Man, not all alive nor dead" (71; *Poems* 126). The uncertainty of the leech gatherer's ontological status here reinforces those earlier fears of distress and poverty that rush upon the narrator again after he hears the leech gatherer's story: "My former thoughts return'd: the fear that kills; / The hope that is unwilling to be fed; / Cold, pain, and labour . . ." (120–122; *Poems* 128).

Like the discharged soldier or the old Cumberland beggar, the leech gatherer's apparition-like presence admonishes the narrator and reader through a stately, and affectively powerful and disturbing, tale. If, as Jonathan Wordsworth claims in *William Wordsworth: The Borders of Vision*, the "borderers" in Wordsworth's poetry "possess a symbolic, not an actual, wisdom" (10), that symbolic wisdom is suffused with the power of normative instruction and thus intends practical consequences. What is the instruction the narrator receives as his fears of "Cold, pain, and labour" press upon him? To persevere in the face of possible misery and failure: "[the leeches] have dwindled long by slow decay; / Yet still I persevere, and find them where I may" (122, 132–33; *Poems* 128–29). Ironically the narrator, who has long lived life as a lark—"My whole life I have liv'd in pleasant thought, / As if life's business were a summer mood" (36–37; *Poems* 124)—receives comfort and consolation from a man whose life's business has been a wintry weight of sickness and labor.

Like Scott's minstrel, Coleridge's ancient mariner, or Turner's liminal shamans, the leech gatherer speaks with a severe intention, a moral power beyond the ken of ordinary men and women: "there was, while he spake, a fire about his eyes" (98; *Poems* 127). His feeble but "solemn" words "With something of a lofty utterance drest" (101; *Poems* 127) mark him as a sage whose voice issues forth

> Choice word, and measured phrase; above the reach
> Of ordinary men; a a stately speech!
> Such as grave Livers do in Scotland use,
> Religious men, who give to God and man their dues."
> (102–105; *Poems* 127)

Though the leech gatherer is a borderer who ekes out his subsistence at the periphery of society, his speech is suffused with moral weight and didactic intent. As Hartman describes him, the leech gatherer "is of the purest Protestant stock, a grave and hardy Scotsman who lives by those lines of Scripture [Matthew 6:25] . . ." (202–3). Invested with the moral authority of structure, which is characterized by normative codes and distinctions of rank, gender and wealth, the leech gatherer's presence admonishes the narrator (and reader) with values that only appear to transcend their own worldly conditions. It is no coincidence that he articulates the very imperatives found within the discourse on poverty: industry, perseverance, patience and self-reliance.

If we consider the poem's worldly origins, we find that it silences a crucial fact about the leech gatherer whom Dorothy and William met in October of 1800. In his comments on "Resolution and Independence" to Sara Hutchinson, Wordsworth describes the leech gatherer as a "survivor," a "pious self-respecting, miserably infirm . . . Old Man" (*EY* 367). In the first drafts of the poem, Wordsworth makes clear that the leech gatherer's trade was only summer work. The old man tells the narrator that "in winter time / I go with godly Books from Town to Town" (136–137; *Poems* 323). But Wordsworth suppressed these lines in the revisions begun in May or June of 1802, thus repressing his knowledge that the leech gatherer had in fact abandoned his meager occupation of gathering leeches and had turned to peddling books and begging for survival. As Dorothy Wordsworth records in her Grasmere journal, 3 October 1800, the leech gatherer was no longer strong enough, nor were leeches in sufficient abundance, for him to continue his previous work: "His trade was to gather leeches, but now leeches were scarce and he had not strength for it. He lived by begging and was making his way to Carlisle where he should buy a few godly books to sell" (42).

Ex silentia the leech gatherer's begging haunts this poem, which conflates the "ancient spirit" of dignified begging with the "spirit of independence." Signs of his begging have been completely erased; his peddling of religious tracts—an activity that turns "Choice word, and measured phrase" into commodities—has been transformed into sacred speech. As a result of these historical displacements, the leech gatherer becomes a mythic sign of affective power in the face of economic deprivation. In this substitution of transcendent and positive activities for those with an even grimmer aspect, Wordsworth invokes the discourse on poverty to figure his own activity as a poet whose well being depends upon the sale of "Choice word, and measured phrase." In the historical displacement of the leech gatherer's begging, Wordsworth's poem collapses the distinctions between the "ancient spirits" of begging and independence. The poem thus substitutes for adversity a positive affect that blurs the boundaries between tenuous mendicity and tenacious self-reliance. Surmounting the historical contingencies of the immediate present, laboring instead of begging for the meager leavings of the world, the leech gatherer becomes a sign of the "spirit of independence" whose determining signified constitutes an honored but feared dependence. His independence makes of resolution a necessity, for he can turn to no one but himself to gain his "honest maintenance" and "give to God and Man their dues" (112, 105; *Poems* 127–28). Thus, Wordsworth's "Resolution and Independence" engages dialectically both the positive and negative values of the "spirit of independence" as it negotiates the precarious position of the poet at the turn of the century—a literary producer caught between the "ancient spirit" of charity that would legitimate the deserving dependency of patronage and the "ancient spirit" of independence that would legitimate the self-reliant independence of commercial success. From that negotiation, Wordsworth can only claim the dubious freedom of the marginals with whom he identifies.

V

When Wordsworth addressed the question of the Poor Laws in the *Post-script* of 1835, he reaffirmed the "spirit of independence" and the productive subject it interpellates. The Poor Laws, he argues, had offered a safety net, in today's terminology, that reminded the diligent poor of the benevolence of the state. Such a refuge from possible indigence would maintain the laboring people in that state of "gladness" that the young poet of "Resolution and Independence" had experienced in youth and rescue them from the "despondency and madness" (49) that would result from the absence of paternal charity. As Wordsworth puts it, "Despondency and distraction are no friends to prudence: the springs of industry will relax, if cheerfulness be destroyed by anxiety; without hope men become reckless, and have a sullen pride in adding to the heap of their own wretchedness" (*PrW* 3: 245). Thus, the Poor Laws, in Wordsworth's opinion, strengthen rather than undermine the "spirit of independence" and the incentive to industry and self help that it encompasses. Despite the apparent tempering of Wordsworth's position on self-reliance in the *Postscript*, in 1834 as in 1802 the "spirit of independence" grounds the dignity of the working poor in their productivity, not in any existential quality of being. Yet, as my readings of "The Sailor's Mother" and of "The Old Cumberland Beggar" in the next chapter show, in these poems of 1802 Wordsworth could still find in a certain kind of begging a proud resolution. Moreover, Wordsworth seems to believe, in the words of Margaret Hale from Elizabeth Gaskell's *North and South*, that "God has made us so that we must be mutually dependent. We may ignore our own dependence, or refuse to acknowledge that others depend upon us in more respects than the payment of weekly wages; but the thing must be, nevertheless" (169). The apparent contradiction between these two positions is played out in the equivocal "spirit of independence" within the discourse on poverty, an ambivalence Margaret Hale recognizes when she fails to reconcile Mr. Thornton's "admiration of despotism with [his] respect for other men's independence of character" (171). As I will show in my "Postscript" following Chapter Five, the universalism of this position makes Wordsworth's work available to middle-class and working-class readers as well as opponents of the New Poor Law, who found in Wordsworth's humanism a position of strength from which to argue against the utilitarian degradation of the poor implicit in the theory and practice of that law.

5

The Moral Economy of Charity: The Politics of Exchange in "The Old Cumberland Beggar"

The mutual dependence and reciprocal interest which man has upon man, and all the parts of a civilized community upon each other, create that great chain of connection which hold it together.
Thomas Paine, Rights of Man

Despite the warnings of a few political economists, like J. R. McCulloch, the "spirit of independence," was recast and reified in the theoretical mills of Bentham and his followers into the notorious law of "less eligibility" that governed admittance to the "Poor Law Bastilles" after the New Poor Law of 1834. The *laissez-faire* principles of poor relief discouraged any outdoor relief to the poor and set up the workhouse as a place of last resort, where the poor would be, as stated in the report of the Poor Law Commission of 1834, "subjected to such courses of labour and discipline as will repel the indolent and vicious" (qtd. in Morton 397). Under the principle of "less eligibility," the New Poor Law would enforce men and women to display the "spirit of independence" to avoid the hated workhouse, in which, as Richard Oastler, one of its major adversaries declared, "[p]overty is in England punished with greater severity than crime" (*Fleet Papers* 1: 192). Even in times of scarcity the new dispensation allowed no charity to the poor, for such would interfere with the laws of political economy and further impoverish, as David Ricardo had argued, not just the poor, but the rich as well.[1] To draw upon a literary example, consider again John Thornton, the wealthy manufacturer of Elizabeth Gaskell's *North and South*. Because he considers his workers to be under the disciplinary control of his own "wise despotism," Thornton refuses to offer them provisions at wholesale prices lest he "should be interfering with the independence of [his] men" (167, 445). Thornton does not mean that he would be preempting the rights or freedom of the factory workers; rather, he means that he would be interfering with the free marketplace that interpellates each worker as an individual charged with taking care of himself or herself. Thus, the wise despotism toward the poor that he advocates, unlike the benevolent paternalism that it displaced, rejects charity or assistance to the able-bodied poor, even in times of scarcity.

Thornton's advocacy of self help for the poor was in the spirit of the Poor Law Amendment Act, signed 14 August 1834, which was notoriously severe in denying relief to the able-bodied poor, casting them to their own meager resources for a marginal subsistence. As is well known, in the *Postscript* to *Yarrow Revisited and Other Poems* (1835) Wordsworth joined in the protest against this act, pointing out that the New Poor Law would ultimately degrade and punish many prudent and diligent people who were thrown into desperate circumstances through no fault of their own. Joining radical, Tory, socialist and Christian critics alike, Wordsworth argues that the amendment "proceeds too much upon the presumption that it is a laboring man's own fault if he be not, as the phrase is, beforehand with the world" (*PrW* 3.246). Like most Tory opponents of the essentially Whig policy, Wordsworth objects to centralizing the administration of poor relief. Against the faceless bureaucracy, Wordsworth upholds the local and private charity of a bygone age that promoted the local parish as the chief caretaker of the poor.[2] In Wordsworth's words, the state should stand "*in loco parentis* towards all its subjects, to make such effectual provision, that no one shall be in danger of perishing either through the neglect or harshness of its legislation" (*PrW* 3: 242). Though an apparent classism surfaces in his argument—he writes that poor relief should be "administered under the care of the upper classes, as it ought to be" (*PrW* 3: 244)—Wordsworth never abandons his belief that, within the limits of the benevolent paternalism he advocates, the poor deserve the respect, sympathy and assistance of their social betters. Of course, such benevolent paternalism does imply that the poor, the social equivalents of children, should be under the care of their upper-class "parents."

The knotty position Wordsworth takes on charity gets further entangled when we consider that while he attacks the violence of "less eligibility," he paradoxically praises those poor who, like the leech gatherer in "Resolution and Independence," resolve to subsist by their own means under the most adverse conditions. Indeed, the *Postscript* gives a bathetic account of a couple who carried their dead child with them for four years because "the poor creatures lived in the hope of one day being able to bury their child at their own cost" (*PrW* 3: 245). Wordsworth praises the couple's "spirit of independence" and concludes, "there is not . . . sufficient cause for doubting that a like sense of honour may be revived among the people, and their ancient habits of independence restored, without resorting to those severities which the New Poor Law Act has introduced" (*PrW* 3: 245). Wordsworth's position in the *Postscript*, then, is at best contradictory, for he claims that a relaxation of the Poor Laws, founded on a doctrine of self help, would restore in the "humblest peasantry and mechanics" the "spirit of independence" which, as we have seen in the previous chapter, itself is but an idyllic formulation of self help.[3] In this chapter, I want to disentangle Wordsworth's problematic and contradictory position on charity from the colder, more indifferent and insensitive position of some of his Benthamite contemporaries. Let me begin here by addressing Wordsworth's complicity in the contemporary ideology of poverty, before I move on to show how "The Old Cumberland Beggar" demonstrates a greater compassion and concern for the poor than it may at first suggest.

One of the few early critics to challenge Wordsworth's social text, Edward Bostetter was particularly disturbed by the social implications of "The Old Cumberland Beggar." Conceding that Wordsworth may have been "motivated by the best intentions," Bostetter nevertheless finds that the poem displays "a curious insensitivity" in treating the beggar as an instrument (*Romantic Ventriloquists* 55). More recently, in *Wordsworth's Second Nature* James Chandler observes that the appropriation of the beggar for the benefit of those who give him alms amounts to an endorsement of the social hierarchy that produces abject poverty: "The speaker's claims for the Beggar's 'use' to the villagers has . . . to be seen as serving [the] larger quietistic argument about the limits of human wisdom, the vanity of political science, and the justice of the ways of God to man" (87). In other words, Chandler believes that the poem endorses the prevalent doctrine of the providential inevitability of poverty that we've seen at work in the writings of Burke, Paley and Malthus, among others. An early American critic of Wordsworth's, Orestes Brownson, anticipates Chandler's reading of Wordsworth's contradictory position on poverty. Protesting that the poet's sense of democracy did not go very far to challenge the relations of domination in British society, Brownson writes,"Wordsworth sings beggars, we admit, and shows very clearly that a man who begs is not to be despised; but does he ever fire our souls with a desire so to perfect our social system, that beggary shall not be one if its fruits?" (435).[4]

The answer to Brownson's question is less clear than I once claimed in an early version of this chapter.[5] Certainly, as Mary Moorman suggests, the Wordsworths were known for their hospitality to beggars in the Lake District. In *William Wordsworth: The Early Years*, Moorman points out that "William and Dorothy never refused hospitality or money" to the beggars they frequently met while at Grasmere (470–71). Robert Gittings and Jo Manton praise in particular Dorothy Wordsworth's generosity to the poor in their biography, *Dorothy Wordsworth*. As they put it, "[s]he was a faithful witness to the lot of the poor at a time of exceptional hardship," and they repeat Moorman's claim that William and Dorothy "never refused hospitality or money to the wayfarers . . ." (116). Certainly Dorothy Wordsworth's *Journals* point to numerous incidents of their giving alms—either money or food—to the discharged soldiers, widows and abject beggars at Grasmere.[6] Though she sometimes merely records the numbers of beggars she encounters during a day, Dorothy Wordsworth often gives a few details about their character or about the cause of their poverty. She does not always tell us specifically, yet most readers assume that the beggars received alms from her or her brother.

These assumptions aside, the Wordsworths' attitudes toward the poor do not always appear to reflect the constant admiration and sympathy that Moorman attributes to them. In a letter to William Matthews of 24 October 1795, for example, Wordsworth made this observation about the country laborers at Racedown: "The country people here are wretchedly poor; ignorant and overwhelmed with every vice that usually attends ignorance in that class, viz—lying and picking and stealing &c &c." (*EY* 154). Moreover, even on the occasions described in Dorothy Wordsworth's journals, one sees evidence of what Coleridge described as Wordsworth's tendency to stand at a distance from the poor, an attitude he calls the *spectator ab extra*.[7] This distancing perspective appears in the *Grasmere Journal* of 22 December 1801, in which Dorothy Wordsworth records that "from a half laziness, half indifference and a wanting to *try* [an elderly beggar] if he would speak," she let him pass by silently before feeling a pang of guilt.[8] As we have seen in Chapter Three, Wordsworth describes a similar incident in "Point Rash-Judgment."

Although Dorothy Wordsworth's journals describe moments of apparent sympathy with the poor, her observations should be balanced with the accounts of the working people who knew the Wordsworths. In "Reminiscences of Wordsworth among the Peasantry of Westmoreland," R. H. Rawnsley records this assessment of Wordsworth given by a man who worked as a delivery boy for the local butcher: "as for Mr. Wudsworth, he'd pass you, same as if ya was nobbut a stoan. He niver cared for children, however; ya may be certain of that, for didn't I have to pass him four times in t' week, up to the door wi' meat? And he niver oncst said owt" (164). Another account by a man identified only as George, a waller, corroborates the former delivery boy's view that Wordsworth was a man who paid little attention to the working people he met: " 'He wozn't a man as said a deal to common folk. But he talked a deal to hissen' " (169). As Rawnsley comments, "the secret of Wordsworth's unpopularity with the dalesmen seems to have been that he was shy and retired, and not one who mixed readily or talked much with them" (169). Whatever the reason for Wordsworth's unpopularity, the Wordsworths' reputed affection for the poor must be qualified by these accounts of the working poor who knew them. While willing to give needed alms, as Brownson suggests, the Wordsworths appear to have been motivated both by sympathy and by a regard for their responsibilities as more privileged members of the community.[9] More often than not, it appears, Dorothy and William were importunate questioners into the backgrounds of the beggars, discharged soldiers and widows they met.[10] When Moorman admits that the beggars "were a source of interest and often of compassion to the Wordsworths" (470), she hints that alms from the Wordsworths were often exacted at a certain price—that of satisfying their curiosity. Thus Wordsworth and his sister exacted from the poor at least a small price for their charity—a "homely tale" for a sixpence or a bit of bread.

As I have argued throughout the previous chapters, however, while Wordsworth's attitudes toward the poor are at best contradictory, I remain convinced that we cannot infer that Brownson was right, as David Simpson suggests in his early "Criticism, Politics, and Style in Wordsworth's Poetry," when he asks whether "Wordsworth might have been devoid of certain basic human sympathies for the intrinsic well-being of aging vagrants" (54). Simpson's question assumes that Wordsworth somehow could extricate himself fully from the prevailing attitudes and practices that created what Sarah Trimmer dubbed an "Oeconomy of Charity." No matter how humane or benign in intention, the prevailing economy of charity in the late eighteenth century was determined through discourse in such a way as to reproduce, even further elaborate, the limitations imposed upon it by ideology, as we have seen in the discussion on idleness and industry in Crabbe and Wordsworth in Chapter Three. Further contradictions obtain, however, in discussions of the economy of charity, especially as they complicate Wordsworth's "The Old Cumberland Beggar." While "The Old Cumberland Beggar," rather like Gray's *Elegy Written in a Country Churchyard*, returns Wordsworth to the privileged gaze of the external spectator who naturalizes the death of the poor in an unstoried landscape of universal suffering, the poem does not mark Wordsworth's abandonment of the cause of the poor. Rather it further marks the limits of his critique and a retrenchment into that humanistic liberalism that has earned him, in the eyes of at least one observer, Michael Friedman, the label "Tory Humanist."

I

If we move for a moment to the beginning of the eighteenth century, we note that the boundaries between aesthetic theory and social practice blur or break down altogether when it comes to the question of charity. For some writers, such as Richard Steele, the practice of charity itself should be based upon standards derived from aesthetic conventions. Indeed, the poor were supposed to behave like their ideal models in fiction. Steele's *Tatler* 68 (13–15 Sep 1709), for example, shows how the cultivation of aesthetic taste insinuated itself into the social sphere. In Steele's essay the conventions of philanthropical practice become first a politics, then an aesthetics, of silence; the qualities by which the moral worth of beggars was to be assessed become the criteria of taste that writers should follow in representing the poor in literature. Steele distinguishes the responses of men and women to an object of sympathy. Whereas such an object moves women to tears, the same object moves men to "think how such a one ought to act on that Occasion, suitable to the Dignity of his Nature" (2). A woman errs in sympathizing with those who make public their lamentations, while a man properly sympathizes only with those "whom he observes to suffer in silence" (2). Since for Steele sympathy serves an evaluative function in society, he asserts the priority of "rational" over "emotional" sympathy.[11] Thus, a person with proper judgment would never pity those who are heard to pity themselves—that is, those who utter complaints or lamentations.

Steele illustrates his point with a story about two beggars, "a noisy impudent" one and "a Poor Fellow . . . with a rusty Coat, a melancholy Air, and a soft Voice" (2). The first, of course, "bawls out" his complaint and receives no charity from passersby; the second, the ideal sufferer—clean, deferent, and above all, reticent—"received the charity of almost every one that went by" (2). Interestingly, Steele finds in encounters with the indigent a certain theatrics or poetics of solicitation:

> The Strings of the Heart, which are to be touch'd to give us Compassion, are not so play'd on but by the finest Hand. We see in Tragical Representation, it is not the Pomp of Language, or Magnificence of Dress, in which the Passion is wrought that touches sensible Spirits; but something of a plain and simple Nature, which breaks in upon our Souls, by that Simpathy [*sic*] which is given us for our mutual Good-will and Service. (2)

Since Steele's audience comprised those who would more likely be alms-givers than alms-takers, the poetics of solicitation converts readily into a politics of charity, establishing silence and deference as criteria by which the charitable may judge prospective beneficiaries.

Although elsewhere Steele was capable of arguing that people should be judged solely by their virtue, his essay contributes a standard of taste for potential benefactors which promises to distinguish between the deserving and the undeserving. In *Tatler* 69 (17 September 1709), for example, Steele writes, "he who thinks no Man above him but for his Virtue, none below him but for his Vice, can never be obsequious or assuming in a wrong Place; but will frequently emulate Men in Rank below him, and pity those above him" (1). In *Tatler* 87, 29 October 1709, he praises "the Dignity of human Nature, which often shows itself in all Conditions of Life" (1). Thus, Steele attempts to make the judgment of virtue universally accepted to people of all stations in the social hierarchy. Nonetheless, when it comes to describing an encounter with a beggar, the classist assumptions of the discourse on poverty shift Steele back into a kind of default mode that enjoins the poor man to silence and the privileged man to judgment.

Steele's principle of the pauper's silence as a test of genuine want became commonplace in writings about charity throughout the eighteenth century, especially after the scare of the French Revolution made the silence of the poor an even more desirable quality. In mid-century, Adam Smith's *A Theory of Moral Sentiments* rather innocuously claims that people "are more apt to weep and shed tears for such as . . . seem to feel nothing for themselves, than for those who give way to all the weakness of sorrow" (248). His truism at least could apply to rich as well as poor. Toward the end of the century, however, Joseph Townsend and Thomas Malthus made it eminently clear just what class of people should hold their tongues. Townsend's *A Dissertation on the Poor Laws* (1786) asserts that "modest worth stands at a distance, or draws nigh with faltering tongue and broken accents to tell an artless tale; whilst the most worthless are the most unreasonable in their expectation, and the most importunate in their solicitation for relief" (19). Similarly, the fifth edition of Malthus's *Essay on Population* emphasizes the need to discriminate the deserving from the undeserving by applying the test of silence. By abolishing public relief and relying solely upon private charity, Malthus intends to "check the hopes of clamorous and obtrusive poverty, with no other recommendation but rags" and to "encourage with adequate relief the silent and retiring sufferer laboring under unmerited difficulties" (qtd. in Owen 547–48). With these statements, Townsend and Malthus sum up the "Catch 22" implicit in the discourse on poverty: those who call attention to their suffering should not receive alms; those who suffer silently should receive alms graciously.[12] Of course, those who suffer in silence are likely to remain invisible to the potential benefactor.

Importantly, Steele's practical advice extends into a maxim for representational poetics and in so doing reverses the relationship between theory and practice. The practice that Steele would regulate according to an arbitrary test of silence had already been shown to be the foundation for aesthetic practice: art imitates reality—but here that reality first is established according to a set of artificial principles: "the true art seems to be, that when you would have the person you represent pitied, you must show him at once in the highest grief, and struggling to bear it with decency and patience"—the very formula by which the sentimental novel, such as Henry Mackenzie's *Man of Feeling*, would sketch the deserving poor. Moreover, Steele bases his claim on a theory of literary identification: "Self-love, and a Sense of the Pain we ourselves should suffer in the Circumstances of any whom we pity, is the Cause of . . . Compassion" (*Tatler* 68.2).

This aesthetic silencing of the poor appears to have been a major project of the eighteenth century —a project that coincided with a similar attempt to domesticate the working classes by means of limited literacy. The idea that the deferent poor are those who excite the most pleasant response in the reader derives from the belief that the silence of the poor was a sign of authentic want, and its corollary that importunity was a sign of fraud. Yet, by the late eighteenth century, many writers and critics began to question the relationship between the aesthetic representation of the poor and the actual poor. Sarah Trimmer and Anna Barbauld, for example, questioned whether the poor would actually benefit from readers' encounters with the idealized paupers, beggars and abandoned widows who made up some of the stock characters in sentimental fiction and poetry. Would the representation of the poor as pastoral shepherds, dainty milkmaids or cherubic children in clean but tattered rags do anything at all to remedy the suffering of the actual poor or to improve the disposition for generosity among those who must relieve them?

Trimmer was one of the first to be troubled by the apparent distance between the "objects of pity in romance" and the actual women she knew who suffered from various injustices, including poverty . In her *Oeconomy of Charity* (1787) Trimmer speculates that literature, especially the novel, had adversely influenced social affections between the rich and the poor. As she puts it, the "great cultivation of literature in this kingdom" had made the rich and the poor "as unintelligible to each other as if they came from different regions of the world" (11). "The objects of pity in romance," she writes, "are as different from those in real life as our husbandmen from the shepherds of Arcadia; and a girl who will sit weeping the whole night at the delicate distresses of a lady Charlotte, or lady Julia, shall be little moved at the complaint of her neighbour, who, in a homely phrase and vulgar accent, laments that she is not able to get bread for her family" (228). Similarly, as we have already seen in Chapter Two, Barbauld points out in "An Enquiry into those Kinds of Distress which Excite Agreeable Sensations" that the literature of sensibility, in which beggars and other vagrants appear to elicit an emotional response from the reader, risks engaging the reader's sympathy for ideal objects for whom there are no prototypes in the world of social relations. This literature, then, may actually have limited acts of charity, because most people in real need bore little or no resemblance to their literary proxies.

Given the discrepancy between representations of virtue in distress and the actual beggars, prostitutes, paupers and cripples who depended on charity for their survival, literature and art probably contributed to few acts of benevolence toward those in most need. The "moral tendencies" of representations of the indigent, as Barbauld contends, "are generally thought to improve the tender and humane feelings; but this, I own, appears to me very dubious" (*Works* 2: 227). Lacking the appropriate dress, proper virtues and polite speech of their literary prototypes, real beggars did not fit the models of virtue-in-distress upon which the sympathies of the middle-class reader had been rehearsed. Barbauld argued strongly that the radical difference between the objects of pity in literature and their counterparts in life would in fact produce callousness on the part of those who indulged their passions in fictional representations of sufferers. She writes: "Another reason why plays and romances do not improve our humanity is, that they lead us to require a certain elegance of manners and delicacy of virtue which is not often found with poverty, ignorance and meanness" (*Works* 2: 228–29). One might appreciate Barbauld's telling frankness in noting the indifference to real suffering that literature could impose upon its readers, when she writes: "We are less moved at the description of an Indian tortured with all the dreadful ingenuity of that savage people, than with the fatal mistake of the lover in the *Spectator*, who pierced an artery in the arm of his mistress as he was letting her blood" (2: 219). The poor, in other words, could not rely for charity upon an audience whose sympathy was spent on a simulacrum of poverty.

Unlike Trimmer, Barbauld raises the question of representing the poor as a caveat for aesthetic rather than social interests—to caution writers against violating the taste of their readers. Barbauld advises the prospective writer to protect her or his readers from such shocking pictures of the poor altogether. "A judicious author," she warns, "will never attempt to raise pity by anything mean or disgusting" (200)—an idea that informed critics of Wordsworth's poetry, such as Francis Jeffrey, for at least another half century. Such beggars were more likely to be scorned with disgust, a fact George Canning turned to use in his parody of Southey's "The Widow" (1797).

In "The Friend of Humanity and the Knife Grinder," which appeared in the 27 November 1798 edition of the *Anti-Jacobin*, Canning criticizes not only Southey's poem, but the principle of "universal benevolence" that it praises.[13] For Adam Smith universal benevolence meant the providential wisdom of an omniscient being which persons from all ranks of life should "submit to with resignation" (*Moral Sentiments* 236). But it also suggested a person's responsibility to look out for his or her own welfare and that of friends, family and country. Though Smith himself had little truck with beggars, considering them primarily as objects whose misery might inspire sympathetic horror or contempt, the general import of the *Theory of Moral Sentiments* spawned a sort of frenzy of almsgiving—especially of the fictional kind found in the sentimental novel. Typically, Smith's attitude toward beggars was conflicted. On the one hand, he would write: "We despise a beggar; and, though his importunities may extort an alms from us, he is scarce ever the object of any serious commiseration" (144). At the same time, however, Smith could imply that a beggar by the side of the road—a proleptic version of Wordsworth's old Cumberland beggar—enjoys an equal or even greater peace of mind than those who stand even far above him in social rank: "In ease of body and peace of mind, all the different ranks of life are nearly upon a level, and the beggar, who suns himself by the side of the highway, possesses that security which kings are fighting for" (185). Thus, for Smith, the beggar presents the same kind of contradictory spectacle that Wordsworth and Cowper find in gypsies and that Godwin finds in bandit society: they are signs of both weakness and strength, spectacles of a feared misery and a desirable equanimity. By the end of the century, Smith's universal benevolence became associated with "injudicious and indiscriminate generosity," which, according to Archdeacon Paley's *The Principles of Moral and Political Philosophy* (1785)—a book which represents the middle ground in debates over charity—encouraged idleness and vagrancy (214).

In Paley's hierarchy of kinds of charity, giving alms to beggars was the last and "lowest" form, though he dismisses what he calls the "indiscriminate rejection of all who implore our alms this way" (*Principles* 208). Mary Wollstonecraft and Charlotte Smith go even further than Paley when they advocate to their young readers the giving of alms without subjecting the recipients of their charity to what we would call today a "needs" test. In Smith's *Rural Walks*, for example, Mrs. Woodfield points out to Elizabeth and Caroline that since she cannot distinguish "common beggars from poor men disabled by illness from working, or accidentally distressed in a strange country, where they have no claim to parochial relief," she advises giving alms to anyone who solicits her help as the practice "which may [best] afford a chance of doing good." Though she may risk encouraging an "idle vagabond," she is as likely to relieve "an unfortunate fellow creature" (2: 45). Similarly, Wollstonecraft's Mrs. Mason recommends giving to all persons who appear to be in distress, though giving "[but] a trifle when you are not certain the distress is real. . . ." She would "rather be deceived five hundred times, than doubt once without reason" (*Original Stories* 441). Nonetheless, the beggars we meet with in the stories of Smith and Wollstonecraft, like the distressed stationer of the last example, who "was one of the most sober, industrious young men in London" (442), tend to be from among the deserving poor. It appears that what Simpson calls "an element of real confusion" in Wordsworth's attitudes toward the poor and poor relief reflects fairly accurately a similar element of confusion among his contemporaries (*Wordsworth's Historical Imagination* 173). While advocating universal benevolence and rejecting the objectification of the poor as mute aesthetic objects, Wordsworth and other late eighteenth-century writers and artists at both ends of the political spectrum drew upon the most conventional stereotypes as they praised the virtuous and vilified the profligate.

Simpson argues that Wordsworth's system of charity questions the "propriety" of the categories of "deserving and undeserving" that many of his peers—and especially the utilitarian followers of Bentham—insisted upon as a test for beggars (*Wordsworth's Historical Imagination*

173). Certainly Wordsworth did not completely reject industry and independence as elements in a litmus test for valuing the self- and public worth of the poor; but in view of the recent charges of reactionary conservativism against Wordsworth's poetry, I think it is worth pausing one more time to consider how Wordsworth's view of charity and his use of the discourse on poverty is much more conflicted than that found among many of his contemporaries.

II

Before turning directly to "The Old Cumberland Beggar," I want to elaborate upon a point of apparent contradiction in Wordsworth's particular inflection of the discourse on poverty which celebrates the "spirit of independence" even as it looks favorably upon begging. This contradiction may be shown in contrasting a passage from Cowper's *The Task* (1785) with Wordsworth's "The Sailor's Mother" (1802). In both cases, the poems invest the effectively powerless with, to use Michael Friedman's term, affective power.[14] Moreover, both poems attribute normative value—moral integrity—to the poor. Yet Cowper's poem holds up the independent poor as exemplars of dignity and moral rectitude, while Wordsworth's attributes these qualities to the dependent thus subverting the common assumptions about the deserving and undeserving.

Cowper's *The Task* (1785) frequently posits the gentlemanly narrator observing picturesque scenes of agricultural laborers or families at work. Among these sociological miniatures is a scene from "The Winter Evening" in which the narrator describes a peasant family at home and praises them for their industriousness, modesty, frugality and, most importantly, the spirit of independence that keeps them from appealing to the parish for assistance:

> They live, and live without extorted alms
> From grudging hands, but other boast have none
> To soothe their honest pride, that scorns to beg;
> Nor comfort else, but in their mutual love.
> I praise you much, ye meek and patient pair,
> For ye are worthy; choosing rather far
> A dry but independent crust, hard earn'd,
> And eaten with a sigh, than to endure
> The rugged frowns and insolent rebuffs
> Of knaves in office, partial in the work of
> Of distribution. . . . (*Task* 4.403–13)

The "spirit of independence" is writ large in this passage, for this family demonstrates a willingness to submit to deprivation rather than to the bullying overseers of the parish. Like Crabbe and Wordsworth, Cowper impugns the callousness and incompetence that social observers frequently noted among the parish overseers of the poor, yet it is hard to reconcile his idyllic presentation of such stubborn resistance to needed charity with the more critical position expressed in *Hope* (1782). In that poem he notes that the poor, "inured to drudgery and distress" (7), were able to feel happiness and pleasure "nowhere but in feign'd Arcadian scenes" (9; *Works* 1: 85). Cowper's contradictions are characteristic in the discourse on poverty, in which the "spirit of independence" dignifies the poor at the same time that it abandons them to their indigence—all under the sign of some moral freedom.

This contradiction appears with particular force in Wordsworth's "The Sailor's Mother," which celebrates the virtues of private charity. Invoking a trace of the moral economy that supported the agrarian poor, the poem sets up dependency as an act of communal dignity, a vestige of a past in which paternal obligations bound the rich to supplement the provisions of their laborers in times of scarcity. Thus, perhaps rather unexpectedly, the sight of an old woman begging activates the narrator's pride:

> The ancient Spirit is not dead;
> Old times, thought I, are breathing there;
> Proud was I that my country bred
> Such strength, a dignity so fair:
> She begg'd an alms, like one in poor estate;
> I look'd at her again, nor did my pride abate.
>
> (7–12; *Poems* 77)

The poem evokes the plaintive dignity of the "ancient spirit," that is, the spirit of feudal obligations that purportedly cemented the bonds of domestic affection in the pastoral community of rural England. Wordsworth's romantic feudalism condones begging under certain austere circumstances as a necessary component of raising the domestic affections of the community, as in "The Old Cumberland Beggar." Thus, "The Sailor's Mother" produces an image of a begging woman who has been strengthened by her troubles, a woman who has accepted her misfortune with patience and resilience. She demonstrates the same stoic fortitude as Cowper's peasant family, and her proud demeanor marks her as one of the deserving poor—that is, those who deserve to receive alms.

In the works of Cowper, Crabbe and Wordsworth, the industrious poor, like the sailor's mother, should turn to voluntary private charity for relief when their industry fails to meet their needs. Voluntary charity reaffirms the ties between rich and poor and requires something like a face-to-face encounter between benefactor and recipient, in contrast to the involuntary poor relief that the Poor Laws demand and that further distances the rich from the poor under the canopy of bureau-cratic anonymity. We can recall here Crabbe's protest against the unde-serving poor "who take from our reluctant hands / What *Burn* advises or the Bench commands" (*Parish Register* 1.271–72). Though Crabbe's poem associates insensitive bureaucracy with Richard Burn, a Westmor-land native who took an active role in reorganizing Poor Law administra-tion, Burn was critical of the workhouse system and argued in his *Obser-vations on the Bill . . . for the Better Relief and Employment of the Poor* (1796), that proposed changes in the administration of poor relief would uproot people from their homes, abuse their liberty and isolate them in virtual prisons (22–23).

Wordsworth directly echoes Crabbe's protest against obligatory charity and Burn's concern for the liberty of the poor in his Fenwick note on "The Old Cumberland Beggar" and in the *Postscript* of 1835, respectively. In the Fenwick note, Wordsworth distinguishes between voluntary private charity and what he calls alms "robbed of their Chris-tian grace and spirit, as being *forced* rather from the benevolent than given by them" (*PW* 4: 446). Describing Wordsworth's position in the *Postscript*, Simpson notes that, like Burke, Wordsworth commends self-reliance among the poor, but—unlike Burke—not at the cost of punish-ing the virtuous poor for their distress *(Wordsworth's Historical Imagina-tion* 173). Certainly it is true that in 1835 Wordsworth would have the legislation of poor relief err on the side of humanity; as Wordsworth writes in the *Postscript*, "with regard to the Poor Laws . . . it is better for the interests of humanity among the people at large, that ten undeserv-ing should partake of the funds provided, than that one morally good man, through want of relief, should either have his principles corrupted, or his energies destroyed; than that such a one should either be driven to do wrong, or be cast to the earth in utter hopelessness" (*PrW* 3: 246–47). I don't agree, however, that Wordsworth here denies the "propriety of any attempt to distinguish the deserving from the undeserving poor" (*Wordsworth's Historical Imagination* 173); rather, he questions the prac-ticality of putting such distinctions into practice in any large-scale system of poor relief. While, as Simpson reminds us, Wordsworth in his later years may have been equivocal about the practical consequences of officially distinguishing between the "deserving" and "undeserving" poor, in the early poems it is the industrious, virtuous, "ennobled" poor who appear worthy of attention—and relief. Just as Cowper's narrator in the passage cited from "The Winter Evening" takes satisfaction in leaving unsolicited alms with the poor family, Wordsworth's narrator in "The Sailor's Mother" is moved by the woman's resolution to accept her condition stoically—"like a Roman matron's was her mien and gait" (6). Such resolution numbers her among the "deserving" poor, such as Cow-per's "meek and patient pair" whose modesty, patience and "spirit of independence" paradoxically make them worthy of receiving alms.

The apparent contradiction between "The Sailor's Mother" and "Resolution and Independence," between Wordsworth's praise of dignified begging and self-reliance, can be resolved in this paradox. For in Wordsworth's ideal solution to the problems of poor relief, the local "gentlemen and substantial proprietors" acting *in loco parentis* on behalf of the poor would be able to distinguish on an individual basis between the deserving and undeserving. Paley's influential *Principles of Moral and Political Philosophy* may have guided Wordsworth's assessment of the value of private charity over bureaucratic systems of relief. Paley divides charity into three kinds, in descending order: giving pensions or annuities "to individuals or families with whose behaviour and distress we ourselves are acquainted"; contributing to public charity; and relieving beggars (208). The degree of familiarity between the benefactor and the recipient of his or her charity stands out as Paley's primary concern here. In Wordsworth's "The Old Cumberland Beggar," this emphasis upon the local and the familiar stands out as a means by which even those who would be deemed undeserving under an anonymous bureacracy may be judged worthy of relief. Like Paley's treatise, Wordsworth's poem, as we'll see, discounts the "indiscriminate rejection" of all beggars (*Principles* 208) and urges the preservation of private charity in order to preserve the bonds of familiarity between members of the local community and, to use Goldsmith's phrase, the "long remember'd beggar" (*Deserted Village* 1.151). In the both "The Sailor's Mother" and "The Old Cumberland Beggar,"—and one might include also "Alice Fell," "Simon Lee," "Goody Blake and Harry Gill" and "The Last of the Flock," all of which appeal to the need for private charity and point to the injustice of the Poor Laws—Wordsworth attempts to restore dignity to those degraded by the material practices of a *laissez-faire* system of poor relief.

Like these other poems, "The Old Cumberland Beggar" draws upon elements of the discourse on poverty even as it appears to reject some of the premises underpinning that discourse. Wordsworth's poem, as if drawn up according to Steele's advice, maintains a certain propriety about the origins of the old Cumberland beggar's indigence and presents him as one of Steele's model paupers—deferent, grateful (at least unwittingly so), and nonthreatening. Indeed, the beggar's speechlessness seems to serve as paradigmatic example of those indigent deemed worthy of charity according to the principles set down by Steele, Smith and Townsend. Moreover, as both Bostetter and Chandler agree, "The Old Cumberland Beggar" makes the beggar's adversity seem inevitable and natural, while it maintains strict silence about the probable social causes of his poverty. As we have seen, because the poem appeals to the readers' sympathy for the beggar's intrinsic worth and his social utility, critics like Bostetter and Chandler, emphasizing the latter, read the poem as a concession to the Benthamite engineers of Poor Law reform. In my view, however, the poem places the beggar's humanity into a creative tension with his utility, so that ultimately "The Old Cumberland Beggar" attempts to redeem the basic humanity of the beggar by showing, contra Bentham and his followers, that the beggar's use must be measured not in economic, but in spiritual terms.

The narrator begins his vindication of the beggar with the well-known appeal, "Deem not this Man useless.—Statesmen!" (67). The statesmen Wordsworth has in mind, as he reminded Isabella Fenwick in his 1843 note to the poem, are political economists, such as Bentham and Malthus, who were advocating the centralization of management over the poor, detention in workhouses and compulsory labor. In the Fenwick note to "The Old Cumberland Beggar" Wordsworth says that the poem was written in response to the political economists' "war on mendicity." He further explains that with the passage of the Poor Law Amendment Act of 1834, the "heartless process [had] been carried as far as it can go . . . though the inhumanity that prevails in this measure is somewhat disguised by the profession that one of its objects is to throw the poor upon the voluntary donations of their neighbours . . ." (*PW* 4: 446). He further complains that the Poor Law Amendment Act, because it made charity compulsory, is robbing alms of "their Christian grace and spirit . . ." (*PW* 4: 446). Thus, in contrast to the natural law theorists, who wanted to harness the able-bodied poor to the labor force, Wordsworth argues that begging already has a useful place in the moral economy of society.

The logic of "The Old Cumberland Beggar" compels us to see that the apparently useless rounds of begging constitute a kind of regular industry that manufactures good will and acts of kindness among the villagers:

> Where'er the aged Beggar takes his rounds,
> The mild necessity of use compels
> To acts of love; . . . (98–100; *PW* 4: 237)

Since the distribution of charity in the late eighteenth century was regulated by the test of industriousness, Wordsworth's conception of the beggar's usefulness attempts to offset his apparent idleness by linking him to those industrious, honest people whose accidental misfortune made them the darlings of the philanthropists. As we have seen in Chapter Four, Wordsworth saw in beggars and vagabonds a troubling double for the poet—a marginal whose questionable value to society needed to be justified. In "The Old Cumberland Beggar" this identification once more becomes quite apparent, in that the beggar's offices to the community, like those of the ancient bards, provide people with a tablet of memory—at once a historical record and a spur to their better feelings. Wordsworth was convinced that, like the old Cumberland beggar, poets provide the community with "a record which together binds / Past deeds and offices of charity, / Else unremembered" (89–91; *PW* 4: 237). Assigning the beggar an important, if not crucial, role in society was in part a function of Wordsworth's own need to come to terms with his chosen profession, which, like the beggar's, was subject to questions of authenticity and value.

Wordsworth attributes the beggar's social instrumentality to a natural law that directly contradicts the cold calculus of the utilitiarians, and the poem includes him in a larger group of marginals or outcasts whose value to society, though not immediately apparent, is significant:

> 'Tis Nature's law
> That none, the meanest of created things,
> Of forms created the most vile and brute,
> The dullest or most noxious, should exist
> Divorced from good— . . . (73–77; *PW* 4: 236)

In the scheme of the poem, which claims that every "mode of being" offers some benefit to the community as a whole, Wordsworth deftly invokes Adam Smith's doctrine of universal benevolence as an argument against the contempt or at least indifference toward beggars expressed in the theories of charity perpetrated by Smith's followers. When discussing universal benevolence in the *Theory of Moral Sentiments*, Smith argues that God, the great administrator of the universe, visits loss and misfortune upon people in order to serve the greater interests of community, society, country, or even "as necessary for the prosperity of the universe" (235–36). Therefore, "in the greatest public as well as private disasters, a wise man ought to consider that he himself, his friends and countrymen, have only been ordered upon the forlorn station of the universe; that had it not been necessary for the good of the whole, they would not have been so ordered; and that it is their duty, not only with humble resignation to submit to this allotment, but to endeavour to embrace it with alacrity and joy" (236). While Bentham, Malthus, and later Chadwick and the New Poor Law Commission might see in this principle a justification of poverty and of their objectification of the poor, Wordsworth's poem turns our attention to the power and goodness that such a doctrine invests in the beggar. "The Old Cumberland Beggar" asks us to admire the purposiveness of the beggar's position in the community, and it seeks to establish between beggar and benefactor a common identity. Thus, the poem attempts to reclaim for the beggar a place and function within the community, to conflate the center and the periphery as common space. While its appeal to utility may appear to rationalize the old man's suffering, "The Old Cumberland Beggar" rather serves to remind the reader that, in Smith's words, the wise and virtuous person must attend to "the care of his own happiness, of that of his family, his friends, [and] his country" (237)—a care that should extend to those apparent marginals who are, despite appearances, contributing members of that community and certainly functioning components of "the immense machine of the universe" (236).

Wordsworth's position in "The Old Cumberland Beggar" anticipates Georg Simmel's analysis of poverty in "The Poor" (1908). Simmel, without resorting to the benevolent paternalism characteristic of Wordsworth's attitudes toward the poor, notes that assistance to the poor may proceed, as in Wordsworth, from "an organic link" between the poor and their benefactors or, as in Bentham, "teleologically from a goal one hopes to pursue," in particular the preservation of the state (153). In the first case, Simmel argues, "the *rights* of the poor are more highly emphasized" (153), because the benefactors perceive the poor as a part—albeit a necessarily marginal part—of the community as a whole. Almsgiving, in this case, becomes an end in itself rather than a means to an end, and the poor person participates in the community as an active subject rather than as an instrumental object. In "The Old Cumberland Beggar" the aged beggar's actions do indeed involve him in an active give-and-take with the community. Rather than an instrumentality, he is a catalyst for action, and so interacts with the community as a vital member of the moral economy.

One way to show the radical humanitarianism of Wordsworth's position is to compare his view of the beggar's use to that of Eden's in *State of the Poor*, a treatise which anticipates the utilitarian approach to poor relief. Though lamentable, Eden argues, the pains endured by the poor are insignificant when compared to their ultimate benefit to society in general. Paving the way for the argument that would be made frequently throughout the nineteenth and twentieth centuries to legitimate social oppression of the working classes, Eden writes:

> the only point of view, in which a nation can regard such schemes of reform, is to consider how far they do or do not promote the general weal, by raising the largest quantity of provisions, or materials for manufacture, at the least cost, their inconvenience to individuals will be softened and mitigated, indeed, as far as it is practicable, but by no means be suffered to counteract any new plans of improvement, of great and real national unity. (1: xiv)

For Eden, as well as for Malthus, a "portion, at least, of the society must be indefatigably employed, (and, happily, in every well-regulated state, a portion is sufficient), to supply the necessary wants of the whole" (1: 1).

In contrast to Eden and Malthus who rest the relative idleness and leisure of the many upon the labor of the few (in a rather skewed sense of what was really taking place), Wordsworth places the old

Cumberland beggar within a system of gift exchange into which all members contribute something. The old Cumberland beggar's indigence serves those who give him alms and those who give him alms serve his basic needs. In exchange for a small subsistence, the beggar returns to the villagers the calling to do good and the satisfaction of having done so:

> Let him bear about
> The good which the benignant law of Heaven
> Has hung around him: and, while life is his,
> Still let him prompt the unlettered villagers
> To tender offices and pensive thoughts.
>
> (166–70; *PW* 4: 239)

The beggar's poverty allows the community members to practice their charity and thereby keep alive the social sentiment that binds their society together. Moreover, the villagers

> —all behold in him [the beggar]
> A silent monitor, which on their minds
> Must needs impress a transitory thought
> Of self-congratulation, to the heart
> Of each recalling his peculiar boons,
> His charters and exemptions; . . . (122–27; *PW* 4: 238)

Thus, the beggar is a boon to the local community, for his indigence prompts his benefactors to exercise their virtue. Moreover, as a "silent monitor" of the villagers' good offices, the beggar serves as the tablet upon which the villagers inscribe their history by means of individual acts of charity. In his service as a kind of mirror of charity, we must ask whether the gifts he receives serve to mark him as the exempted Other or whether those gifts include him as a chartered member of the community of benefactors. While the beggar rewards those who can give with a heightened sense of complacent virtue, one wonders whether he must wear the "good" hung around him rather in the way that the Ancient Mariner wore the albatross—as a mark of difference.

As we've seen, readers from Brownson to Bostetter have been bothered by the self-satisfaction that the villagers acquire at the expense of the beggar's poverty. Such obvious rationalization of self-congratulatory behavior at another's expense is seldom so explicit in Wordsworth's poetry, and some critics, like Harold Bloom, have asked us to ignore the political implications the poem makes so clear.[15] Nevertheless, in the context of the discourse on poverty, Wordsworth's doctrine would have seemed rather commonplace.

At its most innocent, the discourse on poverty produced a sentimental vision of assistance to the poor, expressed in typical form in "Of the Poor in Scotland," an essay appended to Eden's *State of the Poor*. This essay fondly remarks charity's role in raising domestic affections within a local community: "The humble and modest supplicant . . . finds much less pleasure in the enjoyment of the alms which are thrown him, (perhaps at second hand,) with the careless fastidiousness of affected superiority, than in the humble pittance which is bestowed with the cordial warmth of social sympathy and unsophisticated nature" (3: ccc). At its more insidious, however, the discourse denounced the Poor Laws (and, by inference, the poor) in favor of returning dominion over charity to those of "affected superiority." Malthus, for example, warned that the Poor Laws, having made charity compulsory, would interfere with voluntary charity and thus deny Christian philanthropists the opportunity to receive God's blessing for giving charity freely. As a contributor to the *Monthly Magazine*, 1 June 1800, put it: "Benevolence may be unbounded; but if it cannot be traced to individual hands, there is but very slender ground for gratitude" (422). The ultimate goal of such giving was to cement bonds within an identifiable community circumscribed by clearly defined spatial and social boundaries—to reinforce, in Burke's words from *Reflections on the Revolution in France*, attachment "to the subdivision" and love of "the little platoon we belong to in society" (135).

Burke links charity with local management of the poor. Poor relief, he writes, must be administered "with a parental solicitude" (202). Furthermore, the superintendence of the poor, he believes, should be like that "sovereign superintendence" over all property. Wordsworth's own stated views about poor relief, as we have seen and as Chandler has persuasively argued, follow Burke's closely.[16] The state, Wordsworth explains in the *Postscript* of 1835, should be *in loco parentis* to the poor. Thus, in his continued opposition to the natural law theorists, who argued for centralized control over the poor, Wordsworth adopted a paternalistic view of superintendence carried out by individual acts of private charity within the strictly defined boundaries of the local community. As Marilyn Butler shows in *Romantics, Rebels and Revolutionaries*, localism of this kind found much favor among many of Wordsworth's contemporaries. Butler notes, for example, that Coleridge's *Frost at Midnight* is a meditation upon the salutary affects of local surroundings and community, and she cites Jane Austen's focus upon "three or four families in a country village" as further demonstration that *in loco parentis* was a favorite romantic doctrine, particularly among those who celebrate the virtues of paternalism centered in a local, landed gentry (84–85). We may recall, however, as David Owen has noted in his study of philanthropy in England from the seventeenth century to the modern era, virtually all of the treatises on philanthropy in the late eighteenth and early nineteenth centuries take for granted the distinctions between social classes, and one of the "ubiquitous theme[s] in the charity literature of the time" was "the deference owed by the poor to the rich" (103). He cautions the cultural critic or historian that to "emphasize the note of class superiority that ran through virtually the whole body of writing on charity would be to criticize the period for not conforming to twentieth-century notions [rather than practices] of social democracy. Even the most devoted and self-sacrificing of those who served the poor never dealt with them on terms of equality, nor did it occur to them to do so" (104).

We can see the validity of Owen's caveat by looking at just a few of the many articles published in the 1790s, a time when writings on charity betray a measure of fear and confusion about changes taking place in the social order and the possibility of serious social disturbances. Owen describes a "certain uneasiness about what is taking place in the British social order" throughout the work of people like William Allen, the editor of *The Philanthropist* (1811–19), Colquhoun, Malthus and Trimmer, among others—and to whom we might add Wordsworth and Coleridge. As Owen puts it: "They were aware, in a greater or less degree, of an economy and society in revolutionary change, but . . . they had not adjusted their thinking to the fact. All pictured their world as a hierarchy made up of classes, each with its special duties and responsibilities highly interdependent" (103). As a result, he observes, some philanthropic activities in the "chilling atmosphere" of the French Revolution "became, to a degree, insurance against revolution, a means of keeping the populace, if not contented, at least reasonably submissive" (97).

The *Monthly Magazine* testifies to the popularity of the view that private charity within a narrowly circumscribed community was a preferred solution to the problems of poverty and would serve as a means to mitigate against revolutionary tendencies.[17] J. Wood, a frequent commentator on the Poor Laws, in letter to the *Monthly*, 1 June 1800, describes the virtues of charity while denouncing a plan to set up a public relief fund for the industrious poor: "Would it [poor relief] operate, as that godlike Virtue [charity] does, to expand the heart; to harmonize the affections; to humanize the temper; and to unite man to his fellow man by that three-fold cord, the sacred band of union which constitutes the grand cement of society?" (425). Mandatory payment of parochial assessments, Wood asserts, "would gradually undermine and ultimately extinguish that cardinal virtue by which this country is distinguished"—private charity (425). Like "The Old Cumberland Beggar," the article claims that charity fosters among benefactors a self-aggrandizing virtue that binds society together, ostensibly for the mutual benefit of both beggars and almsgivers, though Wood's sympathy rather inclines toward the "charitable benefactors" who stand to gain from their own generosity.

Another anonymous writer advocating the revocation of the

poor rates explained to readers of the same issue of the *Monthly Magazine* that private charity not only builds moral character, but stimulates community feeling—the "domestic affections," in Wordsworth's terms: "If the social and benevolent affections are the basis and ornament of society, and if these affections are excited in proportion as we approach nearer to self; it follows that the more this principle is cultivated the higher perfection we are likely to sustain" (422). These charitable acts must take place on a local scale, within a small, identifiable social sphere. Moreover, the anonymous author of this article believes that through such exertions and through the moral example of their benefactors, the poor would be reconciled to the "inequality of fortune" in society, where all ranks would be convinced that "their obligations and dependencies are mutual and indispensible" (422). These precepts were commonplace at the end of the eighteenth century and received particular attention in Trimmer's *The Oeconomy of Charity*.

As we have seen, Trimmer's pamphlet attributes a perceived decline in private charity to the popularity of fiction, and it recommends ways to restore the ancient spirit of benevolence among middle-class women. Although her pamphlet presents a strong appeal for "ladies of rank" to devote time to instructing and aiding the poor, like Wordsworth's poetry about the poor it is based upon the acceptance of poverty as a social given. What is needed to improve society is to instruct the poor in their duties to their superiors, and to ensure that their superiors do their duty to the poor. As she puts it, "the want of concord among the various orders of people must be prejudicial to a nation at large; for, in appointing different ranks among mankind, our all wise and beneficent CREATOR undoubtedly intended the good of the whole" (3).

The duties prescribed to each class anticipate Burke's paternalist description of a society divided between a "spirited nobility" and "a protected, satisfied, laborious, and obedient people" (*Reflections* 124). In Trimmer's formulation, the welfare of the rich and poor are mutually interdependent; therefore, God "has ordained to each peculiar duties: to all in superior stations, justice, humanity, condescension and charity: to the poor, honesty, diligence, humility and gratitude" (*Oeconomy of Charity* 3–4). The economy of charity Trimmer describes crucially depends upon the existence of an impoverished class to receive the "generous offices" of those above them in social rank. Thus, what Brownson wrote in *The Quarterly Review* about Wordsworth might apply equally well to Trimmer and to the vast majority of political economists and philanthropists of the late eighteenth century. To paraphrase Brownson, they too would "compassionate" the poor, but would contemplate measures to "place the means of a comfortable subsistence in hands of all men" with horror (435).

George Dyer was one of the few who advocated anything like a disinterested kind of charity, but it amounted to a kind of *laissez-faire* paternalism. Dyer believed that society, when guided by independent benevolence, would function like an extended family, a family in which the rich were to treat the poor like children—*in loco parentis*. According to Dyer's *A Dissertation on the Theory and Practice of Benevolence* (1795), a benevolent person was one who was free to give charity unencumbered by partiality or prejudice: "a benevolent is an honest man, and he who means to be honest must determine to be independent: he must be no man's retainer, and allow no shackle to be thrown over him, either of interest or friendship, that may interrupt the free circulation of his affections" (12). Nevertheless, like Trimmer's economy of charity, Dyer's principle of benevolence did not mean anything like egalitarianism; his very concept of charity depended upon strict social stratification. He, too, tailored his instructions to meet the peculiar needs of distinct classes: "If a man of fortune, he will put no improper restraints upon his dependents: if he possess not fortune, he will study to maintain by industry, what cannot always be obtained by riches. He will be thankful for civilities, but will depend upon his own endeavours" (12–13). Thus for Dyer, with whom Wordsworth had some contact through Godwin's circle, benevolence and charity result from a free marketplace of circulating affections, but a market set up within the hierarchical structures of patriarchal society.

While we certainly cannot ignore the tacit subordination of the poor implicit in the paternalistic metaphor, we must also consider the idea of mutual affection it suggests in contrast to the bureaucratic alienation and "hedonic calculus" of the Benthamite reformers, who would push through the workhouse test in the Poor Law Amendment Act of 1834. Bentham, of course, believed that local organization and private charity could not keep up with the demands for relief and "pauper management," rightly recognizing that the increase in population and the concentration of people in urban centers offered little opportunity for the familiarity between rich and poor that such systems depended upon. In his classic *A History of English Philanthropy* (1905), B. Kirkman Gray captures well the sense of this changing social landscape when he remarks that "in the towns the rich knew poor streets, in the country they knew poor people" (234); thus, the urban poor lost any status as subjects, and increasingly were known as "charitable objects." Perhaps Bentham's apparent callousness toward the poor results from his reading "things as they are" rather than "things as they ought to be," but many would agree with Charles F. Bahmueller's claim in *The National Charity Company* (1981) that Bentham's policies for Poor Law reform are "replete with a repressiveness so pervasive, so soul-destroying, and with so little regard for either the civil libertics or the emotional sensitivities of those whose health (moral and physical) and happiness it set out to promote and protect, that its administrative progressiveness pales in the comparison" (2).

Bentham wanted to assemble the poor into panopticon-like

"pauper Kingdoms," where a supervisory authority would monitor and observe their every move. The overseers at the center of these octopus-like pauper kingdoms would organize the "hands" and their managers around a pivotal point of command and surveillance. As I suggested in Chapter Two, Bentham's panopticon plan for pauper management was essentially a design to create a middle-class version of the spectacle of poverty, to convert the perspective of the Burkean aristocrat into a bureaucratized gaze—a hidden point of observation from which to observe the management of the poor without being observed. Bentham writes: "Management which is sure to be looked at—and generally looked at—and constantly looked at can scarcely fail of being as good as the managing hands know how to make it" (qtd. in Bahmueller 6). Anticipating the Taylorism of a later century, Bentham imagines that even the hazards of time itself can fall under the calculating dominion of management in the poorhouse, where "not a particle of time shall remain necessarily unemployed: and relaxation shall be measured out by reason and humanity, not commanded by necessity and blind chance" (qtd. in Bahmueller 8). While the object of the National Charity Company was to put the poor to work and eventually restore them to a position of relative independence, the "pauper palaces" Bentham envisions were immediately recognized to be pauper Bastilles. If Bentham thought that the Acts of Settlement had turned all of England into a prison, his proposals basically substituted many prisons for the one.[18]

In contrast to Bentham's attempt to gain an impersonal disciplinary control over charitable objects, Wordsworth, who recognizes the same loss of what he calls "domestic feeling" due to the accumulation of population in the cities, insists upon interpellating Bentham's "objects" as human beings; he wants to rectify their economic status in order to preserve their independence and identity. Whereas Bentham and his followers attend to those "poor streets," Wordsworth desperately wants to preserve relations with "poor people." As early as 14 January 1801, in the famous letter to Fox, Wordsworth complains that the spread of "workhouses, Houses of Industry, and the invention of Soup-shops . . . superadded to the encreasing [*sic*] disproportion between the price of labour and that of the necessaries of life," had severely eroded the "bonds of domestic feeling among the poor" (*EY* 313). Moreover, he adds:

> The evil would be the less to be regretted if these institu-
> tions were regarded only as palliatives to a disease; but the
> vanity and pride of their promoters are so subtly interwoven
> with them, that they are deemed great discoveries and bless-
> ings to humanity. In the mean time parents are separated from
> their children, and children from the parents; the wife no
> longer prepares with her own hands a meal for her husband,

the produce of his labour; there is little doing in his house in which his affections can be interested, and but little left in it which he can love. (*EY* 314)

In the few sentences that follow the passage above, Wordsworth praises the "spirit of independence" that would result from preserving a level of maintenance sufficient to free the poor from the need for any relief other than supplementary gifts or the "kind offices," in his words, of friends and neighbours—the kind of community that he envisions in "The Old Cumberland Beggar," "Simon Lee," and by negation in "Goody Blake and Harry Gill."

Unlike the men and women Wordsworth praises in the letter to Fox—those who own a small parcel of property and "are placed above poverty" (*EY* 314)—the Cumberland beggar exists in utter dependence upon the people among whom he circulates. Nonetheless, the poem celebrates the localism and sense of community we find in the letter and that directly opposes the objectification of the poor in Bentham's discussion of poor relief. However anachronistic it may have seemed to Bentham and his followers, Wordsworth's localism invokes the ancient spirit of charity, a spirit of giving organized around local centers that goes back to the ecclesiastical origins of England's Poor Laws and its parish organization. Moreover, Wordsworth's localism confers upon the beggar—whom the political economists or statesmen see as a "nuisance" (70)— a subject rather than an object position, and treats him as though his solicitation were a right rather than a crime.[19]

If I may elide my argument here with Simpson's similar appeal for the basic humanity of Wordsworth's position in "The Old Cumberland Beggar," while Wordsworth, like his contemporaries writing in the *Monthly Magazine*, "accepts the force of self-interest, which was the standard utilitarian first principle," Wordsworth "turns it against Bentham's case." As Simpson rightly says, "Wordsworthian self-interest is not something that excludes concern for others, but rather includes it; it becomes dignified and positive," though not without contradiction, as we have seen (*Historical Imagination* 169). In fact, I think we can favorably place Wordsworth's position on charity in 1802 next to Godwin's in its aspiration for a society where the question of a beggar's humanity would not be at stake, and where the simple assistance of a passerby would not be so rare that the surprised and excessive gratitude of a Simon Lee would be at all necessary.[20] Criticizing what he called philanthropy "dispersed by the hands of ostentatious charity," Godwin was outraged by the servility of the laboring classes attendant upon such charity (*Political Justice* 730). He proposed a more extensive and mutual system of philanthropy in which, to use Blake's terms, pity (or charity for that matter) would be no more were we not to make someone poor in the first place. One of the "benefits attendant on [Godwin's] system of equality," to paraphrase the chapter title, is that charity would be reciprocal, for "all would have leisure to cultivate kindly and philanthropical affections, and to let loose his faculties in the search of intellectual improvement" (*Political Justice* 730). None would become a mere *object* of charity; each person would become a giving and receiving subject. Such a community Wordsworth envisions in his letter to Fox, and even in "The Old Cumberland Beggar" he gives the beggar and the poorer villagers an active position of competence—if not an identity—within this community of gift exchange, even though the beggar remains on the periphery of that community.

"The Old Cumberland Beggar" accepts the prevalent view that almsgiving should produce a self-congratulatory return, conferring as much or more benefit on the benefactor than on the recipient. "Of the Poor in Scotland," Appendix X to Eden's treatise, further demonstrates this idea. It should be remembered that Eden collected his materials on poverty to bolster his argument against the Poor Laws and in favor of what today might be called community-based programs for relief, particularly private, voluntary charity. "Of the Poor in Scotland" repeats the familiar argument of "The Old Cumberland Beggar" that neither the Poor Laws nor workhouses, but private charity with its implicit demand for deference and gratitude from the poor and social responsibility from the rich would solve the problems of poor relief in Britain. The essay argues that establishing poor rates and workhouses in Scotland would only hide the "squalid and unsightly appearance of poverty and infirmity" from society (*State of the Poor* 3: 300). Most importantly, the treatise denounces governmental programs of poor relief because their compulsory and regulated form of charity would ultimately damage the "social virtues" of the poor:

> [T]he social virtues, among those whose virtue is almost their only portion, would suffer much. Thousands, who are now kindly and comfortably supported at home by the charity of their relations and neighbours, would then find the endearing ties of gratitude and natural affection broken at once; the honest peasant and his family would miss the *bennisons* [sic]of "the long-remember'd beggar" who had been their guest; they would feel themselves deprived in a great measure of that most pleasing satisfaction that results from relieving a fellow-creature. . . . (3: 300)

This passage could be described as "The Old Cumberland Beggar's thesis written in prose. Like the poem, the treatise shows the Lucretian return of virtue for almsgivers. As in the poem, the almsgivers number primarily among the poor themselves; the charity of the gentry is thus conspicuously but not unexpectedly absent from "The Old Cumberland

Beggar." The sauntering horseman stands out as the single example of a benefactor who is not himself poor, while the rest comprise a catalogue of the laboring poor: the toll-gate keeper who "turns her wheel" (34) in summer to supplement her income, the post-boy, and the narrator's neighbor, "pressed herself / By her own wants" (156-57; *PW* 4: 239). According to the poem, the beggar performs a spiritual service for those who in critical periods of need would find themselves relying upon charity for support. As in the Scottish community described in "Of the Poor in Scotland," then, the burden of relief rests upon the poor themselves. Indeed, the poem affirms the observation in the treatise that self-help within the community confers upon the laboring poor a tenuous dignity which their dependence upon the rich or upon a mandatory system of relief would deny them:

> [T]he poorer sort are in general strictly attentive to all the duties of religion, strongly impressed with that encouraging and venerable maxim, that "He that giveth to the Poor lendeth to the Lord;" and always ready to contribute, with chearfulness, their mite towards the support of such as may stand in need of it; often consoling themselves, when they are conscious of having stretched beyond their present circumstances, with the reflection that

> > They'll get a blessing w' the leave
> > And never miss't. (3: 300)

The quotation closing the passage is from Robert Burns's "To a Mouse" (1785), a classic testimony to the need for human sympathy, in which Burns compares the lot of the poor to the plight of a mouse occasionally forced to steal grain from a ploughman who has broken up the mouse's nest. In the lines quoted, the ploughmen says that he will be blessed for forgiving his small loss of grain to the starving animal, just as the poor villagers in "The Old Cumberland Beggar" will be blessed for sharing their small portion with the beggar. Wordsworth wants his audience to believe that

> > > the poorest poor
> > Long for some moments in a weary life
> > When they can know and feel that they have been,
> > Themselves, the fathers and the dealers-out
> > Of small blessings. . . . (147–51; *PW* 4: 239)

In the socio-political scheme endorsed by the poem, Wordsworth appropriately calls these benefactors the "fathers" of small blessings, for it suggests that the poor have subsumed the paternalist practice of private charity upon which to establish their community.[21] Because the domestic affections that the community knits together by means of its individual acts of charity imply the existence of a self-sufficient "culture of poverty" separated from the wealthy landlords traditionally held responsible for the overall care of the community, Wordsworth's poem could be appropriated by those who would favor a noninterventionist welfare policy—that is, in nineteenth-century terms, the advocates of self help for the poor. Indeed, Wordsworth's letter to Fox emphasizes "the bonds of domestic feeling among the poor," not between the rich and the poor (*EY* 313–14). Yet few who supported self help for the poor would go as far as "The Old Cumberland Beggar" to make the poor their own masters.

Reverend George Glover's *Observations on the Present State of Pauperism in England* (1817) invokes the familiar "ancient national spirit and independence" to criticize the Poor Laws for degrading the poor and turning "upside down the whole fabric of society" (3). Glover focuses, however, upon restoring a sense of shame and disgrace to those who must turn to relief; he wants the poor to exhibit a humble and deferential gratitude in exchange for alms:

> The poor man, who feels himself necessarily dependent and humiliated, a beggar every week at the door of his overseer for a pittance grudgingly paid; with links that remind him of his strength; with the history of other days yet frcsh in his remembrance; and with the phantom of British liberty and independence yet dancing before his eyes, soon learns to lay aside respect and reverence, where neither gratitude nor affection bind him. (6–7)

Wordsworth, however, does not demand from the Cumberland beggar deference, gratitude or reverence; rather, he asks the statesmen—"Who have a broom still ready in [their] hands / To rid the world of nuisances" (69–70; *PW* 4: 236) with their work-house policies—to show respect for the beggars and the poor, who, like their so-called betters, share in a common pursuit of dignity and honor.

In adopting the practices of their masters, the poor in Wordsworth's idealistic community participate in the self-congratulatory economy of charity inherent in the received practice of poor relief. We can read this participation, or the subsumption of that role, as a mere projection of bourgeois self-indulgence in their own goodness. In his *Authority*, Richard Sennett has called bourgeois paternalism "an authority of false love," in which charity "operates as a parade of benevolence which exists only so far as it is in the interest of the ruler and which requires passive acquiescence as the price of being cared for" on the part of the dependent (131). In the poem, for example, all derive "a transitory thought / Of self-congratulation" (124–25; *PW* 4: 238) from giving alms to the beggar, who himself, as the poem implies, participates in the network of exchange by leaving his few crumbs and scraps to the birds:

> He sat, and ate his food in solitude:
> And ever, scattered from his palsied hand,
> That, still attempting to prevent the waste,
> Was baffled still, the crumbs in little showers
> Fell on the ground; and the small mountain birds,
> Not venturing yet to peck their destined meal,
> Approached within the length of half his staff.
>
> (15–21; *PW* 4: 234)

On the other hand, we may do better to read the poem as an attempt to include the poor in what might be called the charter of charity from which they, like the Cumberland beggar, usually are exempted. In the meager leavings the Cumberland beggar inadvertently gives to the birds, the poem even attempts to include him in the paternalist role, though I agree that it regretably fails to do so. Although the poem expresses admiration for the communal benefit invested in the solitary beggar whose destitution provides the ground for public good, the beggar himself does not share equally in what Marcel Mauss describes as the "pattern of symmetrical and reciprocal rights" within the network of exchange (*The Gift* ll). Of course, the poem attempts to invest spiritual "good" with the exchange value of material "goods," but the beggar remains in fact dependent upon others for his material survival. He relies upon material support from the community and may foster in its members a transcendental "good," but his own involuntary charity connects him more directly to the natural than the human world. Nonetheless, as Burns's "To a Mouse" implies, the connection to the natural world provides a link to the human, at least in the eyes of Wordsworth and his contemporaries. Like Burns, Wordsworth here establishes the "organic link" that Simmel describes in "The Poor," that guarantees some consideration of the poor as individuals with the same rights as others in the community. To quote, now, Simmel's passage in full:

> Where assistance to the poor has its *raison d'etre* in an organic link between elements, the *rights* of the poor are more highly emphasized, whether their religious premise derives from a metaphycial unity or their kinship or tribal basis from a biological unity. We will see, in contrast, that when assistance to the poor derives teleologically from a goal one hopes to pursue in this way, rather than from the causal basis of a real and effective unity among all the members of the group, the rights of the poor dwindle to nothingness. (153)

Under the conditions of the participative community in the poem, the gifts given to the old Cumberland beggar do not mark him, finally, as an excluded Other, as Heather Glen has argued, even though they do mark him as poor.[22] But in Simmel's view the poor are both outside *and* inside the group; as recipients of charity they are necessarily objects, but as part of the collectivity they are necessarily, as well, subjects. In his words, "the poor are located in a way outside the group; but this is no more than a peculiar mode of interaction which binds them into a unity with the whole in its widest sense" (158). In its contradictory stance toward its principal figure, Wordsworth's "The Old Cumberland Beggar" demonstrates, even as it does not resolve, this paradox. The only way out of the paradox, according to Simmel, would be the end of assistance altogether, which would mean the abolition of poverty by a complete and radical redistribution of wealth—a possibility that Wordsworth, like other liberal reformers of his age, does not imagine.

The very maintenance of a gift economy, as Lewis Hyde explains in *The Gift*, requires an imbalance that defies the necessary equilibrium of exchange in a market economy. Gifts must always be kept in motion, as when the old Cumberland beggar passes on his crumbs to the birds; they subvert the weights and measures of capitalist economy because, in Hyde's terms, they "pass beyond the control of the personal ego, and so each bearer must be a part of the group and each donation is an act of social faith" (16). Indeed, as Hyde points out, unlike the commodity which alienates relationships between the buyer and seller, the gift "tends to establish a relationship between the parties involved" (xiv).

Unlike the exchange of property and commodities, which requires a system of equivalence, a materialist quid pro quo, the gift economy virtually insists upon disequilibrium and imbalance. Thus, although the old Cumberland beggar does not return material gifts directly to his benefactors, his indigence provides an essential part of the collective exchange of *good* as well as goods. In fact, and this is the main point in the poem, his role as receiver of gifts is essential to make the system of gift exchange work. In a passage that could have been written of "The Old Cumberland Beggar," Hyde offers what could be another paraphrase of the central tenet of the poem:

> The gift is a pool or reservoir in which the sentiments of its exchange accumulate so that the more often it is given away, the more feeling it carries, like an heirloom that has been passed down for generations. The gift gets steeped in the fluids of its own passage. . . . What gathers in it is not only the sentiment of generosity but the affirmation of individual good will. ("Some Food" 57)

As in Wordsworth's theory of poetry, what circulates in "The Old Cumberland Beggar" and in the system of gift exchange is feeling—hence, Hyde speaks of the *eros* of gift exchange, in opposition to the *logos* of commodity exchange (*Gift* xiv). What the beggar leaves behind for the community is precisely that "sentiment of generosity and the affirmation of individual good will" Hyde describes; by means of his regular rounds, the beggar

> so keeps alive
> The kindly mood in hearts which lapse of years,
> And that half-wisdom half-experience gives,
> Make slow to feel, and by sure steps resign
> To selfishness and cold oblivious cares.
>
> (91–95; *PW* 4: 237)

By exchanging a moral surplus for the few provisions he receives in turn from private members of the community, the old Cumberland beggar participates in a network of exchange that suggests in the poem a critique of the industrial society and its practices. While Heather Glen and others, including myself, have read this imbalanced exchange only as a form of exploitation, these readings neglect to point out that the valorization of gift exchange—as opposed to economic exchange—in the poem is an affront to the modalities of the capitalist market economy in which it is placed.[23]

Without idealizing the gift economy as a pure or primitivist form of exchange—for example, Mauss has shown how gift-based systems of exchange form a market in which transactions are "based on obligation and economic self-interest" (1)—I follow Michel De Certeau's suggestion in *The Practice of Everyday Life* that when gift exchange is insinuated into a socio-economic system based on money, it challenges the assumptions of that system by violating its "code of generalized equivalence," that is, money (27). De Certeau argues that within a capitalist economic system, a network of gift exchange functions as what he calls a *perruque*—that is, a tactic that takes advantage of the dominant system's mechanisms while simultaneously resisting its hegemony. The gift exchange, like other such "diversionary tactics"—sleight of hand, covert borrowings from factory surplus or work time to supplement one's private store—function to "subvert the law that, in the scientific factory, puts work at the service of the machine and . . . progressively destroys the requirement of creation and the 'obligation to give' " (28). In presenting private charity as a community responsibility, "The Old Cumberland Beggar" marks the "return of a socio-political ethics" into a system of poor relief based primarily on the transfer of money and increasingly under the management of a remote, centralized bureaucracy. Moreover, the poem criticizes those theories of political economy that suggest money is the basis of all exchange and that human beings accrue value only through the commodities they produce. Despite the inherent paternalism of Wordsworth's system, the "moral economy" of local community it invests in the old Cumberland beggar—the "long remember'd beggar" of this not yet deserted village—evinces a critical power turned against both the Burkean form of callous paternalism and the utilitarian *laissez-faire* attitude toward poor relief.

In enacting a form of exchange that rejects the intermediation of a fetishized sign—money or the commodity—the poem reestablishes in the midst of economic alienation a mark of similitude between the old beggar and the community. Because the beggar's benefactors come exclusively from the lower-class villagers, the poem at once calls attention to the widening gulf between the social classes and reminds the polite reader of his or her common link to people on the periphery of society. The beggar's visit suggests the return of the repressed Other in such a way that it invites, if it does not demand, that he be reintegrated into the community: his exclusion, in other words, suggests the exclusion of people of all classes. Though archetypes left over from the feudal past, the old Cumberland beggar and the ancient spirit of charity that he embodies contain a utopian surplus—in Bloch's terms, the hint of a "yet-to-be-worked-out" system of exchange that does not dehumanize or exploit its participants (*Principle of Hope* 1: 162). As Simpson has noted, while the poem lacks a careful "analysis of the general fate of the vagrant poor," it nonetheless remains "coherent in its negative address to the utilitarian aspirations" that motivated specifically Bentham's, but more broadly, progressive plans for the reform of poor relief that culminated in the infamous Poor Law Amendment Act of 1834 (*Wordsworth's Historical Imagination* 171–72).

Having identified the critical perspective of "The Old Cumberland Beggar," it remains to acknowledge that Wordsworth concludes the poem with an act of historical displacement; the strategy of the conclusion is, in the terms of Jerome McGann's *The Romantic Ideology*, "to replace an image and landscape of contradiction [and one might add conflict] with one dominated by 'the power / Of harmony' " (86). Though the old Cumberland beggar serves the spiritual needs of the community, his only comfort is to die quietly and alone: "As in the eye of Nature he has lived, / So in the eye of Nature let him die!" (196–97; *PW* 4: 240). Like the old man of "Animal Tranquility and Decay," the old Cumberland beggar at last becomes a sign of an ever evasive and ambiguous Nature. In his death, that radical absence that defies social order, the beggar at last finds the equality he could not have in life. Thus, the poem repeats yet another idea familiar to the discourse on poverty, that the poor denied community and riches in the present would receive their reward in the afterlife. The move from social being into Nature attenuates the possible callousness of the poem and mitigates against our outrage at the seeming dismissal of, or disregard for, the old man's life. More importantly, from the point of view of the poem, the naturalization of the beggar's life and death cancels the social and political content of the poem in a universalizing moment of affirmation. While "placing sorrow" in the poem, to borrow a term from Ellen Lambert's book of that title on the pastoral elegy, the assimilation into Nature displaces its politics. This displacement was a strategy Wordsworth would later comment upon in the *Essays upon Epitaphs*.

The pastoralism in the final stanzas of "The Old Cumberland Beggar" proposes a setting in which the questions of poor relief are set aside while the questions of immortality and being become central. Landscape and Nature here, as in *The Ruined Cottage* and other poems, offer a setting for pain that promises a transcendent vision of immortality as consolation. In the *Essays*, Wordsworth suggests that consciousness, natural objects and memory are fused to achieve continuity between past and present in a transcendent moment of calm. Remarking the Greek and Roman custom of burying the dead in the countryside, Wordsworth invites his reader to "ruminate upon the beauty which monuments, thus placed, must have borrowed from the surrounding images of nature" (*PrW* 2: 53). From the association among natural objects and the monument, a traveler stopping to notice the stone would have experienced, according to Wordsworth, "strong appeals to visible appearances or immediate impression, lively and affecting analogies of life as a journey . . . of admonitions and heart-stirring remembrances like a refreshing breeze that comes without warning, or the taste of the waters of an unexpected fountain" (*PrW* 2: 54). The epitaph, the monument and the environment, then, fuse in the observer's mind to become a place or spot "which gathers all human Beings to itself, and 'equalises the lofty and the low' " (*PrW* 2: 59).

Playing on the notion that death is the great leveler, Wordsworth suggests in the *Essays* that the locus of sorrow, as mediated through language and landscape, offers a refuge from the political and social order. It does so by indulging the observer in what he might call the "sentiment of being," under which influence the political and social determinants of being are negated in the contemplation of a universalized, transcendent order. The beggar's death, then, naturalizes the distinctions between the beggar and his benefactors upon which the economy of charity in the poem depends. In this final naturalization of poverty, "The Old Cumberland Beggar" invites the existential readings of the poem that have neglected its direct intervention into the politicized debates over the economy of charity.

In the late eighteenth century the idea that death canceled the distinctions between rich and poor was such a commonplace rationalization for the misery of the poor that Elizabeth Inchbald parodied it in *Nature and Art* (1796). The narrator of the novel ironically comments that in death there is "something which so raises the abjectness of the poor, that, on their approach to its sheltering abode, the arrogant believer feels the equality he had before denied, and trembles" (387). In linking the old Cumberland beggar with nature, Wordsworth's poem dignifies and naturalizes poverty as an inevitable condition relieved by death, even as it further underscores, in the threat of the beggar's absence, his organic link to the community. Its final word on indigence, as Bentham put it in his *Essay on the Poor Laws* (1796), is that poverty is "the natural, the primitive, the general, and the *unchangeable* lot of man" (qtd. in Poynter 119), but that does not mean that Wordsworth advocates a passive acceptance of the miseries of the poor. The naturalization of the old Cumberland beggar's death may attenuate, but does not completely neutralize, the social and political concerns about charity and poverty raised throughout the poem. As I will show in the next chapter, moreover, among Wordsworth's readers this naturalized or universalized humanity of which we tend to be so critical gave some working-class readers a sense of their rightful place among the politically dominant classes.

At a time when beggars were commonly expelled from villages as rogues and vagabonds (despite the relaxing of the Acts of Settlement), Wordsworth's "The Old Cumberland Beggar" further develops the nostalgia for Goldsmith's "long remember'd beggar" (*Deserted Village* 1.151), who makes orderly, familiar rounds within his parish. The idyll of agrarian poverty that characterizes the poem was constructed within a discourse on poverty which necessarily limited Wordsworth's vision of the relations between community and poverty. It may be that George Eliot, offers the best answer to Wordsworth's questionable sympathy toward the poor. In *Silas Marner*, George Eliot put it this way: "I suppose one reason why we are seldom able to comfort our neighbours with our words is that our goodwill gets adulterated, in spite of ourselves, before it can pass our lips. We can send black puddings and pettitoes without giving them a flavour of our own egoism; but language is a stream that is almost sure to smack of a mingled soil" (31). In the mingled soil of late eighteenth-century Britain, caught in the discursive network of signs exchanged in the debate over poverty and the Poor Laws, "The Old Cumberland Beggar" stands as one effort, however complicitous in the contradictions of its time, to demand some respect for the poor. Within the limitations of Wordsworth's Tory humanism, the poem attempts to cement the bond between the poor and those who are not poor and attacks directly the proponents of those systems of relief that would dehumanize the poor and treat them as criminals and mere instrumentalities. In many ways, as we'll see, Wordsworth's 1802 poem anticipates the debate over the New Poor Law of 1834 and provides Tory, Whig and Radical alike some of the humanitarian terms on which to base their critique of the alienating bureacratization of poor relief that the New Poor Law entailed.

Postscript
The Poverty and Power of Transcendence:
The Victorian Reception of Wordsworth's Social Text

What though on hamely fare we dine,
That hings his head, and a' that.
Gie fools their silks, and knaves their wine,
A Man's a Man for a' that.
  Robert Burns, "Song—For a' that and a' that"

While the Anglo-American literary institution has canonized a fairly unified "Wordsworth," a Wordsworth who occupies a middle position along the axis of ideology and utopia, reaction and revolution, other interpretive communities have realized both his reactionary and his revolutionary potentials more explicitly. In this postscript, I want to show how interests identified with both the right and the left have appropriated Wordsworth's social text—the text produced through these diverse and often contradictory "readings"—to further their own ends. The social function, like the social value, of a work of art—including a poem—results more from the conditions prevalent at its moment of reception than its moment of production. Once set upon its historical trajectory, the aesthetic object becomes vulnerable to appropriation from various interpretive communities, whose deployment of the work and its construed meanings may also vary to the point of mutual exclusion. Thus, works of art, especially those that use language for their medium, may set certain conditions of limitation upon what we might call their range of variance. Our contemporary critical failure to realize or acknowledge the legitimacy of the critical and utopian positions of Wordsworth's poetry marks the limits of our own critical strategies, which, under the banner of historical critique, have further dehistoricized Wordsworth's poetry and silenced or muted the radical voice to which even the earliest reviewers of Wordsworth's poetry were alert.

We have seen so far that Wordsworth's poetry offers a critique— sometimes more, sometimes less, explicit—of the industrial transforma- tion of the poor and the Poor Laws, even as it reproduces certain features of the discourse on poverty that ultimately reinforce that transformation. Unlike many of the works on poverty at the end of the eighteenth century, Wordsworth's poetry endows poverty and the poor with at least a sym- bolic dignity. In many cases, however, the price of symbolic dignity for the poor, as represented in Wordsworth's and Crabbe's poetry or in Gainsbor- ough's or Constable's landscape paintings, was an image of the poor under the sign of production and inserted into categories defined for the poor by those above them in social standing. As Friedman reminds us, "Wordsworth's growing concern with the humble classes as a usable sub- ject for serious verse . . . was a complex and contradictory gesture with a distinct humanitarian significance, on the one hand, but a gesture that also signified a ratification of the established social structure on the other" (*Tory Humanist* 297). I have argued in previous chapters that the power of Wordsworth's poetry derives from its dialectical modulation between these two gestures. Invoking a different lexicon, a *Monthly Repository* review of Wordsworth's *Yarrow Revisited and Other Poems* puts it this way: "In politics and religion, Wordsworth is the poet of the past, blend- ing sophistical apologies for its outward forms with those aspirations for futurity which are native to him because he is a poet and a philosopher; which he cannot repress if he would, which it is his delight to indulge when he forgets the present condition of church and state; but which are often trammelled in their flight by his veneration for things which are passing away" (423). Thus, even early reviewers noted the tendency for Words- worth's poetry to oscillate between the fixity of the past and the promise of the future—between ideology and utopia. In its negotiation between these two horizons, Wordsworth's poetry appears to inhabit multiple positions along the axis of political reaction and reform. While we tend to identify the Victorian reception of Wordsworth with the Liberal positions of John Stuart Mill and Matthew Arnold, Wordsworth's Victorian reader- ship also included subscribers to the *Chartist Circular*, which reviewed and reprinted portions of his work, and audiences at workingmen's asso- ciation meetings. For some of its working-class readers, despite its com- plicity in middle-class values of which these readers were aware, Words- worth's poetry stood alongside works by Percy Shelley and Ebenezer Elliot in an alternative, radical canon.

When thinking of the way Wordsworth's "middle-class values" might be transformed as they circulate among various interpretive com- munities, we must, as Trygve Tholfsen has cautioned in *Working Class Radicalism in Mid-Victorian England*, distinguish between the middle- class and working-class forms of moral categories and concepts. Even within the working class, we find discursive variation in the deployment and significance of such terms. In discussing the working-class appropriation of "respectability," for example, Tholfsen notes at least two possible inflections of this concept. On the one hand, those who accepted the middle-class definition of the "respectable working man" would define respectability as "one who deferred to his betters, recognised their superior virtue and rationality, and set out to emulate them." On the other hand, those working men and women who refused to accept such deference to middle-class interpellation insisted that their "respectability" was contingent upon "genuine independence" (18). Similar divisions can be found in the way working-class discourse deployed concepts like "industriousness," "thrift" and even "independence" itself. These discursive permutations of *langue* that occur when signifiers or terms become ideologemes within particular discourses contributed to the widely recognized appropriation of middle-class values to serve the interests of the working class in nineteenth-century England.

E. P. Thompson and Thomas Walter Laqueur, among others, have described how the project to inculcate middle-class values among the working classes had the unintentional effect (from the point of view of the moral reformers) of empowering the very class that those values were meant to subdue. In *The Making of the English Working Class* Thompson discusses at length how working-class men and women took advantage of the programs of instruction designed in the morality industry to inculcate the values of thrift, industriousness and hygiene among the poor to serve the interests of their betters.[1] These values and the practices to which they led actually empowered the poor by giving them the means to form a political consciousness. Moreover, despite the conservative content of many Protestant sects and their emphasis upon spiritual rather than material rewards, working-class members of these groups honed their skills in organizing and were exposed to an apocalyptic imagery of reform in what Thompson calls a "slumbering Radicalism" (30). Similarly Laqueur's *Religion and Respectability* describes at length how working-class self-awareness grew partly from the morality industry's attempt to inculcate middle-class values in that sector of society. As an article titled "Tory Literature" in *The Chartist Circular* 3 October 1840 shows, this appropriation was often fully conscious. Practicing a little one-upmanship on *Fraser's* and *Blackwood's*, the *Circular* notes mockingly that "in Tory periodicals one really finds some choice morsels of political truths that are quite refreshing. Many of their principal and cleverest writers are staunch Radicals at heart, and now and then come forth with a few sentences that blow to atoms the fallacies piled up in the rest of their paragraphs" (217). Joseph Arch, farm laborer turned M.P. for Northwest Norfolk, adds some local color as he affirms that the inversion of "Tory" values among working-class readers was a rather widespread phenomenon: "I expect the Tory barley bread I had to feed on got into my bones and made me a Liberal! It has had that contrary effect on more than one man I have come across" (36). Similarly, Francis Place describes how the religious and moral instruction he received gave him the power to serve the interests of people and principles that would have been unsettling for members of the moral tract and Sunday School societies.[2] It should come as no surprise, then, that as it enters what McGann calls its "dialectical life,"[3] Wordsworth's poetry enters various interpretive communities, where it becomes subject to, and is redeployed in, discourses that realize the political potentials allowed within its range of variance. In what follows I hope to show that among the small samples of "official" and everyday practices, Wordsworth's poetry enabled a wide range of inflections, not all of which were solely amenable to the interests of middle-class liberalism or humanism, but to those of working-class radicalism as well.

I

The early reception of Wordsworth's work—Francis Jeffrey's hostility toward his poetry, Coleridge's dissent from his theory of poetic diction, Byron's attack on his political apostasy—is all well known, and I do not intend to review in full those well-known debates here. However, I do want to recall some early readings of Wordsworth in order to show that while some of his contemporaries, like Henry Crabbe Robinson, complacently accepted his representations of the poor as just another spectacle of poverty, the majority of readers raised social, moral and even political questions about them.[4] Much of the early criticism called attention to Wordsworth's use of vagrants and paupers in his work, which, as we know, aroused a considerable amount of negative criticism, if not contempt, from a host of literary *illuminati*. Robert Southey, for example, remarked: "It is the vice of Wordsworth's intellect to be always upon the stretch and strain—to look at pile-worts and daffodowndillies through the same telescope which he applies to the moon and stars, and to find subject for philosophizing and fine feeling in every peasant and vagabond he meets" (qtd. in Newton 84). Like Jeffrey, Southey objected to Wordsworth's use of vagrants and peasants as subjects for philosophical poetry, and especially as subjects who spoke philosophy.[5]

Byron's satiric quatrain from *Don Juan*, though wittier and more comic than most attacks on Wordsworth's violation of poetic decorum, might be said to be typical of the kind of assault Wordsworth had to bear simply for writing serious poetry about "simple" pedlars, idiots and vagrants:

> 'Pedlars' and 'Boats' and 'Wagons'! Oh ye shades
> Of Pope and Dryden, are we come to this?
> That trash of such sort not alone evades
> Contempt, but from bathos' vast abyss

> Floats scumlike uppermost, and these Jack Cades
> Of sense and song above your graves may hiss— . . .
> (3.100.889–94)

Unlikely bedfellows, Coleridge and Byron find a point of agreement in chastising Wordsworth for his lack of decorum. In *Biographia Literaria*, for example, Coleridge objects to "The Idiot Boy" because it shows, in his words, the "disgusting images of ordinary, morbid idiocy" and does not present the ideal, clothed in a palatable veneer of pleasantry more appropriate to polite taste.

Such questions of decorum and realism persisted even through reviews of *The Excursion*. Jeffrey, who reviewed *The Excursion* for the *Edinburgh Review* 24 November 1814, saw Wordsworth's selection of a "superannuated Pedlar" as the vehicle of moral teachings and philosophical discourse as a "perversity of taste and judgment" (29–30). According to Jeffrey, Wordsworth had "willfully debased his moral teacher by a low occupation"; a man "accustomed to higgle about tape, or brass sleeve-buttons," complains Jeffrey, should not be represented using such lofty diction and holding such profound ideas (30). Similarly, Charles Lamb's October 1814 review of *The Excursion* aks why Wordsworth would "put such eloquent discourse in the mouth of a pedlar?" (qtd. in *RBBR* 60). Though Lamb could rationalize, as Wordsworth did, the pedlar's speech as a product of his unusual education and the poetic need to have a character in keeping with the "system and scenery of the poem," he shrewdly advised those readers who might be "scandalized" by the pedlar to substitute for the word pedlar "wherever it occurs . . . silently the word Palmer, or Pilgrim, or any less offensive designation, which shall connect the notion of sobriety in heart and manners with the experience and privileges which a wayfaring life confers" (qtd. in *RBBR* 61). Lamb's conflation of pedlar with palmer or pilgrim anticipates the later Victorian tendency to sanctify Wordsworth as a religious teacher. Despite his objections to Wordsworth's use of the pedlar as a mouthpiece for philosophy, Lamb did praise the poem's dialogue and setting. Overall the poem presents a coherent doctrine of "Natural Methodism," as Lamb famously called it, a faith fostered by nature. "From such a creed," Lamb believes, "we should expect unusual results; and when applied to the purposes of consolation, more touching considerations than from the mouth of common teachers" (qtd. in *RBBR* 57).

Reviews of the collected *Poems* of 1815 show further contempt, not for Wordsworth's use of paupers in his poem, but for the originals upon whom those figures are based. W. R. Lyall, for example, writes in the *Quarterly Review* 14 October 1815 that Wordsworth paints his unluckily selected subjects with fidelity and pathos. But, he goes on, "[i]n themselves . . . they would not appear to be of the most difficult nature; it requires no extraordinary degree of judgment and penetration to discriminate the broad rough lines by which the characters of people in low life are commonly chalked out; nor can it require, considering the few simple objects about which their thoughts must necessarily be conversant, any extraordinary force of imagination to enter into their feelings. . . . " (qtd. in *RBBR* 75).

While most critics objected to Wordsworth's violation of social and poetic decorum in treating seriously "incidents and situations from common life" (*PrW* 1: 123), some questioned his attitudes toward the poor and the implications of his work for social policy. In view of the claim that Wordsworth's poetry has buried its history beneath the smooth surface of a politically neutralized landscape, it's important to remember that among its earliest reviewers, indeed throughout the nineteenth century, Wordsworth's poetry continually raised explicitly political questions, especially with regard to his representation of the poor and his affiliation to what came to be recognized as the working class. As we have seen in Chapter Three, John Aikin's review of *Lyrical Ballads* in the *Monthly Review* 29 June 1799 specifically called attention to the issues of poverty, distress and relief raised by certain poems. Aikin feared that "Goody Blake and Harry Gill" would give the wrong impression about poor relief by arousing readers' pity while insinuating that they had no charitable responsibility to the indigent. Anticipating some contemporary critics, Aikin objected to "The Last of the Flock" because "[n]o oppression is pointed out; nor are any means suggested for his relief. If the author be a wealthy man, he ought not to have suffered the poor peasant to part with the last of the flock" (qtd. in Newton 36).

When we sum up the considerable number of critics, conservative and liberal alike, who dissent from Wordsworth's effort, however modified, to write poetry about "low and rustic life" and to use the language of rustics, no matter how much "purified indeed of what appear to be its real defects" (*PrW* 1: 124), it becomes clearer that Wordsworth's treatment of the poor as a class worthy of note and capable of philosophical utterance and deep feeling really did break through a dominant wall of prejudice—a prevailing ideology or what Raymond Williams might call a "structure of feeling"—about the poor. Unwilling to admit the poor into aesthetic demesnes that had been the privileged space of aristocracy and the middle classes, Wordsworth's contemporaries were disturbed by the radical implications of his work. In its refusal to police the borders of the once privileged space of the poem, Wordsworth's poetry opened the social borders between high and low and exposed their arbitrary nature. Hence, the question of aesthetic decorum was itself a displaced, largely unconscious attempt to maintain a strict division between classes, to refuse to recognize the poverty of the bourgeois self in the impoverished Other. As Glen has argued about the *Lyrical Ballads*, because Wordsworth's poems "refuse to offer a clear-cut moral directive," they "question the unarticulated moral assumption of the polite reader; most centrally, that paternalistic diminution of the other which insidiously structured late eighteenth-century social thinking, even in its conspicuously radical manifestations" (245). Thus, Wordsworth's representations of the poor, however much they may be complicitous in middle-class ideology, were, by the standards of his contemporary readers, unsettling in their potentially revolutionary challenge to middle-class hegemony.

The way to get around such challenges, of course, is to project questions of value and utility onto a neutralizing field of universal value, which is what many of Wordsworth's Victorian and modern readers have done. For such readers, questions about the dignity of the poor become questions about human dignity in general. Conceived of as a universal or transcendental subject, the poor are transformed into signs of the middle-class subject. Wordsworth's poor, severed from their historical relation to production and invested with a kind of transcendental dignity and power, certainly lend themselves to such appropriation. Yet, in elevating the value of the subject, Wordsworth's poetry—like most romantic discourse—projects the image of the well-being and non-alienated subjectivity of people in all classes. Here I draw upon Bloch's insight that the bourgeois subject posited by idealist philosophy contains within it what he calls the "freedom of a counter-move contradicting the badly existing" (*Principle of Hope* 1: 148)—more simply, the hope for a non-alienated existence for humanity as a whole. Thus, early and late Victorian readers of all classes found in Wordsworth's poetry signs of value and a source for empowerment. Wordsworth's poetry of human dignity did not simply serve the interests of the ruling class, for, while couched in the class-bound ideology of its production, it was integrated into the discourse of some working-class readers who went on to challenge, not to promote, the systems of domination implicit in some of Wordsworth's poems.

II

The rise of Wordsworth's reputation coincided with the massive foment of support for reform that surrounded the Reform Bill of 1832 and the equally massive protest against the New Poor Law Amendment Act of 1834. While middle-class and working-class supporters of reform often cooperated with one another, the 1830s also saw increased antagonism between the two classes. As we approach the decade of the Reform Bill, the reception of Wordsworth's text splinters into many overlapping discourses. Early Victorian readers could ignore the social conundrums posed by *Lyrical Ballads* and find clear moral instruction in the explicit didacticism of *The Excursion* or take refuge in the natural landscape of the poems of *Yarrow Revisited, and Other Poems*. The demand for natural settings of refuge and calm expanded in the mid-Victorian period, at the point that Wordsworth's poetry reached its height of popularity in the 1830s and 1840s. As Ann Bermingham has argued, the English countryside at this time became a site of increasingly "specialized investigation" and a space in need of the civilizing influences of urban values. Of the 1830s and 1840s Bermingham observes that "[r]ural life, without the direct experience of the larger world or the indirect experience of this world as manifested in politics, religion, or education, was felt not only to brutalize the individual but also to threaten the social order. . . . Because of government centralization, provincialism had become a national concern; urban values and their intrusion into the countryside came to be seen as necessary and benign civilizing influences" (161). One of those arguing that the city could now morally benefit the country was William Howitt, a fond admirer of Wordsworth's work. One can surmise that Wordsworth's appeal as a "nature poet" for the Victorians was due largely to the demands of Victorian society for a landscape saturated with moral value and a desire for a vision of nature that could renew faith in the rural life that appeared increasingly threatening. George Thomas Smart perhaps typifies the sentimental bathos toward which this tradition could lead; in *Wordsworth: A Lecture* (1902), he claims that from poetry readers want "rest, quietness, a momentary glance into the nobler worlds lying all about us, a brief breathing space before we attack again the earthy breastworks" (9). The appeal of Wordsworth's poetry as a repository of musing on natural beauty and site of natural consolation, refuge and requiem, culminates in late nineteenth-century collections such as *Our English Lakes, Mountains, and Waterfalls, as seen by William Wordsworth* (1864), one of the first collections of photographs (by T. Ogle) of the Lakes; Birket Foster's *Beauties of English Landscape* (1874), one of a series of illustrated gift books that uses selections from Wordsworth's poetry, among others, as companion verses to vignettes of rustic ease engraved after Foster's landscape paintings; and *Wordsworth's Poems for the Young* (1863), an illustrated selection of Wordsworth's poetry whose precious portraits of innocent children soften the harsher edges of the poetry. The illustrations to "Resolution and Independence" and "We Are Seven" (Plates 5 and 6), for example, bear striking resemblance to the sentimentalized versions of poverty we've seen in Francis Wheatley and others at the end of the eighteenth century. Both engravings blur any idiosyncratic features of the rustic figures, who are absorbed into the landscape—a landscape of austerity in "Resolution and Independence" and of quaint simplicity in "We Are Seven."

Carrying out to its fullest degree that process of uprooting Wordsworth's poetry from its historical ground, the compilers of these collections select passages of landscape description from the poetry, leaving out altogether passages that might have some reference to the social turmoil from which they offer sheer escape. The compiler of *Our English Lakes*, for example, informs us that he "has availed himself of

Plate 5: "Resolution and Independence."
Birket Foster, *Beauties of English Landscape*. By permission of
The Huntington Library, San Marino, California.

WE ARE SEVEN.

A SIMPLE child
That lightly draws its breath,
And feels its life in every limb,
What should it know of death?

I met a little cottage girl :
She was eight years old, she said ;
Her hair was thick with many a curl
That clustered round her head.

Plate 6: "We Are Seven."
John MacWhirter and John Pettie, *Wordsworth's Poems for the Young*. By
permission of The Huntington Library, San Marino, California.

such portions, whether smaller pieces or extracts from his longer poems, as refer expressly to the scenery of his beloved native country of Cumberland and Westmorland; and has, as far as practicable, classified these extracts under the heads of the different Lakes or other objects of interest in each locality" (v). The purpose of the books is for the reader "to appreciate more fully Wordsworth's wonderfully true descriptions of the beauties of Nature; but the tourist will have the additional pleasure of identifying with his own favorite spot any of the Poet's verses which refer especially to it" (vi). Wordsworth's text was construed as a supplement to the tour in a strange reversion back to the spectacle of eighteenth-century verse, as discussed in Chapter Two. Thus, by the end of the nineteenth century Wordsworth, especially as mediated through the various gift books and collections of landscape views for which his poetry was excerpted, was for many readers above all the poet and even prophet of nature. While this brief view by no means gives a complete accounting of this process of naturalization—I want to save that project for another occasion—I turn here to the more explicitly political versions of Wordsworth, not constructed as a rarefied poet of nature, but as a teacher of moral, social and political ideas.

In many ways Wordsworth had set up the conditions for, and gladly accepted, his own reception as a moral teacher—among the middle classes and even among the poor.[6] In a letter to Francis Wrangham (5 June 1808), Wordsworth writes that he often wished he "had talents to produce songs, poems, and little histories, that might circulate among other good things, supplanting the bad" in the manner of the half-penny ballads and two-penny histories so widely distributed among the poor (*MY* 1: 248). Wordsworth considers such works "flowers and useful herbs to take place of weeds," and suggests that some of his previously published work was "composed not without a hope that at some time or other they might answer this purpose" (*MY* 1: 248). Wordsworth and Wrangham were discussing the value of religious books in the education of the poor, and while Wordsworth agreed with Wrangham "in chiefly recommending religious Books for the Poor" (*MY* 1: 247), he entertained serious doubts as to their reception among agricultural laborers. Following Adam Smith, Wordsworth found manufacturing laborers in much greater need of religious education than agricultural workers, for unlike the latter, the former were not in daily commune with the permanent forms of nature which nurtured "devout feelings" and steadied their intellectual and moral frame. Given the monotony of their work and the inconstancy of their working conditions, factory workers would find some compensation for the spiritual agitation of their tasks alleviated by a steady diet of religious books: "A select Library . . . in such situations, may be of the same use as a public Dial, keeping every Body's clock in some kind of order" (*MY* 1: 249). In comparing the effects of books upon agricultural and industrial laborers, Wordsworth frames a desideratum for both: a conformity to work rhythms of the public dial. Agricultural laborers, attuned to the diurnal round of nature, could achieve this synchrony without the benefit of books— although books might benefit some individuals "in awakening enterprize, calling forth ingenuity, and fostering genius" (*MY* 1: 248). Without the benefit of nature, industrial laborers, on the other hand, required the moral guidance of printed works and formal instruction.

Wordsworth had worked out this philosophy of education as early as 1803 in the first drafts of the *The Pedlar* (ms. E, 1803/04). The pedlar's education became the model for Wordsworth's subsequent formulation of moral and intellectual development amid the permanent forms of nature. In the country, the written word played a subordinate role to direct experience and the network of oral communication among the native dalespeople. Like the priest of Ennerdale's response to Leonard in "The Brothers," Wordsworth's faith in the spoken word among the rural population leaves him almost complaisant about whether to extend the system of education to the countryside. A library in agricultural districts, Wordsworth told Wrangham, would be of little general use, though a few individuals might acquire some knowledge which would spread "by being dealt about in conversation among their Neighbours, at the door, or by the fireside . . ." (*MY* 2: 248). These few remarkable individuals recall the pedlar's acquisition of natural lore from immediate impressions of nature and the spoken word of the local community:

> Thus inform'd
> He had small need of books; for many a Tale
> Traditionary round the mountains hung;
> And many a legend, peopling the dark woods,
> Nourish'd Imagination in her growth
> And gave the mind that apprehensive power
> By which she is made quick to recognise
> The moral properties and scope of things.
> (ms. E 157–64; *RCP* 396)

In the 1805 version of *The Prelude*, Wordsworth affirmed the opposition between the culture of the city and that of the country. Contrasting London's Bartholomew's Fair to the rural Grasmere Fair, Books 7 and 8 evaluate the difference between the entertainments of the laboring classes in the absence of, and in the midst of, the ordering influences of nature. According to Wordsworth's view, the urban mechanical laborers, lacking the mediating and instructive influence of nature, indulged in a carnivalesque cacophony that reflected moral chaos. Only by means of reading the right books would they be able to compensate for their early loss of natural influence; books offered a corrective and surrogate "natural lore" in the absence of nature, which for Wordsworth was the great moral teacher.[7] Wordsworth here in some sense blurs the distinctions between books of religious instruction and books of "natural lore": both would provide an adequate substitute for the direct experience of nature, both could in the absence of direct experience of the great teacher nature effect the moral and spiritual development of the reader. For Matthew Arnold, John Stuart Mill and the founders of the Wordsworth Society (September 1880), Wordsworth's poetry of human suffering and feeling were transformed into those "flowers and useful herbs" that he had hoped would instruct and awaken moral sentiment among factory laborers, in particular, and among middle-class readers, in general.

Matthew Arnold's tribute to the powers of Wordsworth's poetry to console, heal and inspire its readers to moral sentiments in the "iron time" of Victorian England is well known. Arnold perhaps best sums up the prevalent attitude toward Wordsworth among the Victorian middle classes in "Memorial Verses" (1850): "But where will Europe's later hour / Again find Wordsworth's healing power" (62–63; *Poems* 109). That healing power could take at least three forms: a balm to soothe personal suffering, a poultice to cover over the injuries of class conflict, or a sedative to be administered to the victims of social injustice in order to help them cope with the status quo. All three kinds of Wordsworthian anodyne were managed by those who wanted to ease the growing tension between the classes and maintain some form of superiority—moral or intellectual—over the laboring poor, who had been gaining intellectual and moral ground over their so-called "betters" throughout the 1830s and 1840s. Thus, Wordsworth's poetry was highly valued for the quality of its moral instruction and religious sentiment, and editors seized the opportunity to put it to work as an instrument of instruction for all classes.

Despite efforts on the part of people like Howitt to encourage the laboring classes to read Wordsworth, his work circulated far more— partly perhaps due to the high cost of his books—among the middle classes.[8] In the 1830s and 1840s, Wordsworth's poetry was among those works, including Burke's *Reflections* and Paley's *Moral and Political Philosophy* that contributed to what David Roberts calls an "unprecedented efflorescence of paternalist ideas" (28). Receiving especially wide circulation among Tory periodicals like *Blackwood's*, *Fraser's*, and the *British Critic*, Wordsworth's name appears in a parade of "Tory humanist" writers, including two of Byron's favorite targets for satire, Southey and Coleridge.[9] Indeed, Wordsworth became the darling of those journals that adamantly opposed the New Poor Law, as Gertrude Himmelfarb explains, on both humanitarian and paternalist grounds.[10] In these Tory periodicals, the critical appreciation of Wordsworth's poetry among early reviewers gave way to uncritical, even doting, hero-worship. J. D.

Blackie, an Edinburgh professor of belles-lettres and a reviewer for *Black-wood's*, for example, reported a "fit of Wordsworthian fervour" in 1832; W. H. Smith, also of *Blackwood's*, experienced through Wordsworth "a sort of moral conversion" (qtd. in Roberts 67). From such fits of revelation, we move more soberly to the *Quarterly's* John Lockhart, who, according to his biographer, "bent low at the shrine of Wordsworth" (qtd. in Roberts 67). While Dean Lake was promoting Wordsworthian lore at Oxford, more reservedly (and more familiarly) the twenty-two-year-old John Stuart Mill experienced a conversion of his own while reading *Poems in Two Volumes*. In his *Autobiography* (1853) Mill describes Wordsworth's poetry as "medicine for my state of mind," a palliative that reintroduced him to the "culture of feelings" from which he had been alienated (104). Most importantly, however, Mill identifies a Wordsworthian version of universal sympathy as the source of the poetry's power of renovation: "In [the poems] I seemed to draw from a source of inward joy, of sympathetic and imaginative pleasure, which could be shared in by all human beings; which had no connection with struggle or imperfection, but would be made richer by every improvement in the physical or social condition of mankind" (104). In locating his source of refuge and renovation in Wordsworth's transcendental humanism, Mill announces what would be the central tenet of the middle-class appropriation of Wordsworth's poetry. For these readers, Wordsworth's poetry exemplifies the power of mind and will to overcome pain, deprivation or loss. Through Wordsworth's poetry, for example, Mill was "made to feel that there was real, permanent happiness in tranquil contemplation" (104), even for a person who had suffered a stultifying, Gradgrindian repression of all faculties but the analytical. Thus, Wordsworth's poetry awoke in Mill, as in Arnold and other middle-class readers, an abstract concern for the "common feelings and common destiny of human beings" (104), a concern which does not necessarily promote, but which equally does not necessarily deny, a sense of social responsibility and active regard for real men and women who might be in pain or in need.

Rather than deploying Wordsworth's poetry in the interests of the poor, the Victorian dons and sages sometimes deployed poverty in the interests of Wordsworth—adopting the ideology of poverty as a source of moral value. In accepting his nomination as President of the Wordsworth Society on 2 May 1883, Arnold compared his admission into this austere society to entering a monastery. As recorded in *Transactions of the Wordsworth Society*, Arnold told the members that a "monastery is under the rules of poverty, chastity and obedience. Well, and he who comes under the discipline of Wordsworth comes under those same rules. Wordsworth constantly both preached and practised them" (5: 5). For Arnold, Wordsworth himself had lived under such a rule, which meant virtually (though not actually) taking a vow of poverty and seeking refuge from "a world which sometimes . . . may almost seem to us . . . to have set itself to be as little poor as possible . . ." (5: 5) He enjoined other members to do as Wordsworth had done, and under the philosophical tutelage and shelter of Wordsworth's corpus to take a similar vow to live under the rule of poverty. For those "oppressed" with thoughts that the world is "as little poor as possible, as little chaste as possible, and as little obedient as possible," advised Arnold, "let him seek refuge in the Wordsworth Society" (5: 7).

Under the guiding discipline of the Wordsworth Society, the poet was transformed into a Victorian sage and teacher, the great ethical leader and comforter of a nation in search of some sanctuary from Byronism, industrialism, Darwinism and the rest of it. In the meeting on 2 May 1883, none other than John Ruskin described the "grand function" of the Wordsworth Society as "to preserve, as far as possible, in England the conditions of moral life which made Wordsworth himself possible" (*Transactions* 5: 3). Distinguished members of the society thought of Wordsworth in terms of empire and dominion. The Rev. Dean of Salisbury, for example, praised Wordsworth's role in healing such troubled spirits as John Stuart Mill and added that surely "all lovers of Wordsworth have, or ought to have, [*Ode to Duty*], by heart"; the Dean wrote in the *Transactions* that he was "loath to believe that the hour of Wordsworth's empire as an ethical teacher and as a great poet is coming to an end . . ." (5: 41–42).

By the 1850s the empire of Wordsworth's ethical teachings was fairly extensive, and from the great Victorian lights like Mill and Arnold for whom Wordsworth's poetry was personal anodyne, we move into the world of moral reformers who harnessed his writings into actual "missionary" interventions among the rural and industrial laborers— children and adults alike. One of the first to recommend Wordsworth's work—along with Cowper's, Southey's and Bloomfield's—to the poor was William Howitt. In *The Rural Life of England* (1840), a book steeped in Wordsworthian feeling and naturalism and dotted with quotations from Wordsworth's poetry, Howitt recommended that the poet's writings be distributed among the rural population in order to purify their otherwise rude sentiments. Moral instruction, not enlightenment, was Howitt's intention; as he declares, "whoever has his mind well stored with the pure and noble sentiments of such writers will never condescend to debase his nature by theft, idleness, and low habits" (593–94). Quoting from "Resolution and Independence," Howitt vows that laborers ennobled by benefit of Wordsworthian instruction will learn, like Burns, to walk "in glory and in joy / Following [their] plough along the mountain's side" (594).

Howitt's (and Wordsworth's) goal to deploy Wordsworth's writings as a moral anodyne for the poor was perhaps partly realized in the use of Wordsworth's work in religious and moral instruction. Richard Altick has noted that Wordsworth's poetry appeared in Wesleyan popular magazines like the *Youth's Instructor* and *Methodist Magazine*, while Annabel Newton has shown how Wordsworth's poetry in the United States found its way into Presbyterian readers. Altick also notes that Wordsworth's *The Excursion* was one of the works that applicants to the Church of England Training Schools for Schoolmasters in 1851 had to tackle in order to prove their mastery of grammar (162). More pointedly, perhaps, Howitt disseminated Wordsworth's poetry and ideas—often in snippets and reviews—by means of popular journals, such as *Howitt's Journal* and *The People's Journal*, and lectures to the Working Men's Associations. Affiliated with reformers like William Howitt, John Saunders and W. J. Fox, who were solidly middle class in their values, these journals and lectures demonstrate what Trygve Tholfsen calls a "total commitment to the social predominance and moral pre-eminence of the middle classes in relation to a subordinate working class" (43). Including essays from Harriet Martineau, Samuel Smiles, W. J. Linton, Mary Howitt and William Howitt himself, on subjects ranging from political economy to modern poetry, these journals continued the work of the late eighteenth-century morality industry; they inherited the legacy of John Aikin, Hannah More and Sarah Trimmer, to mention only a few. *The People's Journal*, for example, edited by John Saunders, attempted to gloss over class antagonisms by defining "the people" as a homogeneous national body. In its first number, published 3 January 1846, the editor emphasizes that in its title "People's" should be understood "in its widest and most legitimate sense, to express a nation, and not a class" (1).

In an essay titled "William Wordsworth" appearing in the 24 January 1846 issue of *The People's Journal*, Howitt reminds his readers that "by the people, we mean the national, including all classes" and so translates his opening question, "What has Wordsworth done for the People?" to "What has he done for mankind?" (44). Taking a cue from Hazlitt, just as W. J. Fox had done in his lectures (as I will discuss below), Howitt remarks of Wordsworth that "[t]his grand old conservative is at the same time, unknown to himself, the grandest of levellers . . ." (44). His leveling amounted to the momentous humanist project to break down distinctions between classes: Wordsworth, writes Howitt, "was amongst the very first to assert the dignity of man by selecting his subjects from amongst the lowliest of the human family; and as to that liberty without which no social good or moral greatness can flourish, there is no man who has spoken out so boldly as he" (44). So far as Howitt is concerned, Wordsworth's subject matter, the spirit he infuses in his works, and his sonnets to liberty, in particular, promote republican principles.

Another person associated with *The People's Journal* was W. J. Fox, a frequent lecturer on Wordsworth's "republicanism" to the working-class audiences at the Working Men's Associations.[11] Like

Howitt, Fox recognized Wordsworth's professed conservatism, the reactionary stance of his late politics, and the moral didacticism and institutional apologetics of poems like *The Excursion*. Nonetheless, again like Howitt, Fox realized—and with the same universalist limitations—the democratic principles that were implicit in Wordsworth's work. Acknowledging the need to combat Wordsworth's image as a reactionary, in his lectures to the Working Men's Association of Holborn in 1834, Fox describes the poet as a modern version of the prophet of Balaam, for "when he intends to curse democracy, he is obliged, from the power of truth within him, to bless it" (141). This truth, Fox believes, lies in the essence of poetry itself, which, in his view, is "essentially and vitally democratical: it deals with the universal; it appeals to the common heart of man: it is feeling, thought, and passion, and not external rank, glitter, or station" (138). After describing Wordsworth's characterization of the dignity of human beings sketched in the paupers and laboring poor of his poetry, Fox exuberantly declares himself to be indifferent to Wordsworth's practical politics, which he believes contradict the view of human nature manifest in the poetry. He writes: "Why, in Wordsworth's poems, the lowliest man that walks the streets of a town, or climbs the hills of Cumberland—even the poorest of them all—is good enough not only to be a voter, but to wear a coronet; or rather, perhaps, to trample a coronet in the dust" (143). For his working-class audience Fox presents Wordsworth's pedlars and agricultural laborers as prototypes of revolutionaries. Moreover, since the person who can trample the coronet can also wear one, Fox spells out the political implications of Wordsworth's humanism. His comments show how the incendiary traces of revolutionary content within Wordsworth's poetry had not been fully extinguished, either in the post-revolutionary waters of Wordsworth's own disenchantment, or in the turgid wash of Byron's satire.

In their distinctive use of Wordsworth's work to support their own ideological positions, Arnold's respectability and cultural elitism may not seem too remote from the moral propaganda of middle-of-the-road reformers like Howitt and Fox. We can see in these uses of Wordsworth's text the apparent cost of the ambiguity involved in the agrarian idyll as a form of critique, for it was easily appropriated by Arnold and adopted by Howitt and Fox as an agency of containment. Despite their slightly different approaches, Arnold and the moral reformers share a paternalist program to reconcile the rural and industrial poor to their conditions of labor and scarcity. For these writers Wordsworth's poetry represents the poor as models of middle-class morality and signs of middle-class subjectivity, thereby contributing to an ideology of poverty in which the suffering of the poor is naturalized as a sign of a universalist human dignity and virtue. In their hands, Wordsworth's poor are reduced to signs of equivalence, which, as Max Horkheimer and Theodor Adorno have noted, make "the dissimilar comparable by reducing it to abstract qualities" (*Dialectic* 7). By emphasizing the transcendental subject that Wordsworth's representations of the poor invite, these readers make the indigenous poor over into mythological representations of the enlightened self, thereby blurring the distinctions between classes and creating a comforting illusion of the fundamental unity of all human beings and the equivalence of their suffering. One of Wordsworth's American readers, William Ellery Channing, perhaps sums up this position best, when he writes in "The Present Age":

> The works of genius in our age breathe a spirit of universal sympathy. The great poet of our times, Wordsworth, one of the few who are to live, has gone to common life, to the feelings of our universal nature, to the obscure and neglected positions of our universal nature, for beautiful and touching themes. . . .
> He has revealed the loveliness of the primitive feelings of the universal affections of the human soul. . . . Wordsworth is the poet of humanity; he teaches reverance for our universal nature; he breaks down the factitious barriers between human hearts. (*Works* 6: 155–56)

This myth of the universal Man, which was part and parcel of the project of moral indoctrination in which William Howitt and W. J. Fox were engaged, did not sway all of Wordsworth's working-class readers into accepting the terms handed down to them from above or from rejecting other possibilities in Wordsworth's work. Indeed, the very idea of "universal sympathy" can be and was construed by working-class writers as a demand not for pity, but for respect and even for an equal vote. If for the middle classes universal sympathy meant a kind of one-sided peace between the classes, for some working-class readers universal *sympathy* translated into universal *suffrage*. Indeed, the passage quoted above was excerpted in the *Chartist Circular* for 14 August 1841, not as a device to inculcate some quietude among its readers but to suggest that Wordsworth's poetry (and Channing's interpretation of it) might inspire further enthusiasm and justification for political action against the very classes with whose interests we have tried to affiliate Wordsworth's "romantic ideology."

For at least some working-class readers, the laborers, pedlars and vagabonds in Wordsworth's poetry suggested horizontal equivalences, rather than vertical degrees of difference. These readers transformed the Wordsworthian sedative handed to them from above into a fourth kind of medicine, not mentioned earlier—a vitalizing elixir that emboldened their resistance to middle-class imperatives and strengthened their class solidarity. In the industrious and frugal poor and in the exhausted vagrants, some Victorian working-class readers recognized the possibility of a class identity and the possibility of their own social and political, as well as moral, improvement. For these readers, Wordsworth's poor were empowering figures whose knowledge and wisdom suggested their own; whose industry suggested the possibility for the improvement of their miserable conditions; and whose independence meant independence of will and values, not deference to institutional authority. As it was expressed in the third essay of a series titled "Politics of the Poets" in *The Chartist Circular*, 1 August 1840, Wordsworth poetry is "so almost entirely political, that . . . we cannot but wonder how he came to be called a Tory at all." Indeed, taken as a whole, Wordsworth's poems "are Radical—deeply, essentially, entirely Radical" (182).

Like the middle-class reformers, these more radical working-class readers anticipated the New Criticism's divorce of poetry from the poet, but they did not separate poetry from politics. If we look again at *The Chartist Circular*'s essay on Wordsworth, it becomes evident that Wordsworth's use of concepts like independence, dignity and liberty did not signify for the working-class reader some abstract spiritual quality, as it did for Liberals and Tories. Citing Wordsworth's sonnets to liberty, the *Circular* essay invokes an apocalyptic and Shelleyan metaphor: the tone of these "living, breathing, burning, inspiring, and intoxicating compositions" is that of a "trumpet." Quoting from the sonnets, the writer asserts that they speak a language that would be "most marvellous . . . for a Tory!" Indeed, the idiom represents "nothing less than Republicanism, the purest and highest." What this republicanism means is made quite explicit: "England, in [Wordsworth's view] is a fen of stagnant waters—not that immaculate and unmendable thing Tories usually proclaim her. Reform is needed in all her institutions" (182). Rather than focus on the universality of Wordsworth's "rustics," the author of this piece points out the particularity of Wordsworth's laboring poor, noting that Wordsworth "associated himself in spirit, if not in person with the poor and the suffering" and that his "heroes were waggoners, strollers, pedlars, beggars, hedgers and ditchers, and shepherds" (182).

Among later Victorian readers of "humble" origins who grew up in the 1830s and 1840s and who acknowledged to some degree the influence of Wordsworth's poetry on their life is Thomas Burt, the son of a Northumberland coal miner. A miner himself and trade unionist who eventually took a seat in Parliament, Burt first read Wordsworth in his schoolbooks, where he found poems like "Lucy Gray" and "We are Seven" "charming," but little more. Later in life, however, and under the guidance of another miner, Joseph Fairbairn, Burt began to appreciate especially Wordsworth's shorter poetry, to the point that, as he puts it in his *Autobiography* (1924), he "quickly became a devoted Wordsworthian" (147); in other words, "Wordsworth took firm hold of me, becoming, as it were, part of my moral and intellectual being" (119). Allusions to and quotes from Wordsworth's poetry appear throughout his *Autobiography*, and Burt also quoted from Wordsworth's poetry in his speeches to Parliament.[12] He notes, for example, that his father "in his graver moods" reminded him of Wordsworth's leech gatherer, whose " 'words came feebly," and who " 'gave to God and man their dues' " (126). Assimilating and quoting the familiar epithet, "the child is father to the man," Burt describes, furthermore, how he "was fond of solitary rambles through the fields and country lanes" (126) around Whitley, where he moved because of the shifting conditions in mining, from Murton Row, where he was born in 1837. While Burt was a moderate, rather than a radical—in the 1890s he refused to join the Labour party and though tolerant of socialism he did not support it—his autobiography, especially in the account of John Fairbairn, whom he describes as "a staunch teetotaller, a keen Radical politician, and an ardent trade unionist," shows that Wordsworth's poetry did circulate and speak to at least some working-class readers (147). The value of poetry for Burt, as he says, was not to relieve readers of their cares, but to "ennoble them, making them less trivial and less unworthy of our manhood" (119).

Certainly not all working-class readers took to Wordsworth with such approving enthusiasm as we've seen in the *Chartist Circular* or in Burt, nor am I arguing that we should place Wordsworth in the Chartist panoply of such radical poets as Milton, Blake, Burns, Shelley and Byron; or among the contemporary Chartist poets like Thomas Cooper, William Massey, William Linton, Ebenezer Elliott and Ernest Jones. While more data need to be gathered to make any conclusive statements regarding relative reading habits, it's interesting to note that the Fourth Annual Report of the Blackburn Free Library (1866) shows that between February 1865 and February 1866, borrowers checked out the copy of Wordsworth's poems (unidentified) only six times, compared to Byron's *Hours of Idleness*, ten times; Shelley's poems, eleven times; Bloomfield's, fifteen times; and Burns's (two copies) poems, thirty times. While these figures are hardly sufficient to admit any generalizations, we can see that at least for readers at the Blackburn library, Wordsworth was rather low in priority. Nonetheless, Wordsworth's poetry did have a place, however small, among working-class readers, as we have seen, and it apparently moved some of the more vocal and devoted of them to credit his writing with giving them a sense of personal worth and a sense of identity—both individual and collective.

Despite the wide range of variance in the reception of Wordsworth's work, the liberationist potentials of his representations of the poor were more congenial to Victorian middle-class advocates for the working poor than to working-class radicals themselves. If the Victorian working men and women did not rally around Wordsworth as they did Shelley, whose *Queen Mab* was considered to be the "Chartist Bible," it is because Wordsworth's poetry did not offer an overt call to political organization and resistance to the established power. What Wordsworth's poetry did offer, in all its ambiguity, was the potential for middle-class *and* working-class readers to engage in a literary identification with the itinerant and laboring poor represented there. While it could serve the high-handed moral imperatives of critics like Matthew Arnold and middle-class reformers like William Howitt and W. J. Fox, Wordsworth's poetry could also serve working-class readers, like the audience of *The Chartist Circular*, in their struggle to find a position of moral and political power. If for some readers his representations of the poor parade as a spectacle of innocent suffering, as naturalized signs of a transcendental, ahistorical and politically neutralized human dignity and virtue, for other readers these same representations of the poor serve as models of a politically empowered working class that challenges the assumptions and political hegemony of their so-called betters. Thus, as we have seen, what the Victorian liberals and radicals thought of as the "grand old conservative," in William Howitt's words, "was at the same time the greatest of levellers" (*People's Journal*, 24 January 1846). In recovering the "leveling" voice in Wordsworth's work, I hope to recall attention in our contemporary reading of Wordsworth to the positive utopian potentials of his work that recent criticism has either minimized or completely ignored. In concluding with this survey of the many "Wordsworths" produced by various readers, I hope to point to possibilities for further work in the literary sociology of Wordsworth's reception that might further expand or recover hitherto lost, neglected or suppressed "readings" of his work.

Notes

Notes to the Introduction

1. In *The Idea of Poverty* Gertrude Himmelfarb observes that throughout the 1790s the terms "laborers" and "poor" were, in her words, "used interchangeably, and were often amalgamated in the term 'laboring poor' " (77). She cites Patrick Colquhoun's *Treatise on Indigence* (1806) as typical. Colquhoun, a friend and supporter of Jeremy Bentham's proposals on prison and Poor Law reform, calls poverty "the state of every one who must labour for subsistence" (148; qtd. in Himmelfarb 78). Following Bentham, Colquhoun distinguishes between the indigent—what American culture in the 1980s might have called the "truly needy"—and the poor, which included middle-class men and women without independent means. In his *Essay on the Poor Laws* (1796), Bentham defines indigence as "the state of him who, being destitute of property . . . is at the same time, either *unable to labour*, or unable, even *for* labour, to procure the supply of which he happens to be in want" (qtd. in Poynter 119).

2. For more detailed discussions of these critics, see the chapters below. In general, the works I have in mind are Marjorie Levinson's *Wordsworth's Great Period Poems*, Jerome McGann's *The Romantic Ideology*, James Chandler's *Wordsworth's Second Nature*, Alan Liu's *Wordsworth: The Sense of History*, David Simpson's *Wordsworth's Historical Imagination*, and John Williams's *Wordsworth: Romantic Poetry and Revolution Politics*. While my book represents an intervention into the discussion of Wordsworth's politics, it should become readily clear that I do not intend it as a direct polemic—such as Susan J. Wolfson's "Questioning "The Romantic Ideology": Wordsworth," Peter Manning's "Placing Poor Susan: Wordsworth and the New Historicism," or M. H. Abrams's "*On Political Readings of* Lyrical Ballads"—upon these previous critical perspectives.

3. While it is true, as Simpson has argued, that Wordsworth "often seems to be engaged in an obfuscation of or falling from the position that his polemic . . . would seem to entail" (*Wordsworth's Historical Imagination* 4), that is, that the historical dimension of Wordsworth's work seldom appears explicitly and unproblematically, I think it is necessary to qualify the position of recent critics who suggest that Wordsworth's poetry displaces the historical dimension so completely that the social issues it involves are scarcely recoverable at all. Simpson's and more recently Liu's researches into the minute particulars of Wordsworth's work show that both psycho-sociological materialism and a rhetorically-oriented, materialist formalism can recuperate the historical particulars of Wordsworth's poetry—however incoherent or displaced they may be. My object here, however, is not to lay a new claim upon those recessed (or repressed) contents of the poetry that current methodologies may yield; rather, I am interested in the discursive surfaces of the poetry readily apparent—and seemingly transparent—to Wordsworth's contemporaries.

4. As I will discuss further in Chapter Four, Bentham had raised such a spectre as a possible consequence to idleness: "Indigence is the centre to which inertia alone, that

force which acts without relaxation, makes the lot of every mortal gravitate. Not to be drawn into the abyss, it is necessary to mount up by continual effort; and we see by our side the most diligent and the most virtuous sometimes slipping by one false step, and sometimes thrown headlong by inevitable reverses" (*Theory of Legislation* 127–28). With this caveat in mind, one can see how Wordsworth's vagrants might function as the nexus for a specular literary identification between the idealized vagrants and the spectator whose labor or genius may not suffice to balance him or her at the edge of Bentham's abyss of indigence.

5. Thomas Laqueur's *Religion and Respectability* describes how the education provided by the morality industry unintentionally gave rise to a powerful critical literacy among many working-class men and women. For further discussion, see E. P. Thompson, *The Making of the English Working Class*, especially Chapter 16, and my last chapter here.

Notes to Chapter One

1. The concept of a moral economy has been the subject of recent debate among social historians. Generally it appears that tenants and agricultural laborers did indeed appeal to a "customary moral economy," as Thompson calls it in his influential essay "The Moral Economy of the English Crowd in the Eighteenth Century," as a standard against which to measure and protest change in their relations with landlords. In discussing a tenant protest against Sir William Lowther in Westmorland, C. E. Searle recently concludes that custom "was made up of more than just the formal record as inscribed in manorial court books. . . . It also contained an active and living component, which embraced the experience and collective memory of present and past generations" (120). Given his dependence upon the Lowther estate, Wordsworth would no doubt have had some firsthand knowledge of what Searle calls the "confrontation between an ascendant capitalism and the claims of the customary economy" (121).

   In discussing the effects of industrialism on the popular sense of time and work discipline, David Landes argues that the displacement of agricultural time by factory time especially from the 1770s onward amounted to nothing less than a "revolution in time." The mechanic forms of factory life disrupted the "natural rhythms" of agricultural life and required for laborers a wholesale reorientation of the regulation of the body. Mark Harrison's "The Ordering of the Urban Environment: Time, Work and the Occurrence of Crowds 1790–1835," offers a useful critique of Landes, agreeing that while the everyday life of a factory worker was subject to the mechanical routine of the time clock, the agricultural laborer was still governed by more natural elements, such as the hours of daylight and seasonal fluctuations in weather (139). As I will discuss briefly in the "Postscript," in a letter to Francis Wrangham of 5 June 1808, Wordsworth shows a keen awareness of this transformation of time and work discipline when he recommends that a select library of religious books be set up for factory workers, because these books "may be of the same use as a public Dial, keeping every Body's clock in some kind of order" (*MY* 2: 249). Because the natural forms and rhythms of nature govern the work time of agricultural workers, Wordsworth says that they have little or no need for such books.

   For more general discussions of the role custom played in the relations of production in late eighteenth-century England, see Robert W. Bushaway, *By Rite: Custom, Ceremony and Community in England, 1700–1880*, and E. P. Thompson, "The Grid of Inheritance: A Comment" and his "Time, Work-Discipline and Industrial Capitalism."

2. W. A. Armstrong cites a doubling of per capita relief in many villages by the end of the eighteenth century (97). As an indication of the dimension of the problem, the receipts for parish poor relief increased from under .75 million pounds in the 1750s, to

5.3 million pounds by 1803, and to more than 8 million pounds by 1813, when rates leveled out until after 1834 (Mathias 46).

3. For a fuller discussion of the changes Sayer made to Laroon's plates, see Shesgreen (40–42).

4. See Barrell's *The Dark Side of the Landscape*, Bermingham's *Landscape and Ideology*, Fabricant's "The Aesthetics and Politics of Landscape in the Eighteenth Century," and Alan Liu's chapter titled "The Politics of the Picturesque" in his *Wordsworth: The Sense of History*.

5. See Richard Sha's "Gray's Political *Elegy*: Poetry as the Burial of History" for a discussion of Gray's ambivalent and ideologically motivated treatment of the poor in his *Elegy Written in a Country Churchyard*. Showing the collusion of Gray's elegy and the discourse on poverty in contemporary treatises and debates about the poor, Sha notes that Gray's "compassion [for the poor] is strongly predicated both on the cheerful industry of the poor, and on their acceptance of their place" (338).

6. The formation of the mythic laborer has its origins in the primitivist doctrines of the eighteenth century as they intersect or overlap with what Clifford Geertz calls the "uniformitarian" concept of human nature that pervades Enlightenment thought. For the Enlightenment, nature and human nature appear to be homological—entirely congruent, ordered and governed by consistent, indisputable and timeless natural laws ("Concept of Culture" 35–36). Hayden White's "The Noble Savage Theme as Fetish" offers a more complex analysis of eighteenth-century primitivism that can be applied to the mythic agrarian laborer. While perhaps less widely applicable than "the noble savage" concept, the trope of the agrarian laborer nonetheless exhibits some of the same fetishistic qualities that White finds in the latter. White describes how the myth of the noble savage, which is really a remaking of the wild man image, arose "only *after* the conflict between the Europeans and the natives had already been decided and when, therefore, it could no longer hamper the exploitation of the latter by the former" (186). Moreover, through a dialectical encounter with both the wild man and the noble savage, Europeans worked through (but did not resolve) their basic confusion (and fear) about "the nature of their own humanity" (189). A similar displacement and dialectic are at work in the opposition between the profligate, urban poor and the virtuous, rural laborer. The mythic agrarian laborer arises well after the decision to exploit labor had been made, and the oppositions between profligacy and virtue, idleness and industriousness (as I will show in more detail in Chapters Two and Three) indicate that the middle classes especially, but also members of the higher orders, were working out through the myth of the agrarian laborer and its spectral other—the urban manufacturing worker—their uncertainty about the nature of their own morality, utility and value.

7. See Karl Polanyi, *The Great Transformation*, on the devaluation of labor due to the Speenhamland system of relief that was introduced in Berkshire in 1795 (79). In his *Work and Authority in Industry*, Reinhard Bendix draws out the significance of Polanyi's observation (41–43). While both Polanyi and Bendix exaggerate the influence of the Speenhamland system on blurring the distinction between wages and relief— Speenhamland was primarily limited to the south and eastern counties of Kent, Sussex and Essex—other forms of relief throughout England in the late eighteenth century, such as the workhouse and the roundsman system (in which out-of-work laborers had to "go the rounds" in the parish to find work for a subsidized wage), similarly lowered the self-respect of rural laborers, who in a customary agricultural economy would not have been stigmatized by periods of unemployment. As W. A. Armstrong recently comments, the " 'roundsman' system . . . appeared to involve an undesirable element of wage subsidisation calculated to lower the recipients' self-respect and make for indifferent standards of performance" ("Countryside" 97).

8. McGann's distinction between romantic ideology and romantic work offers a crucial distinction here, for the utopian writers may not themselves be aware of the discrepancy between their nostalgic utopian vision and the actual social practice or habitus, in Pierre Bourdieu's terms, in which they are immersed. McGann calls those works "primary," which "do not bring their own dialectical stance into question" (*Romantic Ideology* 108). Among these works we may include Goldsmith's *The Deserted Village*, much of Cowper's *The Task*, and Wordsworth's *Tintern Abbey* and "The Old Cumberland Beggar." From the retro-view of the cultural critic, however, the uncritical idealism of these primary texts exemplifies a society in conflict, a society in which the pastoralisms seem forced and out of complementarity with the turbulent agrarian transformations taking place in the English countryside. The reflexive displacement and idealization, even escape, that such poems transact (and even subsequent ones from a later, more self-critical phase of English romanticism, like Shelley's and Byron's, in McGann's view), however, reveal the troubled source from which these poems attempt to withdraw. In McGann's words, "The poetry supplies a reflection of the world, . . . but the image is generated from the poetry's 'reflex' or response to that world and its own act of observation. In this way the poetry draws itself into the world it is reflecting" (130). Or, perhaps more clearly: "The grand illusion of Romantic *ideology* is that one may escape such a world through imagination and poetry. The great truth of Romantic *work* is that there is no escape, that there is only revelation (in a wholly secular sense). . . ." (131). I cannot resist noting that Bloch anticipates our post-structuralist "discovery" of a self-conscious critique of romantic ideology, inasmuch as he observes: "Romanticism does not understand utopia, not even its own, but utopia that has become concrete understands Romanticism and makes inroads into it, in so far as archaic and historical material, in its archetypes and works, contains a not yet voiced, undischarged element" (*Principle of Hope* 1: 141).

9. In *Socialism: Utopian and Scientific*, a pamphlet derived from three Chapters of *Against Dühring*, Engels distinguishes between what he calls utopian and scientific socialism:

> The socialism of earlier days certainly criticized the existing capitalistic mode of production and its consequences. But it could not explain them, and, therefore, could not get the mastery of them. It could only simply reject them as bad. The more strongly this earlier socialism denounced the exploitation of the working class, inevitable under capitalism, the less able was it clearly to show in what this exploitation consisted and how it arose. But for this it was necessary (1) to present the capitalistic method of production in its inevitableness during a particular historical period, and therefore, also, to present its inevitable downfall; and (2) to lay bare its essential character which was still a secret. This was done by the discovery of *surplus value*. (89)

10. Other critics have noted the new demands that Wordsworth's poetry made upon its earliest readers. Mary Jacobus, for example, argues in *Tradition and Experiment in Wordsworth's* Lyrical Ballads, that Wordsworth's poetry involved a new kind of imaginative engagement with the vagrants, deserted mothers and aged figures otherwise commonplace in much of the magazine poetry of the 1790s. In its redefinition of the ballad, the "ballad reader's expectations are aroused, disappointed—and redirected towards what were for Wordsworth more significant aspects of human experience" (233). Most importantly, and perhaps the cue to Heather Glen's elaboration of this concept, Jacobus notes that like Hannah More, Wordsworth was linking instruction (hers religious, his ethical) to popular forms; but while More aimed at inculcating religious doctrine to the semi-literate, Wordsworth aimed to awaken his literate readers from their everyday torpor. In Jacobus's words, he wanted them to "think about their own code" (239). For further discussion on Wordsworth's "novelty" see John E.

Jordan, *Why the Lyrical Ballads*, especially the chapters on *"Lyrical Ballads* and Innovation" and "The Originality of the *Lyrical Ballads.*"

11. Descriptive accuracy, as Jordan has noted in his discussion of Wordsworth's *Lyrical Ballads*, must not be confused with "precise literalness" (159). Jordan notes that Wordsworth strove to find a narrative technique that would convey "the essential verity of feeling, not the literal historicity of the action" (161). While it appears to some critics that Wordsworth succeeds all too well in substituting feeling for action, I am arguing here that the Wordsworthian combination of literalness and literariness that infuses his marginal figures with affective and objective power leads to the possibility of identification with those figures and offended Wordsworth's early critics.

Notes to Chapter Two

1. Smith writes:

> When I endeavour to examine my own conduct, when I endeavour to pass sentence upon it, and either to approve or condemn it, it is evident that . . . I divide myself, as it were, into two persons; and that I, the examiner and judge, represent a different character from that other I, the person whose conduct is examined into and judged of. The first is the spectator, whose sentiments with regard to my own conduct I endeavour to enter into, by placing myself in his situation, and by considering how it would appear to me, when seen from that particular point of view. The second is the agent, the person whom I properly call myself, and of whose conduct, under the character of a spectator, I was endeavouring to form some opinion. The first is the judge; the second the person judged of. (*Moral Sentiments* 113)

2. Foucault discusses "Las Meninas" in *The Order of Things* 3–16.

3. In *Wordsworth: The Sense of History*, Liu sees the banishment of narrative figures from the picturesque landscape as a characteristic tendency of the picturesque to institutionalize repose as a "total arrest of experience in form, of passion in topoi" (82). In focusing here upon the arresting function of the sublime in Wordsworth's poetry, I am suggesting that Wordsworth's sublime vagrants transfer the policing power that resides in the picturesque spectator to themselves as agents, not objects, of interpellation. If, as Louis Althusser suggests in "Ideology and Ideological State Apparatuses: Notes Towards an Investigation," interpellation acts as an agency of ideology in which human beings represent "their relation to [their] conditions of existence," this reversal of the power of naming the Other indicates a significant leveling, if not the erasure, of the vertical distance between classes (164). To adapt a phrase from Clifford Siskin's *The Historicity of Romantic Discourse*, the imposition of Wordsworth's vagrants on the formerly complacent spectator results from "the increasing insecurity of hierarchical position" that Siskin links to generic change in the late eighteenth century (141).

4. In a further elaboration of the politics of the picturesque, Liu's *Wordsworth: The Sense of History* finds in the politically motivated debates over picturesque theory that "the picturesque . . . was a political platform whose declaration of British constitutional freedom gravitated increasingly leftward in the period that most concerns us toward an idea of revolution cognate with the American or very early French Revolution. The lasting effect of such politicization, no matter a writer's final stance after the French Revolution, was that picturesque landscape became an almost automatic second language of politics" (113). I offer my analysis of the picturesque as an aesthetic that further distances the poor from the polite spectator as an important qualification of

these views, but as a qualification that shows the limits of that leftward drift. See his chapter "The Politics of the Picturesque" (esp. 84–115).

5. In "Edmund Burke's Natural Aristocrat: The 'Man of Taste' as a Political Ideal," Frans De Bruyn argues that Burke's aesthetic studies "confronted him with fundamental questions about human nature and the moral order," questions that involved contradictions that Burke resolved by appealing to an essentialist vindication of aristocracy. As De Bruyn writes, "The natural aristocrat, by virtue of his education and his position in society, is uniquely qualified to cultivate and to act properly upon his natural feelings; his education in taste . . . transforms this hitherto private individual into the very cynosure of his society's prejudices, himself now become an object of moral and aesthetic appreciation" (49).

6. Malcolm Andrews notes the contradiction between Gilpin's and Price's preference for the "low" as objects for the picturesque and their political sympathies. In his view, Price and Gilpin are cool to any kind of social leveling, as suggested in their insistence that the picturesque display *order* in variety (65). More specifically, Liu argues that "the picturesque was the imaginary ground on which the rights of old property could be adjusted to the demands of new money" (*Wordsworth* 91). Liu links the liberal trend in the picturesque and the wilding of English gardens—the gardens of liberalism—to Price's and Knight's affiliations with the Foxite Whigs, which made them subject to Humphry Repton's Burkean assaults on their ideas for "theoretical improvement." As Liu shows, their detractors, who included Anna Seward, Horace Walpole and William Wordsworth, decried the purported "Jacobinism" of Price and Knight (111–12).

7. Siskin describes the ideological service of personification as a "strategy of exclusion" that reaffirms the naturalized "truths" of social hierarchy by speaking exclusively to a reader who identifies his or her social position as being above labor (71).

8. For this critical play on the terms "overlook" and "oversee" I thank Marc Briggs, University of California, Santa Barbara, who first presented it in "The Isolation of the Poet in *The Prelude*." Unpublished essay, 1989.

9. In using the term "aristocratic hegemony" to describe the set of relations Cowper's poetry insinuates, I follow J. C. D. Clark's *English Society 1688–1832,* which argues that the case for middle-class consolidation of power in the eighteenth century has largely been overstated. For Clark, the "values of rural society," meaning the values of a propertied elite whose wealth derived primarily from landholdings, persisted throughout the eighteeenth century. As Clark describes the hegemony of aristocratic values:

> If the landed and mercantile elites were specialised and distanced by function, they were still united in deferring to a common code of manners and values: that of the traditional elite. New men were accepted; but on terms set by the aristocracy and gentry. . . . The mercantile, financial and professional elite, like the landed elite, increasingly became " 'amphibious' " between town and country, money and status: the emerging social divide was a cultural one, between the patrician landowner, banker, lawyer, clergyman or merchant on one hand and the plebeian tradesman and manufacturer on the other, not a Marxist one between an aristocracy and a bourgeoisie, and the challenge to the ancien regime, when it came, was from culturally defined groups, not from economically defined classes. (70–71)

See also Clark (38–41) and his Chapter 2.

10. Largely because of his celebration of liberty and the overt attacks on slavery in his work, Cowper has sometimes been identified with a more liberal position than he occupies. In *William Cowper: Humanitarian*, Lodwick Hartley, one of Cowper's early twentieth-century critics, has cautioned: "However revolutionary Cowper's social passion may

seem to be, it is always well to remember that in his way of thinking class distinctions were an indispensable part of the social order and were not indiscriminately to be broken down" (39). Cowper attributes social distinctions to Providence, as is evident in his comments on the French Revolution to Lady Hesketh: "Princes and peers reduced to plain gentlemanship, and gentles reduced to a level with their own lacqueys, are excesses of which they [the French] will repent hereafter. Difference of rank and subordination are, I believe of God's appointment, and consequently essential to the wellbeing of society" (*Letters* 3: 396). See Richard Feingold's *Nature and Society* for a more general discussion of Cowper's idealization of the *ancien régime*, the moral authority of which Cowper believes to have been corrupted by the rise of a state based on illegitimate—that is, commercial—rather than hereditary, wealth and power (143–53).

11. Hazlitt's perceptive observation, while often cited, seems little credited by critics who otherwise attempt to historicize readings of Wordsworth. For his contemporaries, Wordsworth's muse was "a levelling one," as Hazlitt explains, that "proceeds on a principle of equality, and strives to reduce all things to the same standard" (132).

12. Cowper's infamous lines describing the poet as a cloistered voyeur who sees but does not feel the busy hum of the world offer an important footnote to the surveying eye of his narrator as opposed to the sympathetic eye of Wordsworth's: "Tis pleasant through the loopholes of retreat / To peep at such a world; to see the stir / Of the great Babel, and not feel the crowd" (*Task* 4.88–90).

13. In *Landscape and Ideology*, Bermingham describes a "project of knowing the countryside" which involves an increasingly systematic and urban-centered classification of the poor in the juridical discourse that governs the debates about the Poor Law Amendment Act of 1834 (160). In adopting her concept of a *terra cognita* for my analysis of Cowper, I am suggesting that the loco-descriptive and picturesque genres equally offer a mode of perception that presumes to know the landscape and its rustic population as categorical types. Moreover, the discursive terms and features in these genres reify in natural lore the social relations of inclusion and exclusion practiced in eighteenth-century rural society.

14. In the *Critique of Judgment* Kant describes boundlessness as a concept that obtains metonymically to those formless objects in nature which trigger our ideas of the sublime. He believes that the sublime is at odds with the purposiveness of nature and so grounded "in ourselves and in our attitude of thought" (82–84). If so, the boundlessness of the sublime, in the case of Wordsworth's encounters with vagrants, exposes the arbitrary and social grounds of class distinction. (For Lyotard on the Kantian sublime, see *The Differend* 161–71.)

15. Eagleton writes that the Kantian sublime "centres the human subject in an imaginary relation to a pliable, purposive reality, thereby granting it a delightful sense of its own inner coherence and confirming its status as an ethical agent. Yet it does this without ceasing to discipline and chastise the subject . . ." (98).

16. In "Rephrasing the Political with Kant and Lyotard: From Aesthetic to Political Judgments," David Carroll comments that Lyotard "makes of this 'sorrow' an activism in pursuit of the Idea of community" (87). For Lyotard, the failure of the enlightenment and postenlightenment narratives of liberation has led us to an impasse, but one which may,' in the very heterogeneous possibilities of its own liminality, lead to a more just society. One may sense a certain romantic utopianism in such a position, a utopianism to which political realities of the 1990s offer a serious challenge. Nonetheless, as Carroll goes on to explain, Lyotard finds in the liminal state of the postmodern a vision of the future, but one with a pressing sense of the present need to renew our human obligations to one another. In Carroll's words, Lyotard "sees in the signs of 'our history,' in these refutations of all the classical theories of the political, indications not of future victories, . . . but of the continuing obligation to the idea of humanity, of

the obligation to resist those forces attempting to regulate and resolve the differends basic to such an Idea" (87).

Notes to Chapter Three

1. See John Mullan's *Sentiment and Sociability* for an extended discussion of the cult of sensibility, which in his view emerges when politic culture finds problematic the nature of its relations among those who occupy different stations, or when, as Mullan puts it, people have difficulty in "conceiving society as a community of moral and material interests" (4). For Mullan, the sentimental novel becomes the site of "signs of sentimental fashion," and the discourse of the sentimental novel generates "new representations of social instinct" (6). He recognizes, however, that the fashionable language of sensibility—especially in the later part of the century, when the novelty began to wear thin—could easily become an affectation. Most importantly, however, Mullan notes how the project to construct an enlightened sociability finally turned back upon the self, and so the initial focus upon benevolence gave way to a rather more self-interested focus upon the benevolent. In particular, illness became a sign of "privileged delicacy"—the "last retreat of the morally pure" (160). When the illness and even death of the delicate and refined become signs of distinction, as Mullan claims, "[w]hat was originally posed as a capacity for sociability was eventually realized in the most private of experiences" (16).

2. In *The Historicity of Romantic Discourse*, Siskin argues that early romantic poetry collapses questions of "kind into degree"; that is, questions of genre become entangled with questions of intensity of feeling. This collapse "functions to naturalize the transformation of hierarchy from a structure based on inherited, unchanging distinctions to one that posits an initial equality subject to psychological and developmental difference" (46). As will be apparent throughout my argument here—in Siskin's terms, perhaps yet another example of romantic discourse infiltrating a critical project—the emphasis upon sympathetic identification in literature that results from the romantic conflation of kind and degree makes it possible for readers of romantic and post-romantic poetry to disturb rather than affirm the uncontested assumptions and ideological formations that ground relations between the poor and those who are not poor.

     Robert Mayo's "The Contemporaneity of the *Lyrical Ballads*" demonstrates that the vagrant subjects of Wordsworth's poetry would have seemed almost commonplace among contemporary readers of popular and magazine poetry, where the indigent, aged and desperate appeared with alarming frequency. In Mayo's words: "The strains of 'nature' and 'simplicity' in the *Lyrical Ballads* deeply blend with those of humanitarianism and sentimental morality, as they did in a great deal of popular verse. . . . However much they may be rendered fresh and new by poetic treatment, it must be recognized that most of the objects of sympathy in the volume belong to an order of beings familiar to every reader of magazine poetry—namely, bereaved mothers and deserted females, mad women and distracted creatures, beggars, convicts and prisoners, and old people of the depressed classes, particularly peasants" (495).

3. Under his stage name Courtney Melmouth, Pratt abandoned his star-crossed stint as an actor and turned to writing for his living. "Sympathy, A Poem," which was published anonymously in 1788, went through four editions in its first year and was reprinted as late as 1807. In 1797, Pratt's "Letter to the 'Tars' of Old England" went through six editions in just a few weeks. *Bread*, first appearing in 1801, saw a third edition by 1803; and "John and Dane" was even more successful. Two collections of his works appear as *Pity's Gift* (1798) and *A Paternal Present* (1802).

4. Barrell discusses the concept of "blissful toil" in his discussion of Thomas Gainsborough's blending of the pastoral and georgic. As he notes, the concept appears throughout the eighteenth century in pastoral, georgic and combined forms, both in poetry and in painting. Such phrases as "blissful toil," happy labour" or "grateful toil," according to Barrell, "are the phrases whereby the producers of Britain's agricultural wealth are seen to work as hard as they are required to do by the moral imperatives of the georgic tradition, but to be as happy as the idle shepherd is in the tradition of Pastoral" (49).

5. As Ronald Paulson has noted in *Emblem and Expression*, the twelve plates of *Industry and Idleness* construct a "simple pattern of a morality—right and wrong, reward and punishment, action and consequence, strengthened by the stark blacks and whites of the design" which is devoid of any grey area of ambiguity: "the greys are largely absent visually as well as morally" (59). Among the many critics who have noted the similarity of Crabbe's narrative technique and Hogarth's "progress," Ronald Hatch has made the specific link between this scene and Hogarth's *Industry and Idleness* (53).

6. In his *Romantic Narrative Art*, Karl Kroeber observes in general that "the basic pattern of all Crabbe's narratives . . . is that of the Progress, which enumerates in defined stages the course of punishments attendant upon a particular vice" (118–19). As Beth Nelson argues in *George Crabbe and the Progress of Eighteenth-Century Narrative Verse*, however, Kroeber's definition of the progress is "too narrow," in that the progress also shows the rewards attendant upon a particular virtue. Moreover, in Nelson's view, he underestimates the ability of the progress tale to construct a complex characterization (65). For further discussion of Crabbe's progress narratives see also Peter New (27–30).

7. McGann argues that Wordsworth engages social life and history through the calming medium of the "One Life," while Crabbe engages them more directly. Where Crabbe writes "a poetry of truths," Wordsworth writes "a poetry of Truth" ("Anachronism" 303). McGann's appraisal of Crabbe's focus, rather like Elizabeth Barrett-Browning's of her own work in *Aurora Leigh*, suggests that Crabbe, in Browning's terms, "exert[s] a double vision" (5.184). Such vision leads to a "living art / Which thus presents and thus records true life" (5.221–22). McGann writes: "Crabbe's nature and history are fields of betrayal, places where one can and must expect adversity, disaster, even malevolence" ("Anachronism" 299). While I agree that in "Tintern Abbey" and in the poetry after 1802 Wordsworth tempers the *truths* of his earlier poetry with some reified *Truth*, in his early poetry—and perhaps especially in the *Salisbury Plain* poems—the world indeed is marked as a site of vexation, disaster and political terror. We need, perhaps, to be careful of constructing out of the diversity of Wordsworth's poetry a "one Wordsworth."

8. Taking Jacobus's observations one step further, Nicholas Roe, following Thompson, argues that in the early 1790s the transformation in the structure of feeling among the poor provided "an enabling pattern for Wordsworth's poetic development after 1793" (129; see Thompson's *Making* 127). Both Jacobus (144-46) and John Williams (10–18), for widely different purposes, connect the *Salisbury Plain* poems to the humanitarian protest found in William Crowe's *Lewesdon Hill* (1788) and John Langhorne's *The Country Justice* (1774–75). Williams seems to minimize the radical potentials of Wordsworth's poem by overemphasizing the pastoralism it shares with Crowe's work, while Jacobus more accurately notes that Wordsworth's protest is "much more far reaching" than Langhorne's (144).

9. One discerns a disappointing attenuation of the social critique in Wordsworth's revisions after 1799. While the 1795 revisions emphasize and name specifically the social causes of the female vagrant's suffering, the later revisions lose sight of the causes as they refocus the poem on the complex psychology of suffering. While Wordsworth shifts the emphasis in the final version of the poem, retitled *Guilt and Sorrow*, from

social critique to personal tragedy in the face of destitution arising from ambiguous but nonetheless external causes, in this version as well, in Stephen Gill's words, the "attack on the oppression of the poor is the center from which all of the poem's questioning radiates" (5).

10. Clive Emsley notes that the "departure of married men for the regular army or the navy could . . . put additional burdens on the poor rate; when the principal breadwinner was gone and once any bounty money left them (and a substantial part of the bounty was often required for necessaries in the army) had been spent, many families had no other recourse but the parish. In September 1793, the overseers of the poor of Sunderland estimated that their poor rate would increase from the usual L1000 a year to about L3000 a year and 'the difference in the expence . . . arises totally from the families of impressed men' " (40).

11. See Deleuze and Guattari's chapter, "Treatise on Nomadology—The War Machine"; nomadism, itself a utopian construct, imagines a perpetual state of absolute liminality, an assemblage that confounds all boundaries rather more by ignoring than in reacting against centers of power (*A Thousand Plateaus* 360).

12. Wordsworth and Godwin were not the first to associate gypsies with liberty. In *The Country Justice*, John Langhorne writes: "The gypsy-race my pity rarely move, / Yet their strong thirst of liberty I love" (qtd. in Simpson, *Wordsworth's Historical Imagination* 44). Like Wordsworth, Cowper finds among the gypsies reason for both attraction and repulsion. In Book One of *The Task* Cowper describes the gypsies as a "vagabond and useless tribe" and further claims that they have compromised their basic humanity: "Strange! That a creature rational, and cast / In human mould, should brutalize by choice / His nature, and . . . prefer / Such squalid sloth to honorable toil" (1.559, 575–79). Cowper nonetheless concedes that there is something appealing in their "health and gaiety of heart," for they spend their sylvan lives "breathing wholesome air, and wand'ring much" (1.88–89).

13. In light of Robert's remaindering of his human presence for the "sack of gold" in *The Ruined Cottage*, Liu goes on to explain how that poem transforms the conventional semiotic relationship between sign and signified in that the poem enacts a major structural transformation in the rural economy: "in the moment of economic crisis, labor became part of a sign-structure displaced from the independent household—an industrial sign-structure in which, as Saussure has suggested, wages became the signifier and labor itself the signified" (34). In the case of this transformation: "Labor . . . became intertextual, and what was once the value of domestic humanity opened out into the inhuman value or cash of the economic other" (341). Liu's deft reading of the poetics of economy in *The Ruined Cottage* does not, I think, mean that we should expect to find such transformations throughout cultural production—even Wordsworth's—after 1798 when, in Liu's words, "[w]eaving and writing: the partners of textualization together entered the economy of debt" (341). While this observation may apply to some of Wordsworth's works—*The Ruined Cottage* in particular—later poems, like "Resolution and Independence" and "Point Rash-Judgment," for example, rely upon the earlier equation that labor equals humanity.

14. In describing the shallow education she received from her English aunt, Aurora Leigh concludes the list with,

> And last
> I learnt cross-stitch, because she did not like
> To see me wear the night with empty hands,
> A doing nothing. (1.14–15)

15. The history of the crisis in the textile industry at the end of the eighteenth century is, perhaps, familiar to most readers. In general, new technology and the application of

water and steam power to spinning and then weaving transformed the everyday practices of thousands of workers in wool and cotton. The flying shuttle, for example,
which enabled weavers to increase production, led in the 1730s to an increase in
demand for yarn and hence to a rise in the cottage industry of spinning, by which wives
and children of many agricultural laborers supplemented otherwise meager incomes.
With the advent of the jenny and mule in the 1770s and 1780s, however, spinning
became concentrated in towns like Manchester. While regional variations make such a
generalization imprecise, the conclusion of G. D. H. Cole and Raymond Postgate
sums up accurately enough the contemporary perception in the 1790s: "The spinning
wheel began to disappear from the cottages of the poor all over the country; and the
most important source of supplementary earnings for families in the rural areas went
with it" (123).

16. Mary Jacobus has noted how *Salisbury Plain* introduces the equation between
    "employment and happiness" that Wordsworth intensifies in *The Ruined Cottage*.
    See her discussion of the poem in *Tradition and Experiment in Wordsworth's* Lyrical
    Ballads (148).

17. The textual history of *The Ruined Cottage*, like that of most of Wordsworth's major
    poems, leads one along a complex trajectory of revisions. For a detailed analysis of
    this trajectory, see James Butler's introduction to his edition of the poem for The
    Cornell Wordsworth (3–35).

18. In setting up an equivalency between poetic and manual labor, according to Liu,
    Wordsworth's image making in *The Ruined Cottage* creates an object to exchange for
    the reader's labor. "Thus," in his terms, "is the original bond of labor in 'The Ruined
    Cottage' at last redeemed: as an act of imagination whose labor is to be valued on a
    par with any other species of human work" (*Wordsworth* 357). Of course, the problem
    is that products of poetic labor, the objects produced by Dove Cottage industry, if you
    will, like those produced by domestic cottage industries, themselves are subject to the
    alienating forces of the marketplace from which the poem purportedly rescues them.
    See Liu's full discussion in Chapter 7 of *Wordsworth: The Sense of History*.

19. Indeed, as Simpson notes in his discussion of "Beggars" and "Alice Fell," and as I
    discuss further in Chapter Five, Wordsworth often seems to advocate charity toward
    those who would have been considered unqualified for relief under the standards set
    by the Poor Laws and by their utilitarian adversaries, like Bentham. See *Wordsworth's
    Historical Imagination*, Chapter 6, (esp. 175-76).

Notes to Chapter Four

1. I am invoking here Barrell's observation that a hybrid form, the pastoral-georgic,
   appears in much of the loco-descriptive poetry and painting of the eighteenth, especially
   the late-eighteenth, century, since these works depict rural life as "a blend of work and
   play"—with work primarily designated for the poor; play, for the well-to-do. As Barrell
   observes: "Pastoral and Georgic are intertwined in a way that is of distinct benefit to all
   classes, so that the swain may well smile as he works, and the gentleman will feel his
   leisure justified by his practical concern for rural affairs" (*Dark Side* 48). See Barrell's
   discussion in his chapter on Thomas Gainsborough (esp.48–53).

2. Benjamin describes two "archaic types" of storyteller, "the resident tiller of the soil,
   and the . . . trading seaman," who embody, respectively, those who are rooted in one
   place and know intimately the local tales and those who have travelled afar and hence
   circulate such stories from place to place. Upon the contact between these two types,
   Benjamin believes, the very life of storytelling devolves: the "actual extension of the

realm of storytelling in its full historical breadth is inconceivable without the most intimate interpenetration of these two archaic types" (85).

3. In a notable exception to the rule, Alan Bewell reads the leech gatherer's activity as "a prototype for the task of a post revolutionary poet" (272). While noting the complex motives for the poem in Wordsworth's financial predicament, as well as in residual anxiety from childhood trauma, Peter J. Manning's " 'My Former Thoughts Returned': Wordsworth's *Resolution and Independence*," describes the leech gatherer as a composite figure onto which Wordsworth projects his "untoward thoughts" in order to tame them (401). Manning and I disagree only in the degree to which we think Wordsworth's poem successfully domesticates this spectral Other, and the degree to which the leech gatherer embodies social, not just personal, trauma. More often than not, however, critics tend to ignore or dodge the question of Wordsworth's financial insecurity; they read "Resolution and Independence" as a poem addressing purely metaphysical concerns. In "Process and Permanence in 'Resolution and Independence,' " Alan Grob argues that the leech gatherer represents for Wordsworth "a spiritual existence alien to and transcending the very processes of nature themselves, a source of permanence in the midst of flux" (97). Similarly, in *Wordsworth's Poetry*, Geoffrey Hartman concludes that the leech gatherer's "example persuades the poet that faith in nature can survive maturation and even decrepitude" (203). See also " 'Resolution and Independence': Wordsworth's Answer to Coleridge's 'Dejection: An Ode,' " in which George W. Meyer examines the poem as a self-affirming reply to Coleridge's despair over the apparent loss of his imaginative power. In *Romanticism and the Forms of Ruin*, Thomas McFarland similarly describes "Resolution and Independence" as a response to Coleridge's "Dejection: An Ode" (74-78). In my view, these essays underemphasize Wordsworth's state of uncertainty about his future as a poet and, like Manning's, overvalue Wordsworth's power successfully to displace his anxieties onto a figure that he can manipulate from a safely mediated distance. Though he agrees that "The Leech Gatherer" shows Wordsworth at the gates of what he calls the "romantic Hell of the wasted imagination, "Anthony Conran goes so far as to read "Resolution and Independence" as a comic poem written by a man who "had achieved a *modus vivendi*" ("The Dialectic of Experience" 68). While this could possibly have been true of the poet after 1807—the date Wordsworth erroneously assigns to the composition of the poem in the Fenwick note to the poem—it could hardly be said of the poet in 1802 when his work, to quote Manning, "lay uncertainly ahead" (398).

4. See Mary Moorman, *William Wordsworth: A Biography* (1: 523) and Kurt Heinzelman, *The Economics of the Imagination* (215). More recently Marjorie Levinson, Alan Liu, David Simpson and Annabel Patterson have affirmed Wordsworth's tendency to identify poetic with manual labor. See Levinson's analysis, for example, of the economic themes in "Michael" in *Wordsworth's Great Period Poems*, (esp. 74–79). In a discussion of *The Ruined Cottage*, Liu notes Wordsworth's identification of poetic labor with peddling in his *Wordsworth: A Sense of History*. Simpson's chapter on "Gipsies" in *Wordsworth's Historical Imagination* describes Wordsworth's displacement of his anxieties about his poetic labor in the poems of 1807. In particular, he compares "Resolution and Independence," a "meditation on poetic labour," to Wordsworth's "Gipsies," another poem that attempts to work out Wordsworth's "embarrassment and guilt of dependence" and his "insecurity of his vocation as an unestablished writer" (38, 36). See also Patterson's *Pastoral and Ideology* which argues that in Wordsworth's version of the pastoral the Virgilian antinomies of painful and pleasurable labor collapse into the composite figure of a mythic, Lake District shepherd, in whose occupation Wordsworth "was able to reconcile his own poetic program with a philosophical view of the work that transcended and obscured the social issues" (281).

5. In *The Formal Method in Literary Scholarship*, Bakhtin defines the ideological environment as the "realized, materialized, externally expressed social consciousness of a

given collective" which is unique to the network of social relations specific to any given historical moment (14).

6. For a detailed analysis and description of Wordsworth's composition and revision of "Resolution and Independence" see Jared Curtis's notes to The Cornell Wordsworth edition of the poem (*Poems* 123) and his *Wordsworth's Experiments with Tradition* (97–113).

7. See also Hartman (202–3).

8. Hartman points out the allusion to Matthew in *Wordsworth's Poetry* (202). See Don H. Bialostosky's comparison of "The Discharged Soldier" and "Resolution and Independence" in his *Making Tales* (162–67). Willard Spiegelman also compares these two solitaries in *Wordsworth's Heroes* (134–36).

9. As Bialostosky notes in his analysis of "Resolution and Independence," where we expect a clear lesson we get further ambivalence: the narrator "does not say on what occasions he will think of [the leech gatherer] or, more significantly, what thoughts the recollection of the leech-gatherer will bring to mind or what form those thoughts will take" (151). Similarly, in "Beyond the Imaginable: Wordsworth and Turner," Kroeber adds: "The moral [the narrator] draws, while comprehensible, is dubious enough and at least potentially so inadequate to what has gone before that we pause to question his summation . . ." (210).

10. The Wordsworths originally claimed their inheritance from Lowther in 1786. Although they first received word in June 1802 that Sir William Lowther, the cousin and now recent heir to Sir James Lowther, was willing to settle the Wordsworths' claim to the estate, their case was not resolved until 1803. Wordsworth was revising what Dorothy Wordsworth called "The Leech Gatherer" in June and July 1802. See her *Grasmere Journals* of 18 June 1802 and 2 and 4 July 1802 (138, 144–45).

Notes to Chapter Five

1. See David Ricardo, *Principles of Political Economy and Taxation*. Ricardo attacks the outdoor relief of the Old Poor Law thus: "The clear and direct tendency of the poor law, is in direct opposition to these [*laissez-faire*] obvious principles: it is not, as the legislature benevolently intended, to amend the condition of the poor, but to deteriorate the condition of both poor and rich; instead of making the poor rich, they are calculated to make the rich poor . . ." (126). Ricardo's treatise was originally published in 1817. Long before Ricardo and the workhouse test, Joseph Townsend's *Dissertation on the Poor Laws* had argued that the fear of scarcity offered the greatest incentive to industry: "To promote industry and economy, it is necessary that the relief given to the poor should be limited and precarious" (62).

2. In *Industrial England 1776–1851*, Dorothy Marshall notes that the Poor Law Amendment Act of 1834 weakened the power of parish authorities to determine who would receive poor relief (187-88).

3. Ivanka Kovacevic's *Fact into Fiction: English Literature and the Industrial Scene 1750–1850* demonstrates that throughout the nineteenth century what she calls the "gospel of self help" became a means to reduce the obligations of the rich to the poor by encouraging *laissez-faire* attitudes toward the problems of poor relief.

4. I am indebted to Professor Jay Fliegelman of Stanford University for this observation.

5. See my "Wordsworth's 'The Old Cumberland Beggar': The Economy of Charity in Late Eighteenth-Century Britain."

6. See, for example, her entries in the *Grasmere Journals* of 14 and 15 May 1800; 10 and 20 June 1800; 12 February 1802; and 30 June 1802.

7. Coleridge was aware of Wordsworth's propensity for condescension and hasty generalization about the poor. In *Biographia Literaria*, Coleridge complains that Wordsworth's "Gipsies" displays an insensitive indignation toward the gypsies' apparent idleness (259). Moreover, in *Table Talk* of 16 February 1833, Coleridge writes that Wordsworth shares with Goethe the "peculiarity of utter non-sympathy" with the rustic subjects of his poetry; Coleridge defines Wordsworth's narratological presence in the poems as that of the *spectator ab extra* who feels "for, never with" his characters (qtd. in Lindenberger 206). See Herbert Lindenberger's discussion of the *spectator ab extra* in his chapter "Visionary Aloofness" (205–31)

8. See *Journals* (71,121). Roger Sales, in *English Literature in History 1780–1830: Pastoral and Politics*, interprets the encounter described in the 22 December 1801 entry as an illustration of the Wordsworths' paternalistic attitudes toward the poor (64–65). Like Simpson's early essay "Criticism, Politics and Style in Wordsworth's Poetry," Sales's analysis does not consider the weight of ideological discourse in setting limits upon the practice of charity. In a related discussion of "Point Rash-Judgment," Michael Friedman discerns Wordsworth's uncritical acceptance of an "internalized code" that governs social relations and gives rise to his apparent condescending treatment of the old laborer in the poem. See Friedman's argument in *The Making of a Tory Humanist* (191–92).

9. Such duty, as I will discuss, was advised in Sarah Trimmer's *Oeconomy of Charity*, which, as Gittings and Manton point out, guided Dorothy Wordsworth in her Sunday school and in her plans for setting up a School of Industry (24–25).

10. Wordsworth's "obstinate questioning" of the poor is often reflected in the moments of encounter between a narrator and a vagrant in his poetry. This characteristic feature of Wordsworth's poetry led Lewis Carroll to parody in the Knight's song of *Through the Looking Glass* Wordsworth's poetic treatment of the beggar in "Resolution and Independence." The Knight's song begins:

    > I'll tell thee everything I can,
    >   There's little to relate.
    > I saw an aged aged man,
    >   A-sitting on a gate.
    > 'Who are you, aged man?" I said.
    >   And how is it you live?'
    > And his answer trickled through my head,
    >   Like water through a sieve.

    The Knight's song suggests that the narrator is less interested in the beggar's tale than in how that tale may further the narrator's own intentions. The quoted stanza appears in *Through the Looking Glass and What Alice Found There* (133).

11. In distinguishing between reason and feeling, Steele splits into two distinct categories what later in the century will be fused in what R. F. Brissenden calls the "reasonable feeling" of the sentimental. As Brissenden comments in *Virtue in Distress*, the idea of a "necessarily reasonable feeling" found in sentimentalism "helped to provide the basis for a liberal and a revolutionary ideology—humanist, anti-authoritarian and compassionate . . . but at the same time, in the flattering picture it offered of man both as essentially benevolent and good natured and as potentially weak, it provided a means of evading the very problems to which it apparently offered a solution and of evading them in a peculiarly subtle and self-gratifying manner" (55). Compare Wordsworth's use of the term "rational sympathy" in the Preface to *Lyrical Ballads*.

12. Henry Fielding recognized that contempt for the poor stemmed from the relative invisibility of those who were not in need. In a pamphlet of 1753 describing a plan for relief of the poor in houses of industry, Fielding writes: "The sufferings of the Poor are

indeed less observed than their mis-deeds; not from any want of compassion, but because they are less known; and this is the true reason why we hear them so often mentioned with abhorrence, and so seldom with pity. They starve, and freeze, and rot among themselves; but they beg, and steal, and rob among their betters" (qtd. in Eden 1: 329). Closer to Wordsworth's time, John Coakley Lettsom echoes Fielding's concerns in his *Hints Reflecting the Distresses of the Poor* (1795). Lettsom defends the poor against accusations of improvidence, noting that one drunk brings more attention than a thousand deserving and industrious poor. He adds, "cruel would it be, as it is injust, to censure a whole class for the misconduct of a few individuals" (4).

13. In this parody, a "friend of humanity," like one of those prying Wordsworthian narrators, solicits a sentimental tale from a somewhat incredulous (and as it turns out, undeserving) knife grinder:

> Drops of compassion tremble on my eyelids,
> Ready to fall as soon as you have told your
> Pitiful story. (18–20)

To his utter disgust, the friend of humanity learns from his new acquaintance that there is no pitiful story to tell. Upsetting the philanthropist's expectations, the knife grinder replies that his troubles come from drinking and not from the injustice of an abusive task-master:

> Only last night a-drinking at the Chequers,
> This poor old hat and breeches, as you see, were
> Torn in a scuffle. (22–25)

Outraged, the friend of humanity, in Canning's satiric endnote to the poem, "[k]icks the Knife-grinder, overturns his wheel, and exit[s] in a transport of Republican enthusiasm and universal philanthropy" (16). Canning's parody reflects the reaction against reformist and radical challenges to private charity and the system of paternalistic deference on which it depended. Nevertheless, it calls out a basic contradiction in those advocates of "universal benevolence" who nonetheless expected the poor to deport themselves in a manner appropriate to middle-class expectations.

14. In *The Making of a Tory Humanist*, Friedman uses these terms to distinguish between the "actual material power to influence and change events and people" and the imaginative power to "alter the world not by changing it physically, but by projecting emotional colorations outward onto the world" (61).

15. In *The Visionary Company*, Harold Bloom claims that "Wordsworth's best poetry has nothing to do with social justice, as Blake's or Shelley's frequently does" (176). In *Wordsworth's Second Nature*, James Chandler rightly argues that Bloom's position on "The Old Cumberland Beggar" "emerges from and contributes to" an erroneous reading of Wordsworth that has "been too intent on seeing him as a prophetic visionary to recognize certain earthly facts about his political and intellectual allegiances" (84).

16. See Chandler's fine analysis of Wordsworth's adoption of Burkean principles in "The Old Cumberland Beggar" in *Wordsworth's Second Nature* (85–89).

17. The *Monthly Magazine*, edited by Dr. Aikin, was one of the most popular of the moderate reformist periodicals of the 1790s. In 1797, for example, it had a circulation of 5,000—equaled only by the *Monthly Review*—and it numbered Wordsworth and Coleridge among its contributors. See Richard Altick's *The English Common Reader* for more on the *Monthly Magazine* (392). Moorman describes Wordsworth's interest in the *Monthly Magazine* in *William Wordsworth* (1: 347). Wordsworth's own comments on the *Monthly Magazine* appear in the letters collected in *EY* (167, 186n. and 218n.)

18. Charles F. Bahmueller points out that Bentham attacked the Acts of Settlement for setting up obstacles to the movement of labor and violating the personal liberty of

workers. Nonetheless, Bentham advocated that infant children of the poor should be tattooed with their place of residence—stamped with an official birth mark, as it were, in the interests of social control. Moreover, with respect to a pauper's feelings, Bentham says that when a place of settlement is in doubt he or she should be allowed to choose between the two. Bahmueller explains the contradictions in Bentham's position: "Bentham . . . was capable of exquisite sensitivity to the privations and injustices inflicted on the poor; but he could be equally callous and manipulative. In this instance the feelings of the pauper would, he tells us, be respected. . . . But what was that choice to be? He could choose which of Bentham's workhouses he wished to enter—workhouses where he would be held prisoner and in most cases under conditions of the most intense discipline" (28).

19. In *Stress and Stability in Late Eighteenth-Century Britain*, Ian Christie emphasizes the Poor Law was generally conceived to provide education, comfort, reformation and work rather than punishment for the poor, despite the punitive and disciplinary language of some of its clauses. Moreover: "Of a piece with this general conception of the Poor Law was the fact that receipt of public relief was an accepted part of life for a large minority of the population, was regarded as a right, and carried little of the stigma later fixed upon it as a deliberate policy by the poor-law reformers of the nineteenth century" (98).

20. I don't see "Simon Lee" as a poem in which the narrator celebrates the servile gratitude of the incapacitated old man. Simon Lee's gratitude arises, in my way of reading the poem, from the sheer rarity of the charitable action. Thus, his "tears . . . / And thanks and praises" (89–90; *PW* 4: 64) lead the narrator to think of "hearts unkind, kind deeds / With coldness still returning" (93–94; 4: 64)—that is, to think of a community in which reciprocal acts of kindness do not occur at all, because people, like Harry Gill, act only out of self-interest. Simon Lee's gratitude leaves the narrator mourning, because its excess suggests that such acts of kindness are the exception rather than the rule.

21. In *The World We Have Lost*, Peter Laslett points out that those subordinate to patriarchal authority, whether exercised by a father, landlord, parson or parish magistrate, adopted the practices of their masters. Thus, independence from higher authority was only possible within the framework of practice established by that authority. Laslett writes: " 'Subsumption' . . . was a very widespread characteristic of traditional society and it could well be extended to cover the relationship between the great household in a village community and the ring of smaller households ranged around it, sited on the landlord's estate, engaged for the most part in working his land" (20–21).

22. In *Vision and Disenchantment*, Heather Glen argues that the beggar becomes a cipher of difference suggesting the impossibility of community. In her view, the villagers share only the illusion of community, since their private acts of charity, motivated by habit and not conscious choice, simply reproduce the "paternalistic distancing" of a society based upon individual, not communal, acts of self-congratulating charity. Glen notes that "The Old Cumberland Beggar" attempts "to trace some way in which, even in a society based on inequality, unconsidered and habitual acts of individual charity might lead without conflict towards positive social feeling on a wider scale" (83).

23. See Glen (83).

Notes to the Postscript

1. See *The Making of the English Working Class*, especially chapters 2, 11 and 16.

2. In his *Autobiography*, Place gives tribute to his moral instructor Mr. Bowis:

How much I owed to my good master Mr. Bowis for his moral instruction, for the confidence he taught me to repose in myself and especially in
whatever I believed to be true; for the notions of perseverance he caused me to
imbibe, of perseverance under difficulties and a reliance on honest industry it is
impossible for me to determine, but I regard his instructions as laying the
foundation of much of the happiness and prosperity I have enjoyed. (61)

3. In his introduction to *Historical Studies and Literary Criticism,* McGann conceives the
socio-historical project as an attempt to recuperate two interlocking histories of a text;
the first derives from the author's expressed decisions and purposes; the second, from
the critical and I would add practical reactions to and uses of the poem's various
audiences (see esp. 4–5). We need to attend to the poem's "point of origin," in
McGann's view, and to its "point of reception" (16). On the latter end: "Once the
poem passes entirely beyond the purposive control of the author, it leaves the pole of
its origin and establishes the first phase of its later dialectical life, what we call its
critical history" (17). In this brief postscript I present a broad overview of Wordsworth's social text in terms of its *critical* and, one might say, its *practical* receptive
history.

4. In a letter to Thomas Robinson, 6 June 1802, Henry wrote of Goody Blake: "The
following stanza, 'Oh joy for her,' is exquisite as well as the whole a most pathetically
poetical display of poverty" (qtd. in Newton 60).

5. John O. Hayden has noted that some reviewers rose to defend Wordsworth's representations of the poor based on their sense that "northern rustics were of a different breed
from the lower orders to the South . . . " (*Romantic Reviewers* 89). Hazlitt, however,
tried to settle that issue in an *Examiner* essay, where he presented firsthand testimony
that "[i]f the inhabitants of the mountainous districts described by Mr. Wordsworth,
are less gross and sensual than other, they are more selfish" (*Examiner,* 2 October
1814, 638; qtd. in *Romantic Reviewers* 89).

6. Historians and critics have already given us a glimpse at some of the influences of
Wordsworth on the Victorian reading public. In *Paternalism in Early Victorian England*
(66–67), for example, David Roberts describes briefly Wordsworth's influence on the
Young England movement. Amy Cruse's *The Victorians and Their Reading* (174–86)
offers a short but broad survey of Victorian readers' comments on Wordsworth, and
Herbert Lindenberger's "The Reception of *The Prelude*" summarizes in detail the
Victorian reaction to the publication of that poem. See also Leon Howard, *MLN* 48
(1933) and Lewis Leary, *MLN* 58 (1943), and more recently Carl Woodring's "Wordsworth Among the Victorians" and David Simpson's "Wordsworth in America."

7. In *Wordsworth's Second Nature*, Chandler convincingly argues that Wordsworth's
theory of education differs from Rousseau's. Whereas Rousseau believes that reason
must guide the direction of human culture toward natural principles, Wordsworth
believes the reverse. Chandler shows that Wordsworth fears that "the very effort to
systematize culture" will subvert the providential order (118). Nonetheless, Wordsworth does believe that books can mediate such natural lore—especially here, as we
see, for educating industrial workers to moral sentiments. See Chandler's Chapter 6
(esp. 140–44).

8. Altick suggests that the price of books would have kept Wordsworth's works primarily
in the homes of the middle and upper classes, at least until after the mid-nineteenth
century. While low-priced editions of the classic English poets were available by mid-
century, Altick claims, "nineteenth-century writers [such] as Hood, Shelley, Coleridge, Wordsworth, and Moore . . . seldom turned up on the stalls" (253).

9. See also Thomas Raysor, who notes that conservative journals like *Blackwood's*, the
Quarterly Review, *The Critical Review* and *The British Critic* were more sympathetic
to Wordsworth's poetry than the more liberal journals (62).

10. In her chapter titled "The Tory Opposition: Paternalism and Humanitarianism," Himmelfarb explains that *Blackwood's* and the *Quarterly*, the journals which engineered Wordsworth's makeover into a Victorian don, denounced the New Poor Law on grounds similar to those we've seen Wordsworth taking here. Despite small differences among the journals, the Tory position against the New Poor Law was unified in its humanitiarianism and paternalism. As an alternative to the New Poor Law, which in the Tory view was turning poverty into a crime and paupers into dehumanized criminals, *Blackwood's*, the *Quarterly* and other Tory mouthpieces advocated a return to that "ancient spirit" of charity described in Chapter Four. As Himmelfarb explains it,

> To the traditional-minded Tory, poverty, so far from being a crime, was . . . a natural condition to be alleviated by the charity of those who, by the grace of God and their own efforts, were happily able to afford it, and by a public system of relief which testified to the obligation of society to care for those who were so unfortunate as to be unable to care for themselves. This paternalistic creed survived long after political economy had pronounced it dead. It was a creed which spoke of "rights" and "obligations" as uninhibitedly as it spoke of "rich" and "poor." (182–83)

11. In his autobiography, William Lovett, secretary for the London Working Men's Association and drafter of the People's Charter, claimed that W. J. Fox was "among the most prominent and talented of our [the Working Men's Association's] lecturers" (*Life* 239).

12. Altick points out that Burt often read from Wordsworth's poetry to small audiences gathered near the House of Commons Library (249).

Works Cited

Abrams, M. H. "*On Political Readings of* Lyrical Ballads." *Doing Things With Texts: Essays in Criticism and Critical Theory*. Ed. Michael Fischer. New York and London: W. W. Norton, 1989. 364–91.

Adorno, Theodor. "Lyric Poetry and Society." *Telos* 20 (Summer 1974): 56–71.

Aikin, John. *A Description of the Country from Thirty to Forty Miles Round Manchester*. London, 1795.

———. Rev. of William Wordsworth, *Lyrical Ballads. The Monthly Review* 29 (June 1799): 202–10.

Althusser, Louis. "Ideology and Ideological State Apparatuses: Notes Towards an Investigation." *Lenin and Philosophy and Other Essays by Louis Althusser*. Trans. Ben Brewster. New York and London: Monthly Review, 1971. 127–86.

Altick, Richard. *The English Common Reader: A Social History of the Mass Reading Public 1800–1900*. Chicago: Univ. of Chicago Press, 1983.

Andrews, Malcolm. *The Search for the Picturesque: Landscape Aesthetic and Tourism in Britain, 1760–1800*. Stanford: Stanford Univ. Press, 1989.

Arch, Joseph. *The Autobiography of Joseph Arch*. 1898. Reprint. London: MacGibbon and Kee, 1966.

Armstrong, Alan. *Farmworkers in England and Wales: A Social and Economic History, 1770–1980*. Ames: Iowa State Univ. Press, 1988.

Armstrong, W. A. "The Countryside." *Regions and Communities*. Vol. 1 of *The Cambridge Social History of Britain 1750–1950*. Ed. F. M. L. Thompson. 3 vols. Cambridge: Cambridge Univ. Press, 1990. 87–185.

Arnold, Matthew. Address to the Wordsworth Society, 2 May 1883. *Transactions of the Wordsworth Society* 5 (n.d.). Reprint. London: Dawson and Sons, 1966. 4–8.

———. *The Poems of Matthew Arnold*. Ed. Kenneth and Miriam Allott. 2nd ed. 1965. London and New York: Longman, 1979.

Austen, Jane. *Emma*. Ed. James Kinsley and David Lodge. 1971. The World's Classics. Oxford and New York: Oxford Univ. Press, 1980.

Bahmueller, Charles F. *The National Charity Company: Jeremy Bentham's Silent Revolution*. Berkeley: Univ. of California Press, 1981.

Bakhtin, M. M. *The Dialogic Imagination: Four Essays*. Ed. Michael Holquist. Trans. Caryl Emerson and Michael Holquist. Austin: Univ. of Texas Press, 1981.

———. *The Formal Method in Literary Scholarship: A Critical Introduction to Sociological Poetics*. Trans. Albert J. Wehrle. Cambridge: Harvard Univ. Press, 1985.

Barbauld, Anna Laetitia. "An Inquiry into Those Kinds of Distress Which Excite Agreeable Sensations." *Miscellaneous Pieces in Prose*. Ed. John and Lucy Aikin. London: 1775. (Reprinted in *Works*. Vol. 2. 214–31.)

———. *The Works of Anna Laetitia Barbauld*. 2 vols. London, 1825.

Barrell, John. *The Dark Side of the Landscape: The Rural Poor in English Painting 1730–1840*. 1980. Cambridge: Cambridge Univ. Press, 1985.

———. *English Literature in History: 1730–80. An Equal, Wide Survey*. London: Hutchinson, 1983.

Baudrillard, Jean. *The Mirror of Production*. Trans. Mark Poster. St. Louis: Telos, 1975.

Beattie, James. *The Minstrel*. 1771. Reprint. London: George Routledge, 1858.

Belsey, Catherine. *Critical Practice*. London: Methuen, 1980.

Bendix, Reinhard. *Work and Authority in Industry: Ideologies of Management in The Course of Industrialization*. 1956. Berkeley: Univ. of California Press, 1974.

Benjamin, Walter. "The Storyteller." *Illuminations*. Ed. Hannah Arendt. Trans. Harry Zohn. 1955. New York: Schocken, 1968. 83–109.

Bentham, Jeremy. "Observations on the Poor Bill, introduced by the Right Honourable William Pitt." [1797; published 1838.] (Reprinted in *Works*. Vol. 8. 440–61.)

———. *The Theory of Legislation*. Ed. C. K. Ogden. Trans. Richard Hildreth. 1931. Reprint. London: Routledge and Kegan Paul, 1950.

———. *The Works of Jeremy Bentham*. Ed. John Bowring. 11 vols. 1838–43. Reprint. New York: Russell and Russell, 1962.

Bermingham, Ann. *Landscape and Ideology: The English Rustic Tradition, 1740–1860*. Berkeley: Univ. of California Press, 1986.

Bernard, Thomas. *Of the Education of the Poor; Being the First Part of A Digest of the Reports of the Society for Bettering the Condition of the Poor*. 1809. Reprint. London: The Woburn Press, 1970.

Bewell, Alan. *Wordsworth and the Enlightenment: Nature, Man and Society in the Experimental Poetry*. New Haven and London: Yale Univ. Press, 1989.

Bewick, Thomas. *1800 Woodcuts by Thomas Bewick and His School*. Ed. Blanche Cirker and the Editorial Staff of Dover Publications. New York: Dover, 1962.

Bialostosky, Don H. *Making Tales: The Poetics of Wordsworth's Narrative Experiments*. Chicago: Univ. of Chicago Press, 1984.

Blackwell, Thomas. *An Enquiry into the Life and Writings of Homer*. London, 1735.

Bloch, Ernst. *The Principle of Hope*. Trans. Neville Plaice, Stephen Plaice and Paul Knight. 3 vols. London: Basil Blackwell; Cambridge: Mass.: The M.I.T. Press, 1986.

Bloom, Harold. *The Visionary Company: A Reading of English Romantic Poetry*. Ithaca: Cornell Univ. Press, 1971.

Bostetter, Edward. *The Romantic Ventriloquists: Wordsworth, Coleridge, Keats, Shelley, Byron*. Seattle: Univ. of Washington Press, 1975.

Briggs, Marc. "The Isolation of the Poet in *The Prelude*." Unpublished essay, 1989.

Brissenden, R. F. *Virtue in Distress: Studies in the Novel of Sentiment from Richardson to Sade*. London: Macmillan, 1974.

Browning, Elizabeth Barrett. *Aurora Leigh: A Poem in Five Books*. New York: C. S. Francis, 1857.

Brownson, Orestes A. "Wordsworth." *The Boston Quarterly Review* (April 1839): 137–68. (Reprinted in *The Transcendentalists: An Anthology*. Ed. Perry Miller. Cambridge: Harvard Univ. Press, 1950. 434–36.)

Burke, Edmund. *An Appeal from the New to the Old Whigs, in Consequence of Some Late Discussions in Parliament, Relative to the Reflections on the French Revolution*. London, 1791.

———. *A Philosophical Enquiry into the Origin of Our Ideas of the Sublime and Beautiful*. Ed. J. T. Boulton. Notre Dame: Univ. of Notre Dame Press, 1958.

Works Cited

————. *Reflections on the Revolution in France*. Ed. Conor Cruise O'Brien. 1968. Harmondsworth: Penguin, 1982.

————. *Thoughts and Details on Scarcity, Originally Presented to the Right Hon. William Pitt in the Month of November, 1795*. London, 1800. (See also *Works*. Vol. 7. 373–419.)

————. *The Works of the Right Honourable Edmund Burke*. 16 vols. London, 1826–27.

Burn, Richard. *Observations on the Bill Intended to be offered to Parliament for the Better Relief and Employment of the Poor*. London, 1776.

Burns, Robert. *Poems and Songs*. Ed. James Kinsley. 1969. Oxford and New York: Oxford Univ. Press, 1990.

Burt, Thomas. *Thomas Burt: An Autobiography*. London: T. Fisher Unwin, 1924.

Bushaway, Robert W. *By Rite: Custom, Ceremony and Community in England, 1700–1880*. London: Junction Books, 1982.

Butler, James. "Introduction." *The Ruined Cottage and The Pedlar by William Wordsworth*. Ed. Butler. The Cornell Wordsworth. Ithaca: Cornell Univ. Press, 1979. 1–35.

Butler, Marilyn. *Romantics, Rebels & Reactionaries: English Literature and Its Background 1760–1830*. Oxford: Oxford Univ. Press, 1981.

Byron, George Gordon. *Don Juan*. Ed. T. G. Steffan, E. Steffan, and W. W. Pratt. 1973. New Haven and London: Yale Univ. Press, 1982.

Canning, George. "Sapphics: The Friend of Humanity and the Knife Grinder." *The Anti-Jacobin* 1 (27 November 1798): 15-16.

Carlyle, Thomas. *On Heroes, Hero Worship, and the Heroic in History*. 1897. Reprint. New York: AMS Press, 1969.

Carroll, David. "Rephrasing the Political with Kant and Lyotard: From Aesthetic to Political Judgments." *Diacritics* (Fall 1984): 74–88.

Carroll, Lewis. *Through the Looking Glass and What Alice Found There*. New York: Random House, 1965.

Chandler, James. *Wordsworth's Second Nature: A Study of the Poetry and Politics*. Chicago and London: Univ. of Chicago Press, 1984.

Channing, William Ellery. *The Works of William E. Channing, D.D.* 10th ed. 6 vols. Boston, 1849.

Christie, Ian R. *Stress and Stability in Late Eighteenth-Century Britain: Reflections on the British Avoidance of Revolution*. The Ford Lectures Delivered at the University of Oxford 1983–1984. Oxford: Clarendon, 1984.

————. *Wars and Revolutions: Britain 1760–1815*. The New History of England 7. Ed. A. G. Dickens and Norman Gash. London: Edward Arnold, 1982.

Clark, J. C. D. *English Society 1688–1832: Ideology, Social Structure and Political Practice During the Ancien Regime*. Cambridge Studies in the History and Theory of Politics. Ed. Maurice Cowling, G. R. Elton and J. R. Pole. Cambridge: Cambridge Univ. Press, 1985.

Cole, G. D. H. and A. W. Filson, eds. *British Working Class Movements: Select Documents 1789–1875*. London: Macmillan; New York: St. Martin's, 1967.

Cole, G. D. H., and Raymond Postgate. *The British Common People 1746–1938*. New York: Alfred Knopf, 1939.

Coleridge, Samuel Taylor. *Biographia Literaria*. Ed. George Watson. 1906. Reprint. London: J. M. Dent; New York: E. P. Dutton, 1965.

Colquhoun, Patrick. *Treatise on Indigence*. London, 1806.

A Compendium of the Laws Respecting the Poor. London, 1803.

Conran, Anthony. "The Dialectic of Experience: A Study of Wordsworth's 'Resolution and Independence.' " *PMLA* 75 (March 1960): 66–74.

Cowper, William. *Letters 1787–1791.* Vol. 3 of *The Letters and Prose Writings of William Cowper.* Ed. James King and Charles Ryskamp. 5 vols. Oxford: Clarendon, 1982.

———. *The Poetical Works of William Cowper.* Ed. George Gilfillan. 2 vols. Edinburgh, 1854.

———. *The Task, A Poem in Six Books.* London, 1785.

Crabbe, George. *The Complete Poetical Works.* Ed. Norma Dalrymple-Champneys and Arthur Pollard. 3 vols. Oxford: Clarendon, 1988.

———. *The Parish Register. The Complete Poetical Works.* Vol. 1. 212–80.

———. *The Village. The Complete Poetical Works.* Vol. 1. 157–74.

Cruse, Amy. *The Victorians and Their Reading.* Boston: Houghton Mifflin; Cambridge: Riverside Press, n.d.

Curtis, Jared. *Wordsworth's Experiments with Tradition: The Lyric Poems of 1802.* Ithaca and London: Cornell Univ. Press, 1971.

Davies, David. *The Case of Labourers in Husbandry Stated and Considered with an Appendix Containing a Collection of Accounts Shewing the Earnings and Expenses of labouring Families in Different Parts of the Kingdom.* 1795. Reprint. Fairfield, N.J.: Augustus M. Kelley, 1977.

Davies, Hughe Sykes. *Wordsworth and the Worth of Words.* Ed. John Kerrigan and Jonathan Wordsworth. Cambridge: Cambridge Univ. Press, 1986.

Debord, Guy. *Society of Spectacle.* Detroit: Black and Red, 1977.

De Bruyn, Frans. "Edmund Burke's Natural Aristocrat: The 'Man of Taste' as a Political Ideal." *Eighteenth Century Life* (May 1987): 41–60.

De Certeau, Michel. *The Practice of Everyday Life.* Trans. Steven Rendall. 1984. Reprint. Berkeley: Univ. of California Press, 1988.

DeLeuze, Gilles, and Felix Guattari. *A Thousand Plateaus: Capitalism and Schizophrenia.* Trans. Brian Massumi. Minneapolis, Minn.: Univ. of Minnesota Press, 1987.

Dyer, George. *A Dissertation on the Theory and Practice of Benevolence.* London, 1795.

———. *The Poet's Fate, a Poetical Dialogue.* 2nd ed. London, 1797.

Eagleton, Terry. *The Ideology of the Aesthetic.* London: Basil Blackwell, 1990.

Eden, Frederick Morton. *The State of the Poor.* 3 vols. 1797. Reprint. London: Frank Cass, 1977.

Ehrenpreis, Irvin. "Poverty and Poetry: Representation of the Poor in Augustan Literature." *Studies in Eighteenth Century Culture: The Modernity of the Eighteenth Century.* Ed. Louis T. Milic. Cleveland: Case Western Reserve Univ. Press, 1971. 3–35.

Eliot, George. *Silas Marner: The Weaver of Raveloe.* Harmondsworth: Penguin, 1967.

Emsley, Clive. *British Society and the French Wars: 1793-1815.* London: Macmillan, 1979; Totowa, N.J.: Rowman and Littlefield, 1979.

Engels, Friedrich. *Socialism: Utopian and Scientific. Karl Marx and Friedrich Engels, Basic Writings on Politics and Philosophy.* Ed. Lewis S. Feuer. Garden City, N.Y.: Anchor Doubleday, 1959. 68–111.

Fabricant, Carol. "The Aesthetics and Politics of Landscape in the Eighteenth Century." *Studies in Eighteenth-Century British Art and Aesthetics.* Ed. Ralph Cohen. Berkeley: Univ. of California Press, 1985. 49–81.

Feingold, Richard. *Nature and Society: Later Eighteenth-Century Uses of the Pastoral and Georgic.* New Brunswick: Rutgers Univ. Press, 1978.

Foster, Birket. *Beauties of English Landscape.* London, 1874.

Foucault, Michel. *The Order of Things: An Archaeology of the Human Sciences.* 1970. New York: Vintage Books, 1973.

Fox, W. J. *Lectures Addressed Chiefly to the Working Classes*. 4 vols. London, 1845.

Friedman, Michael. *The Making of a Tory Humanist: Wordsworth and the Idea of Community*. New York: Columbia Univ. Press, 1979.

Gaskell, Elizabeth. *North and South*. Ed. Dorothy Collin. Harmondsworth: Penguin, 1970.

Geertz, Clifford. "The Impact of the Concept of Culture on the Concept of Man." *New Views of the Nature of Man*. Ed. J. Platt. Chicago: Univ. of Chicago Press, 1966. (Reprinted in Clifford Geertz, *The Interpretation of Cultures: Selected Essays by Clifford Geertz*. New York: Basic Books, 1973. 33-54.)

Gill, Stephen. "Introduction." *The Salisbury Plain Poems of William Wordsworth*. Ed. Gill. The Cornell Wordsworth. Ithaca: Cornell Univ. Press, 1975. 3–16.

Gilpin, William. *Observations on the River Wye, and Several Parts of South Wales, &c, Relative Chiefly to Picturesque Beauty; Made in the Summer of the Year 1770*. London, 1782.

———. *Observations on the Western Parts of England, Relative Chiefly to Picturesque Beauty. To Which are Added, a Few Remarks on the Picturesque Beauties of the Isle of Wight*. London, 1798.

———. *Observations, Relative Chiefly to Picturesque Beauty, Made in the Year 1772; on Several Parts of England; Particularly the Mountains, and Lakes of Cumberland and Westmorland*. 2 vols. London, 1786.

———. *Three Essays on Picturesque Beauty; On Picturesque Travel; and on Sketching Landscape: To Which is Added a Poem, on Landscape Painting*. London, 1792.

Gittings, Robert, and Jo Manton. *Dorothy Wordsworth*. Clarendon: Oxford Univ. Press, 1985.

Glen, Heather. *Vision and Disenchantment: Blake's Songs of Innocence and Wordsworth's Lyrical Ballads*. Cambridge: Cambridge Univ. Press, 1983.

Glover, Rev. George. *Observations on the Present State of Pauperism in England, Particularly as it Affects the Morals and Character of the Labouring Poor*. London, 1817.

Godwin, William. *Caleb Williams, or Things as They Are*. Ed. Maurice Hindle. Harmondsworth: Penguin, 1988.

———. *Enquiry Concerning Political Justice and its Influence on Modern Morals and Happiness*. 1976. Harmondsworth: Penguin, 1985.

Goldsmith, Oliver. *The Deserted Village. The Poems of Gray, Collins and Goldsmith*. Ed. Roger Londsdale. London: Longman, 1969. 669–94.

———. *The Traveller, or A Prospect of Society. The Poems of Gray, Collins and Goldsmith*. Ed. Roger Londsdale. London: Longman, 1969. 622–57.

———. *The Vicar of Wakefield*. Ed. Stephen Coote. Harmondsworth: Penguin, 1982.

Gray, B. Kirkman. *A History of English Philanthropy: From the Dissolution of the Monasteries to the taking of the First Census*. 1905. Reprint. New York: Augustus M. Kelley, 1967.

Green, William. *Plans of Economy, or the Road to Ease and Independence*. London, 1803.

Gregory, George. *The Life of Chatterton*. London, 1789.

Grob, Alan. "Process and Permanence in 'Resolution and Independence.' " *ELH* 28 (1961): 89–100.

Harper, George McLean. *William Wordsworth: His Life, Works, and Influence*. 2 vols. London: J. Murray, 1916.

Harrison, Gary. "Wordsworth's Leech Gatherer: Liminal Power and 'The Spirit of Independence.' " *ELH* 56 (Summer 1989): 327–50.

————. "Wordsworth's 'The Old Cumberland Beggar': The Economy of Charity in Late Eighteenth-Century Britain." *Criticism* 30 (Winter 1988): 23–42.

Harrison, Mark. "The Ordering of the Urban Environment: Time, Work and the Occurrence of Crowds 1790–1835." *Past and Present* 110 (February 1986): 134–68.

Hartley, Lodwick C. *William Cowper: Humanitarian*. Chapel Hill: Univ. of North Carolina Press, 1938.

Hartman, Geoffrey. *Wordsworth's Poetry: 1787–1814*. New Haven: Yale Univ. Press, 1964.

Harvey, A. D. *English Poetry in a Changing Society 1780-1825*. Ithaca: Cornell Univ. Press, 1974.

Hatch, Ronald B. *Crabbe's Arabesque: Social Drama in the Poetry of George Crabbe*. Montreal and London: McGill-Queen's Univ. Press, 1976.

Hayden, John O. *Romantic Bards and British Reviewers. A Selected Edition of the Contemporary Reviews of the Works of Wordsworth, Coleridge, Byron, Keats and Shelley*. Lincoln: Univ. of Nebraska Press, 1971.

————. *The Romantic Reviewers, 1802–1804*. Chicago: Univ. of Chicago Press, 1968.

Hazlitt, William. *The Spirit of the Age, or Contemporary Portraits*. 1904. The World's Classics. London: Oxford Univ. Press, 1970.

Heinzelman, Kurt. *The Economics of the Imagination*. Amherst: Univ. of Massachussets Press, 1980.

Himmelfarb, Gertrude. *The Idea of Poverty: England in the Early Industrial Age*. New York: Alfred A. Knopf, 1984.

Horkheimer, Max, and Theodor W. Adorno. *The Dialectic of Enlightenment*. Trans. John Cumming. 1944. New York: Continuum, 1982.

Howard, Leon. *Wordsworth in America. MLN* 48 (1933): 359–65.

Howitt, William. *The Rural Life of England*. 2nd ed. London, 1840.

————. "William Wordsworth." *The People's Journal* (24 January 1846): 43–44.

Hunter, Ian. "Reading Character." *Southern Review* 16 (July 1983): 226–43.

Hyde, Lewis. *The Gift: Imagination and the Erotic Life of Property*. 1979. New York: Random House, 1983.

————. "Some Food We Could Not Eat: Gift Exchange and the Imagination." *Kenyon Review* 1 (1979): 32–60.

Inchbald, Elizabeth. *A Simple Story; and Nature and Art*. London: Thomas de la Rue, 1880.

Jacobus, Mary. *Tradition and Experiment in Wordsworth's* Lyrical Ballads (*1798*). Oxford: Clarendon, 1976.

Jarrett, Derek. *England in the Age of Hogarth*. 1974. Frogmore, St. Albans: Paladin, 1976.

Jeffrey, Francis. Rev. of George Crabbe, *Poems. The Edinburgh Review* 12 (April 1808): 131–51.

————. Rev. of William Wordsworth, *The Excursion. The Edinburgh Review* 24 (November 1814): 1–30.

Jenyns, Soame. *A Free Inquiry into the Nature of Evil*. 2nd ed. 1757. Reprint. New York: Garland, 1976.

Johnson, Samuel. *The Rambler*. Ed. W. J. Bate and Albrecht B. Strauss. Vol. 4 of The Yale Edition of the Works of Samuel Johnson. 15 vols. New Haven: Yale Univ. Press, 1969.

————. Rev. of Soame Jenyns's, *A Free Inquiry into the Nature of Evil. Literary Magazine* 2 (April-July 1757): 131–51, 251–53, 301–4.

Jordan, John E. *Why the Lyrical Ballads: The Background, Writing, and Character of Wordsworth's 1798* Lyrical Ballads. Berkeley: Univ. of California Press, 1976.

Kames, Henry Home. *Sketches of the History of Man*. 4 vols. Glasgow, 1802.

Kant, Immanuel. *Critique of Judgment*. Trans. J. H. Bernard. New York and London: Hafner, 1968.

Knapp, Stephen. *Personification and the Sublime: Milton to Coleridge*. Cambridge, Mass.: Harvard Univ. Press, 1985.

Kovacevic, Ivanka. *Fact into Fiction: English Literature and the Industrial Scene 1750–1850*. Leicester: Leicester Univ. and Univ. of Belgrade Press, 1975.

Kroeber, Karl. "Beyond the Imaginable: Wordsworth and Turner." *The Age of William Wordsworth: Critical Essays on the Romantic Tradition*. Ed. Kenneth R. Johnston and Gene W. Ruoff. New Brunswick and London: Rutgers Univ. Press, 1987. 196–213.

———. *Romantic Narrative Art*. Madison: Univ. of Wisconsin Press, 1960.

Lamb, Charles. Rev. of William Wordsworth, *The Excursion*. *The Quarterly Review* (October 1814): 100–111. (Reprinted in *Romantic Bards and British Reviewers*. Ed. John O. Hayden. 53–64.)

Lambert, Ellen Zetzel. *Placing Sorrow: A Study of the Pastoral Elegy Convention from Theocritus to Milton*. University of North Carolina Studies in Comparative Literature 60. Chapel Hill: Univ. of North Carolina Press, 1976.

Landes, David. *Revolution in Time: Clocks and the Making of the Modern World*. Cambridge, Mass.: Harvard Univ. Press, 1983.

Laqueur, Thomas Walter. *Religion and Respectability: Sunday Schools and Working Class Culture: 1780–1850*. New Haven: Yale Univ. Press, 1976.

Laslett, Peter. *The World We Have Lost: England Before the Industrial Age*. 2nd ed. New York: Charles Scribner's, 1971.

Leary, Lewis. "Wordsworth in America: Addenda." *MLN* 58 (1943): 391–93.

Letter. *Gentleman's Magazine* 67 Part 2 (October 1797): 819–20.

Letter. *The Monthly Magazine* 7 (January 1799): 27.

Letter. *The Monthly Magazine* 10 (Jun 1, 1800): 421–24.

Lettsom, John Coakley. *Hints Reflecting the Distresses of the Poor*. London, 1795.

Levinson, Marjorie. "The New Historicism: Back to the Future." *Rethinking Historicism: Critical Readings in Romantic History*. By Marjorie Levinson, Marilyn Butler, Jerome McGann and Paul Hamilton. London and New York: Basil Blackwell, 1989. 18–63.

———. *Wordsworth's Great Period Poems: Four Essays*. Cambridge: Cambridge Univ. Press, 1986.

Lindenberger, Herbert. *On Wordsworth's Prelude*. Princeton: Princeton Univ. Press, 1963.

———. "The Reception of *The Prelude*." *Bulletin of the New York Public Library* 64 (April 1960): 196–208.

Liu, Alan. *Wordsworth: The Sense of History*. Stanford: Stanford Univ. Press, 1989.

Lonsdale, Roger, ed. *The Poems of Gray, Collins and Goldsmith*. London: Longman, 1969.

Lovett, William. *Life and Struggles of William Lovett*. 1876. Reprint. London: MacGibbon and Kee, 1967.

Lyall, W. R. Rev. of William Wordsworth, *Poems*. *Quarterly Review* 14 (October 1815): 201–25 (Reprinted in *Romantic Bards and British Reviewers*. Ed. John O. Hayden. 71–85)

Lyotard, Jean-Francois. *The Differend: Phrases in Dispute*. Trans. Georges Van Den Abbeele. Theory and History of Literature 46. Minneapolis: Univ. of Minnesota Press, 1988.

McFarland, Thomas. *Romanticism and the Forms of Ruin: Wordsworth, Coleridge and Modalities of Fragmentation*. Princeton: Princeton Univ. Press, 1981.

McGann, Jerome J. "The Anachronism of George Crabbe." *The Beauty of Inflections: Literary Investigations in Historical Method and Theory.* Oxford: Clarendon, 1988. 294- 312.

———. *Historical Studies and Literary Criticism.* Madison: The Univ. of Wisconsin Press, 1985.

———. *The Romantic Ideology: A Critical Investigation.* Chicago: Univ. of Chicago Press, 1983.

Malthus, Thomas. *An Essay on the Principle of Population, as it Affects the Future Improvement of Society, with Remarks on the Speculations of Mr. Godwin, M. Condorcet, and Other Writers.* London, 1798.

Mannheim, Karl. *Ideology and Utopia: An Introduction to the Sociology of Knowledge.* Trans. Louis Wirth and Edward Shils. 1936. New York and London: Harcourt Brace Jovanovich, n.d.

Manning, Peter J. " 'My Former Thoughts Returned': Wordsworth's *Resolution and Independence.*" *Wordsworth Circle* 9 (1978): 398–405.

———. "Placing Poor Susan: Wordsworth and the New Historicism." *Studies in Romanticism* 25 (1986): 351–69.

Margarot, Maurice, and Thomas Hardy. "An Address to the Nation from the London Corresponding Society, on the Subject of a Thorough Parliamentary Reform." *British Working Class Movements: Select Documents 1789-1875.* Ed. G. D. H. Cole and A. W. Filson. London: Macmillan; New York: St. Martin's, 1967. 44–47.

Marshall, Dorothy. *Industrial England 1776–1851.* London: Routledge and Kegan Paul, 1973.

Mathias, Peter. *The First Industrial Nation: An Economic History of Britain 1700–1914.* 2nd ed. London and New York: Methuen, 1983.

Mauss, Marcel. *The Gift: Forms and Functions of Exchange in Archaic Societies.* Trans. Ian Cunnison. New York: W. W. Norton, 1967.

Mayo, Robert. "The Contemporaneity of the *Lyrical Ballads.*" *PMLA* 69 (June 1954): 486- 522.

Meyer, George W. " 'Resolution and Independence': Wordsworth's Answer to Coleridge's 'Dejection: An Ode.' " *Tulane Studies in English* 2 (1950): 49–74.

Mill, John Stuart. *Autobiography of John Stuart Mill.* 1873. New York: Columbia Univ. Press, 1924.

Milton, John. *Paradise Lost. The Poems of John Milton.* Ed. John Carey and Alastair Fowler. 1968. London: Longman; New York: W. W. Norton, 1972. 455–1060.

Moorman, Mary. *William Wordsworth: A Biography. The Early Years 1770–1803.* 2 vols. Clarendon: Oxford Univ. Press, 1957.

More, Hannah. *Strictures on the Modern System of Female Education, with a View of the Principles and Conduct Prevalent Among Women of Rank and Fortune.* 2 vols. London, 1799.

———. *Thoughts on the Importance of the Manners of the Great to General Society.* 4th ed. Philadelphia, 1788.

———. *The Works of Hannah More.* 4 vols. London, 1803.

Morton, A. L. *A People's History of England.* London: Lawrence and Wishart, 1979.

Mullan, John. *Sentiment and Sociability: The Language of Feeling in the Eighteenth Century.* Oxford: Clarendon; New York: Oxford Univ. Press, 1988.

Nelson, Beth. *George Crabbe and the Progress of Eighteenth-Century Narrative Verse.* Lewisburg: Bucknell Univ. Press; and London: Associated Univ. Press, 1976.

New, Peter. *George Crabbe's Poetry.* London: Macmillan, 1976.

Works Cited

Newton, Annabel. *Wordsworth in Early American Criticism*. Chicago: Univ. of Chicago Press, 1928.

Oastler, Richard. *The Fleet Papers*. 4 vols. London, 1841–44.

Our English Lakes, Mountains, and Waterfalls, as seen by William Wordsworth. Photographically Illustrated. (T. Ogle, photographer.) London: A. W. Bennett, 1864.

Owen, David. *English Philanthropy 1660–1960*. Cambridge: Harvard Univ. Press, 1964.

Paine, Thomas. *Rights of Man*. Ed. Henry Collins. 1969. Harmondsworth: Penguin, 1982.

Paley, William. *Natural Theology: or, Evidences of the Existence and Attributes of the Deity, Collected from the Appearances of Nature*. 1802. Boston, 1836.

———. *The Principles of Moral and Political Philosophy*. London, 1785.

———. *Reasons for Contentment, Addressed to the Labouring Part of the British Publick*. 1792. *The Works of William Paley, D.D*. Vol. 4. Boston, 1811. 411–23. 5 vols.

Patterson, Annabel. *Pastoral and Ideology: Virgil to Valery*. Berkeley: Univ. of California Press, 1987.

Paulson, Ronald. *Emblem and Expression: Meaning in English Art of the Eighteenth Century*. Cambridge: Harvard Univ. Press, 1975.

Percy, Thomas. "Essay on the Ancient Minstrels." *Reliques of Ancient English Poetry*. 3 vols. London: Dodsley, 1765. Reprint. *Reliques of Ancient English Poetry . . . By Thomas Percy*. Ed. Henry B. Wheatley. Vol. 1. London: Allen and Unwin, 1927. 345–81. 3 vols.

Phillips, Adam. "Introduction." *A Philosophical Enquiry into the Origin of Our Ideas of the Sublime and Beautiful*. By Edmund Burke. Oxford: Oxford Univ. Press, 1990. ix–xxiii.

Pinkerton, John. "An Essay on the Origin of Scotish [sic] Poetry." *Ancient Scottish Poems, Never Before in Print*. Vol. 1. London, 1786. xxi–lxxiv. 2 vols.

Place, Francis. *The Autobiography of Francis Place (1771-1854)*. Ed. Mary Thale. Cambridge: Cambridge Univ. Press, 1972.

Polanyi, Karl. *The Great Transformation: The Political and Economic Origins of Our Time*. 1944. Boston: Beacon, 1957.

"Politics of the Poets." *The Chartist Circular* 45 (1 August 1840). *The Chartist Circular*. Ed. William Thomson. Glasgow, 1841. Reprint. New York: Augustus M. Kelley, 1968. 182.

Poynter, J. R. *Society and Pauperism: English Ideas on Poor Relief, 1795–1834*. London: Routledge and Kegan Paul; Toronto: Univ. of Toronto Press, 1969.

Pratt, Samuel Jackson. *The Poor; or, Bread, A Poem*. 2nd ed. London, 1802. (Originally published as *Bread, or The Poor*. 1801.)

———. *Liberal Opinions, upon Animals, Man, and Providence*. 6 vols. London, 1775.

Price, Martin. "The Picturesque Moment. *From Sensibility to Romanticism: Essays Presented to Frederick A. Pottle*. Ed. Frederick W. Hilles and Harold Bloom. New York: Oxford Univ. Press, 1965. 259–92.

Price, Uvedale. *An Essay on the Picturesque, as Compared with The Sublime and the Beautiful; and, on the Use of Studying Pictures, for the Purpose of Improving Real Landscape*. 2 vols. London, 1796.

Priestley, Joseph. *Miscellaneous Observations Relating to Education, More Especially as it Respects the Conduct of the Mind. The Theological and Miscellaneous Works of Joseph Priestley*. Ed. J. T. Rutt. Vol. 25. 1831. Reprint. New York: Kraus, 1972. 1–68. 25 vols.

———. "Some Considerations on the State of the Poor in General." *The Theological and Miscellaneous Works of Joseph Priestley*. Ed. J. T. Rutt. Vol. 25. 1831. Reprint. New York: Kraus, 1972. 314–19. 25 vols.

Radcliffe, Ann. *Mysteries of Udolpho.* Ed. Bonamy Dobree. Notes by Frederick Garber. 1966. The World's Classics. Oxford: Oxford Univ. Press,1981.

Rawnsley, R. H. "Reminiscences of Wordsworth among the Peasantry of Westmoreland." *Transactions of the Wordsworth Society* 6, n.d. Reprint. London: Dawson and Sons, 1966. 159-94.

Raysor, Thomas M. "The Establishment of Wordsworth's Reputation." *JEGP* 54 (1955): 61- 71.

Repton, Humphry. *Enquiry into the Changes of Taste in Landscape Gardening.* London, 1806.

———. *Fragments on the Theory and Practice of Landscape Gardening.* London, 1816.

Rev. of Dr. Townson, *The Poor Man's Moralist. Anti-Jacobin Review* (March 1800): 208–10.

Rev. of Mary Wollstonecraft, *A Vindication of the Rights of Man. Gentleman's Magazine* 61 Part 1 (February 1791): 151–54.

Rev. of William Wordsworth, *Lyrical Ballads. The British Critic* (October 1799): 364–69.

Rev. of William Wordsworth, *Yarrow Revisited and Other Poems. The Monthly Repository* N.S. 9, 102 (1835): 430–34.

Reynolds, Joshua. *Discourses on Art.* Ed. Robert R. Wark. San Marino, Calif.: Huntington Library and Art Gallery, 1959.

Ricardo, David. *Principles of Political Economy and Taxation.* Harmondsworth: Penguin, 1971.

Ritson, Joseph. *Ancient Engleish Metrical Romanceës* [sic]. 3 vols. London, 1802.

Roberts, David. *Paternalism in Early Victorian England.* New Brunswick, N.J.: Rutgers Univ. Press, 1979.

Roberts, William. *Memoirs of the Life and Correspondence of Mrs. Hannah More.* 2 vols. New York: Harper and Brothers, 1835.

Roe, Nicholas. *Wordsworth and Coleridge: The Radical Years.* Oxford: Clarendon, 1988.

Rzepka, Charles J. "A Gift that Complicates Employ: Poetry and Poverty in 'Resolution and Independence.' " *Studies in Romanticism* 28 (Summer 1989): 225–47.

Salaman, Malcolm C. "Wheatley's 'Cries of London.' " *Apollo* 10 (November 1929): 251–56.

Sales, Roger. *English Literature in History 1780–1830: Pastoral and Politics.* English Literature in History. London: Hutchinson, 1983.

Salisbury, Dean of . "A Few Words on Wordsworth's Position as an Ethical Teacher." In *Transactions of the Wordsworth Society* 5 n.d. Reprint. London: Dawson and Sons, 1966. 39-42.

Saunders, John. Untitled introduction. *The People's Journal* 1 (3 January 1846): 1.

Sayre, Robert and Michael Löwy. "Figures of Romantic Anticapitalism." *Spirits of Fire: English Romantic Writers and Contemporary Historical methods.* Ed. G. A. Rosso and Daniel P. Watkins. Rutherford: Fairleigh Dickinson Univ. Press; London and Toronto: Associated Univ. Press, 1990. 23–68.

Scott, Sir Walter. *The Lay of the Last Minstrel: A Poem in Six Cantos.* 1805. New York: Thomas Y. Crowell, n.d.

Searle, C. E. "Custom, Class Conflict and Agrarian Capitalism: The Cumbrian Customary Economy in the Eighteenth Century." *Past and Present* 110 (1986): 106–33.

Sennett, Richard. *Authority.* New York: Vintage, 1981.

Sha, Richard C. "Gray's Political *Elegy*: Poetry as the Burial of History." *Philological Quarterly.* (Summer 1990): 337–57.

Works Cited

Shelley, Percy Bysshe. *A Defence of Poetry. Shelley's Prose, or The Trumpet of a Prophecy*. Ed. David Lee Clark. Albuquerque: Univ. of New Mexico Press, 1954.

———. *Shelley's Poetry and Prose*. Ed. Donald H. Reiman and Sharon B. Powers. New York: W. W. Norton, 1977.

Shesgreen, Sean. *The Criers and Hawkers of London: Engravings and Drawings of Marcellus Laroon*. Stanford: Stanford Univ. Press, 1990.

Simmel, Georg. "The Poor." *On Individuality and Social Forms: Selected Writings*. Ed. Donald N. Levine. Chicago and London: The Univ. of Chicago Press, 1971. 150–78.

Simpson, David. "Criticism, Politics and Style in Wordsworth's Poetry." *Criticial Inquiry* 11 (September 1984): 52–81.

———. *Wordsworth's Historical Imagination: The Poetry of Displacement*. New York and London: Methuen, 1987.

———. "Wordsworth in America." *The Age of William Wordsworth: Critical Essays on the Romantic Tradition*. Ed. Kenneth R. Johnston and Gene W. Ruoff. New Brunswick and London: Rutgers Univ. Press, 1987. 276–90.

Siskin, Clifford S. *The Historicity of Romantic Discourse*. New York and Oxford: Oxford Univ. Press, 1988.

Smart, George Thomas. *Wordsworth: A Lecture*. Boston: Samuel Usher, 1902.

Smith, Adam. *The Theory of Moral Sentiments*. Ed. D. D. Raphael and A. L. MacFie. The Glasgow Edition of the Works and Correspondence of Adam Smith. 1976. Indianapolis, Ind.: LibertyClassics, 1982.

Smith, Charlotte. *The Emigrants. The Poems of Charlotte Smith*. Ed. Stuart Curran. Women Writers in English 1350–1850. New York and Oxford: Oxford Univ. Press, 1993. 132–63.

———. *Rambles Farther: A Continuation of Rural Walks: in Dialogues; in Two Volumes*. London, 1796.

———. *Rural Walks: in Dialogues Intended for the Use of Young Persons*. 2 vols. in 1. Dublin, 1795.

Southey, Robert. "On the Means of Improving the People." *Quarterly Review* (April 1818): 79–118.

Spiegelman, Willard. *Wordsworth's Heroes*. Berkeley: Univ. of California Press, 1985.

Steele, Richard. *Tatler* 68 (15 September 1709): 1–2.

———. *Tatler* 69 (17 September 1709): 1–2.

———. *Tatler* 87 (29 October 1709): 1–2.

Stewart, Susan. "Scandals of the Ballad." *Representations* 32 (Fall 1990): 134–56.

Tholfsen, Trygve R. *Working Class Radicalism in Mid-Victorian England*. New York: Columbia Univ. Press, 1977.

Thompson, E. P. "Disenchantment or Default? A Lay Sermon." *Power and Consciousness*. Ed. Conor Cruise O'Brien and William Dean Vanech. London: Univ. of London Press; New York: New York Univ. Press, 1969. 149–81.

———. "The Grid of Inheritance: A Comment." *Family and Inheritance: Rural Society in Western Europe, 1200–1800*. Ed. Jack Goody, Joan Thirsk, and E. P. Thompson. Cambridge: Cambridge Univ. Press, 1976. 328–60.

———. *The Making of the English Working Class*. New York: Vintage, 1966.

———. "The Moral Economy of the English Crowd in the Eighteenth Century." *Past and Present* 50 (February 1971): 76–136.

———. "Patrician Society, Plebian Culture." *Journal of Social History*. 7 (Summer 1974): 382- 405.

———. "Time, Work-Discipline and Industrial Capitalism." *Past and Present* (December 1967): 56–97.

Todd, Janet. *Sensibility: An Introduction*. London and New York: Methuen, 1986.

"Tory Literature." *The Chartist Circular* 54 (October 3, 1840). *The Chartist Circular*. Ed. William Thomson. Glasgow, 1841. Reprint. New York: Augustus M. Kelley, 1968. 217.

Townsend, Joseph. *A Dissertation on the Poor Laws by a Well-Wisher to Mankind*. 1786. Reprint. Berkeley: Univ. of California Press, 1971.

Trimmer, Sarah. *The Oeconomy of Charity, or, an Address to Ladies Concerning Sunday Schools; the Establishment of Schools of Industry under Female Inspection; and the Distribution of Voluntary Benefactions*. London, 1787.

———. *Reflections upon the Education of Children in Charity Schools*. London, 1792.

Turner, Victor. *The Ritual Process: Structure and Anti-Structure*. 1969. Reprint. Ithaca: Cornell Univ. Press, 1977.

White, Hayden O. "The Noble Savage Theme as Fetish." *First Images of America: The Impact of the New World on the Old*. Ed. Fred Chiapelli. Berkeley: Univ. of California Press, 1976. (Reprinted in Hayden White, *Tropics of Discourse: Essays in Cultural Criticism*. 1978. Baltimore and London: Johns Hopkins Univ. Press, 1985. 183–96.)

Williams, John. *Wordsworth: Romantic Poetry and Revolution Politics*. Manchester and New York: Manchester Univ. Press, 1989.

Williams, Raymond. *The Country and the City*. New York: Oxford Univ. Press, 1973.

Wolfson, Susan J. "Questioning 'The Romantic Ideology': Wordsworth." *Revue internationale de Philosophie* 44 (1990): 429–47.

Wollstonecraft, Mary. *Original Stories from Real Life. The Works of Mary Wollstonecraft*. Ed. Janet Todd and Marilyn Butler. Asst. Ed. Emma Rees-Mogg. Vol. 4. London: William Pickering, 1989. 359–450. 7 vols.

———. *A Vindication of the Rights of Woman, with Strictures on Political and Moral Subjects*. Ed. Charles W. Hagelman, Jr. New York: W. W. Norton, 1967.

Wood, J. Letter. *The Monthly Magazine* 9 (1 June 1800): 425.

Woodring, Carl. "Wordsworth and the Victorians." *The Age of William Wordsworth: Critical Essays on the Romantic Tradition*. Ed. Kenneth R. Johnston and Gene W. Ruoff. New Brunswick and London: Rutgers Univ. Press, 1987. 261–75.

Wordsworth, Dorothy. *Journals of Dorothy Wordsworth*. Ed. Mary Moorman. London: Oxford Univ. Press, 1971.

Wordsworth, Jonathan. *William Wordsworth: The Borders of Vision*. Oxford: Clarendon Press, 1982.

Wordsworth, William. *The Letters of William and Dorothy Wordsworth: The Early Years 1787–1805*. Ed. Ernest De Selincourt. 2nd ed. Rev. Chester L. Shaver. Clarendon: Oxford Univ. Press, 1967.

———. *The Letters of William and Dorothy Wordsworth: The Middle Years, Part I, 1806–1811*. Ed. Ernest De Selincourt. 2nd ed. Rev. Mary Moorman. Clarendon: Oxford Univ. Press, 1969.

———. *Poems, in Two Volumes and Other Poems, 1800–1807 by William Wordsworth*. Ed. Jared Curtis. The Cornell Wordsworth. Ithaca: Cornell Univ. Press, 1983.

———. *The Poetical Works of William Wordsworth*. Ed. Ernest De Selincourt and Helen Darbishire. 5 vols. 1940–49. Clarendon: Oxford Univ. Press, 1952–59.

———. *The Prose Works of William Wordsworth*. Ed. W. J. B. Owen and Jane Worthington Smyser. 3 vols. Oxford: Clarendon, 1974.

———. *The Ruined Cottage and The Pedlar by William Wordsworth*. Ed. James Butler. The Cornell Wordsworth. Ithaca: Cornell Univ. Press, 1979.

————. *The Salisbury Plain Poems of William Wordsworth*. Ed. Stephen Gill. The Cornell Wordsworth. Ithaca: Cornell Univ. Press, 1975.

————. *William Wordsworth: The Prelude 1799, 1805, 1850*. Ed. Jonathan Wordsworth, M. H. Abrams and Stephen Gill. New York: W. W. Norton, 1979.

Wordsworth's Poems for the Young. Illus. John Macwhirter and John Pettie. Vignette by J. E. Millais. Engraved by the Dalziel Brothers. London: Alexander Strahan, 1863.

Index

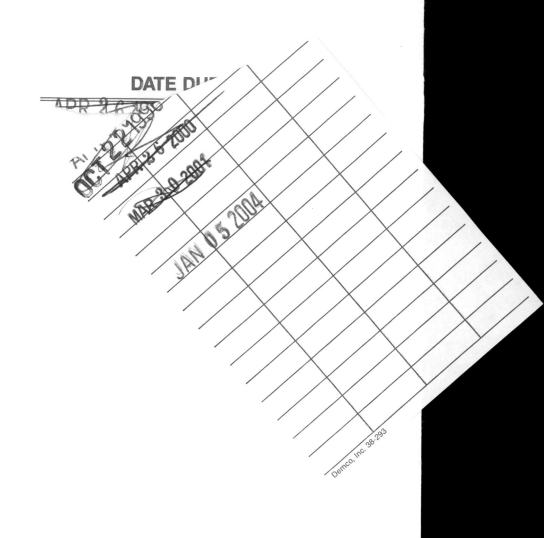

DATE DUE

APR 9 A 1998

AU 2 2 1998

OCT 2 2 D

APR 2 6 2000

MAR 2 0 2001

JAN 0 5 2004